The Valkyries' Loom

UNIVERSITY PRESS OF FLORIDA

Florida A&M University, Tallahassee
Florida Atlantic University, Boca Raton
Florida Gulf Coast University, Ft. Myers
Florida International University, Miami
Florida State University, Tallahassee
New College of Florida, Sarasota
University of Central Florida, Orlando
University of Florida, Gainesville
University of North Florida, Jacksonville
University of South Florida, Tampa
University of West Florida, Pensacola

The Valkyries' Loom

The Archaeology of Cloth Production and
Female Power in the North Atlantic

Michèle Hayeur Smith

UNIVERSITY PRESS OF FLORIDA

Gainesville · Tallahassee · Tampa · Boca Raton

Pensacola · Orlando · Miami · Jacksonville · Ft. Myers · Sarasota

First cloth printing, 2020
First paperback printing, 2023

28 27 26 25 24 23   6 5 4 3 2 1

Library of Congress Cataloging-in-Publication Data
Names: Hayeur Smith, Michèle, author.
Title: The Valkyries' loom : the archaeology of cloth production and female power
in the North Atlantic / Michèle Hayeur Smith.
Description: Gainesville : University Press of Florida, 2020. | Includes bibliographical
references and index.
Identifiers: LCCN 2020017606 (print) | LCCN 2020017607 (ebook) | ISBN
9780813066622 (hardback) | ISBN 9780813057637 (pdf) | ISBN 9780813080116 (pbk.)
Subjects: LCSH: Textile fabrics, Viking—Scandinavia—History. | Women weavers—
Scandinavia—History. | Textile fabrics—Scandinavia—History. | Vikings—Clothing—
Scandinavia. | Women, Viking—History. | Textile fabrics—North Atlantic Region—History.
Classification: LCC DL33.T48 H39 2020 (print) | LCC DL33.T48 (ebook) |
DDC 949.12/01—dc23
LC record available at https://lccn.loc.gov/2020017606
LC ebook record available at https://lccn.loc.gov/2020017607

The University Press of Florida is the scholarly publishing agency for the State University System
of Florida, comprising Florida A&M University, Florida Atlantic University, Florida Gulf Coast
University, Florida International University, Florida State University, New College of Florida,
University of Central Florida, University of Florida, University of North Florida, University of
South Florida, and University of West Florida.

University Press of Florida
2046 NE Waldo Road
Suite 2100
Gainesville, FL 32609
http://upress.ufl.edu

To my mother and daughter,
and all the strong women of the North

Contents

Figures

Tables

Acknowledgments

This book was made possible thanks to funding from the National Science Foundation, Arctic Social Sciences: 2010–2013, Rags to Riches: An Archaeological Study of Textiles and Gender in Iceland, AD 874–1800 (Award no:1023167); 2013–2017, Weaving Islands of Cloth–Gender, Textiles, and Trade across the North Atlantic from the Viking Age to the Early Modern Period (Award no:1303898); 2017–2018, Supplement to Weaving Islands of Cloth. Special thanks to Anna Kerttula, my program officer at the National Science Foundation, who believed in me and my vision of a gendered archaeology of the North Atlantic.

I would also like to thank the Haffenreffer Museum of Anthropology at Brown University for providing me the institutional support I needed to carry out this research and notably its successive directors, Shepard Krech III (Department of Anthropology, Brown University), Steve Lubar (American Studies, Department of History and History of Art and Architecture, Brown University), William Simmons (Department of Anthropology, Brown University) and particularly the current director Robert Preucel (Department of Anthropology, Brown University) for encouraging me and supporting me consistently on these projects.

This work was also made possible thanks to the collaboration and help from the following institutions: National Museum of Iceland (Þjóðminjasafn Íslands), National Museum of Denmark, the Greenland Museum and Archives, the National Museum of the Faroe Islands, the National Museum of Scotland, the Bryggens Museum and the University of Bergen, the Canadian Museum of History, the Institute of Archaeology of Iceland (Fornleifastofnun Íslands), the Fisk Institute, the University of Iceland (Háskoli Íslands), City University New York (Hunter College), Snorrastofa (the cultural and medieval center in Reykholt), the University of Rhode Island, and the University of Tromsø.

I would like to thank the following individuals: Margrét Hallgrímsdóttir, Guðmundur Ólafsson, Ármann Guðmundsson, Lilja Árnardóttir, Ivar Brynjolfsson, and Freyja Hlíðkvist Ómars-Sesseljudóttir (National Museum of Iceland); Jette Arneborg and Karin M. Frei (National Museum of Denmark); Mikkel-Holger Strander Sinding (Trinity College Dublin); Georg Nygaard and Christian Koch Madsen (Greenland Museum and Archives); Símun Arge (National Museum of the Faroe Islands); Martin Goldberg and Lindsay McGill (National Museum of Scotland); Gitte Hansen (University of Bergen); Stacey Girling-Christie, Jean-Luc Pilon, and Karen Ryan (Canadian Museum of History); Douglas Bolender and John Steinberg (Fisk Institute); Gavin Lucas, Steinunn Kristjánsdóttir, Vala Garðarsdóttir, and Helgi Þorláksson (University of Iceland); Guðrún Sveinbjarnardóttir (University College London); Thomas McGovern and Konrad Smiarowski (CUNY, Hunter College); Ramona Harrison (University of Bergen); Mjöll Snæsdóttir, Howell M. Roberts, and Guðrún Alda Gísladóttir (Institute of Archaeology of Iceland); Bergur Þorgeirsson (Snorrastofa); Margaret Ordoñez (University of Rhode Island); Gørill Nilsen (University of Tromsø); Natasha Mehler (University of Vienna); Darden Hood and Ron Hatfield (Beta Analytic); Stuart Jenks (Geschiedenis, Universiteit Leiden); and Marta Kløve Juuhl and Monika Ravnanger (Osterøy Museum).

I would also like to thank Auður Hildur Hákonardóttir for her wise knowledge on weaving and textile work in Iceland, for passionate discussions about women in the past, and for gifting me her warp-weighted loom. I would like to thank Þúry Harðardóttir and Alan Coogan (for the hours spent on the dirty brown rags) and Nathanial Crockett and Guðrún Jóna Rúna Þraínsdóttir for their help with collections, analysis, conservation and friendship; Greg Rebis for his incredible skills as an artist and ability at visualizing the mythic past; and Chris Wolf, Tommy Urban, and Kevin Martin for their help at Gilsbakki and where the textile adventure started. I would like to thank old friends who encouraged me and supported me with fine dining and amazing conversations: Geir Waage from Reykholt, and his wife, Dagny Emilsdóttir, Bryndís Geirsdóttir, Rósa Björk, Sigurbjörg J. Narby Helgadóttir, Nils Kjartan Guðmundsson Narby, Ingegerd Narby, Flóki Kjartansson Narby, Freyja Kjartansdóttir Narby, and Jónas. Special thanks to Jonathan Thomas, who painstakingly read through every bit of this manuscript, editing along the way. I could not have done this without your help!

Finally I would like to thank my family, Arthur Y. Smith, my father; Robin H. Smith, my brother; Alexander and John Smith, my nephews; Bernie Martenson, my sister-in-law; and most of all Kevin P. Smith (Brown University), my husband, who was my biggest fan and support, who pushed me and helped me make this a reality, who endured endless discussions about textiles, who is the best editor one could ask for, and who helped me build my career as an archaeologist, believed in me, and helped me grow as a woman; and my daughter, Emilie Mariette Wilder Smith, along with both of her grandmothers, both strong women: Mary Ann Smith and Mariette Hayeur, my mother, whom she never knew but who taught me to follow my passions, to not fear the fight and fight for what you believe in. Emilie patiently endured hours of archaeological discussions and travel. This book is really for her, because as a member of the next generation of women fighting for equal rights, she and her peers need to know where we came from and what we accomplished in the past. This knowledge can only make them stronger and help them forge their own definition of gender equality based on female ways and female power rather than defining their equality by comparing themselves to men.

Orthography Note

Some Old Norse and modern Icelandic letters in this text will be unfamiliar to English readers. Many letters with accents, such as some of the ones listed here, are long vowels in the medieval language but now represent diphthongs (Karlsson 2000): for example, á (pronounced "ow") é, and ó. Í is pronounced as in "see"; æ is similar to the English "I"; ú is pronounced as in "loom" or "womb" (but **u** has no English parallel); **y** and ý are equivalent to **i** and í; ö is pronounced like the **u** in "but," similar to the French **eu**. Ð (lowercase ð) and þ represent fricative sounds: ð is voiced like the **th** in "brother" or "weather," while þ is pronounced like the **th** in "thin" (see Karlsson 2000:xiii).

Introduction

She soon fell asleep and she had a dream which she related to Pálnir on awakening. "I dreamed," she said, "that I was staying here on this estate and I thought that I had a grey colored cloth in the loom. It seemed as though the weights were attached to the cloth and I was weaving. When one of the weights fell down behind from the middle of the cloth, I noticed that the weights were the heads of men. I took up that head and recognized it." When Pálnir asked whose head it was, she said that it was King Haraldr Gormsson's.

Jómsvíkinga Saga (Blake 1962:10)

The Valkyries' Loom is a book about textiles, specifically textiles from the Scandinavian settlements of the North Atlantic. It is not a descriptive or technological book in nature; rather, it addresses the social archaeology of textiles and textiles as a form of material culture that encodes information about the societies who made them. Textiles are like "text" (which is where the term comes from) and tell a story about hardships and successes and, most importantly, about the lives of the women who made them.

The Valkyries' Loom is the product of nine years' analysis of textiles from the Viking and Norse colonies of the North Atlantic, incorporating the results of three National Science Foundation grants from Arctic Social Sciences: Imagining an Engendered Archaeology of the North Atlantic (NSF 0946247); Rags to Riches: An Archaeological Study of Textiles and Gender in Iceland, AD 874–1800 (NSF 1023167), 2010–2013; and Weaving Islands of Cloth: Gender, Textiles, and Trade across the North Atlantic from the Viking Age to the Early Modern Period (NSF 1303898), 2013–2016. In 2017 I was awarded a one-year supplement to the third grant, which enabled me to complete research on the Norse Greenlandic assemblage.

Archaeological textiles and their social use as a symbol of women's culture have never been addressed in the North Atlantic specifically. Most studies have focused on highly technical overviews of archaeological textiles, including thread counts, weave types, production techniques, tools, fleece type, or were in-depth ethnographic and descriptive analyses examining the finer textiles produced for ecclesiastic centers and religious use. The great majority of these studies in Iceland were performed by the late Else Guðjónsson, a pioneer of Icelandic textile work, but she left to her successors the huge task of tackling a corpus of unexamined archaeological textiles, stored in the National Museum's warehouses. Guðjónsson's work was valuable and comprehensive but discussed only a handful of these archaeological remains in Icelandic journals (for works by this author, see Guðjónsson 1962, 1964, 1973, 1978, 1980, 1989, 1990, 1992, 1994, 1998a, 1998b).

The Faroe Islands had a similar devotee to the study of textiles, Nicolina Jense Bender, whom I had the pleasure of meeting in 2015 and who sadly passed away a year later. Bender published the volume *Seyður ull Tøting* (2010), documenting all manner of textile work and production, from the origins of the Faroese sheep to spinning, weaving, and dyeing and to documenting the extensive knitting traditions that developed in the Faroes. Neither of these women were archaeologists, but both devoted their lives to wool and its various uses in the recent past; both also laid down the path for others, who would pick up where they left off.

In Greenland the most valuable contribution to the study of archaeological textiles came from the Danish National Museum's Else Østergård, who in 2004 published *Woven into the Earth*, the most complete catalog and technical overview of archaeological textiles from Norse Greenland. Her work served as the foundation on which I built my own research. Additional work on archaeological material was performed by Penelope Walton Rogers (1998, 2012), who analyzed Greenlandic textiles from the sites of the Farm beneath the Sand (Gården under Sandet, GUS), Greenland, and the farm at Reykholt, in Iceland. Walton Rogers (and Greaves 2018) also analyzed Inuit material from the Eastern Canadian Arctic and elements from the Faroese collections (Walton Rogers 2001), though these findings from the Faroes have not been published.

Scottish Viking textiles were compiled and analyzed primarily by Lise Bender Jørgensen and published in 1992, followed by Thea Gabra-Sanders (1998), who also passed away leaving unfinished work. I used some of Gabra-Sanders's analyses when recording and consulting the Viking Scottish material, which is largely stored at the National Museum of Scotland, with some collections scattered in regional museums as well as the British Museum.

All of these studies, while essential to the analysis of textiles, have never engaged the material culture as a way to seek an understanding of the social dynamics operating within each of these societies through cloth. What I hope to have achieved here is a social archaeology of textiles. Østergård (2004) did present valuable social insights concerning the emergence of weft-dominant cloth and possible reasons for its proliferation in the Greenland Norse colony. But the work of delving into the deeper motivating factors behind textile work, its symbolic meaning, and what textile work actually meant to the women performing it has been neglected.

I felt that textiles and textile work were a medium as informative as any in understanding important social issues that characterized these North Atlantic Norse societies: environmental stress, economy and trade, and even resistance to Danish colonial oversight. Therefore, after many trips back and forth across the North Atlantic for almost a decade to various museums where I counted threads and otherwise recorded these textiles in minute detail, I can say that this study of the North Atlantic material is by far the most extensive.

An Archaeology of Gender in the North Atlantic

In recent decades, archaeological research in the North Atlantic has made remarkable advances, not only in synthetic analyses (e.g., Bolender et al. 2008; Brewington et al. 2015; Buckland et al. 1996; Church et al. 2007; Dugmore et al. 2007; Harrison and Maher 2014; Harrison et al. 2008; Hayeur Smith 2004, 2012; Lucas 2009, 2010, 2012; Lucas and McGovern 2007; McGovern 1980, 1991; Mann et al. 2009; Smith 1995, 2004, 2009; Sveinbjarnardóttir 2009, 2012, 2016; Zori 2014), but also in reporting basic data from excavations, surveys, and technical analyses. Work linking natural historical sequences with human activity (Adderley et al. 2008; Barrett 1997; Barrett et al. 2008; Church et al. 2007; Hambrecht 2009; Lawson et al. 2007; McGovern et al. 2007; Smiarowski and McGovern 2012) and social histories (Byock 1988, 2001; Durrenburger 1992; Einarsson 1995; Miller 1996; Sigurdsson 1999; Steinberg 2006) provides multifaceted perspectives on social and environmental change, especially in Iceland, the largest of the Norse North Atlantic colonies. Archaeological research on Norse expansion into Greenland and the Faroe Islands has also received more attention in recent years (Arge 2008; Arge et al. 2009; Arneborg et al. 2008; Edwards et al. 2004; Koch Madsen 2014; Nelson et al. 2012; Ogilvie et al. 2009), providing new insights into medieval trans-Atlantic island colonization.

Such works have addressed and continue to address issues of environmental change, human adaptation, sustainability, and human ecodynamics. Relatively less work has been carried out on the social aspects of material culture or economy not directly tied to subsistence or bioarchaeological analyses.

The study of gender has particularly lagged in the North Atlantic and continues to do so despite useful pioneering historical studies on women's roles in the Viking Age in Scandinavia (Friðrikdóttir 2013; Guðmundsson 2016; Jesch 2005; Jochens 1995, 1996) or in mythology (Bek-Pedersen 2013) and more recent work carried out on the roles of women during the Viking Age as warriors (Gardela 2013; Price et al. 2019) and as skalds (Straubhaar 2011). Yet medieval and post-medieval documentary sources imply that women, particularly those involved in the production of cloth, played crucial roles in the economies of the Norse North Atlantic. Thus, women's work was not simply housework—through their engagement and oversight of textile production, women controlled or had a direct hand in organizing one of the most crucial aspects of the North Atlantic economy.

Gender theorists have actively challenged gender stereotypes that relegated women to the role of caregivers and denied (through either commission or omission) their involvement in power relationships and leadership roles (Conkey 2003; Conkey et al. 1997; Gero et al. 1991; Hays-Gilpin 2000). Many pioneering efforts have focused on "finding" women in the past and, more importantly still, on understanding relationships between men and women and how those relationships played out in daily social discourse and changed through time (Conkey 2003; Gilchrist 1999; Hays-Gilpin 2000; Nelson 1997).

Women's roles in North Atlantic societies from the Viking Age to the post-medieval period have been the subjects of several seminal monographs (Friðriksdóttir 2013; Hastrup 1990; Jesch 2005; Jochens 1995, 1996; Mygland 2014; Róbertsdóttir 2008), popular books (Brown 2007), and articles (e.g., Anderson and Swenson 2002; Árnórsdóttir 2010; Burge 2009; Clover 1993; Hedenstierna-Jonson 2015; Magnúsdóttir 1988, 2008; Larsson 2008; Maher 2007; Mygland 2015) that have shaped perceptions about women's roles in these periods. However, these studies—with exceptions—have focused on textual sources, institutional considerations (divorce, marriage, political and legal rights, etc.), and representations of women in literary and visual arts, without considering material culture in any depth. Investigations of the saga literature tend to portray a view of strong Viking Age women able to take matters into their own hands and direct the affairs of men through the context of household politics

(Jesch 2005) or, alternatively, using more subversive methods such as magic to gain power and autonomy in a largely patriarchal society and world "dominated by social structures, male violence and the legal system to which women had no formal access" (Friðriksdóttir 2013:57). This vision of strong Viking Age and medieval women became a foundation through the nineteenth century and on into the twenty-first century for many studies of women's roles in later Icelandic society.

Yet, as Auður Magnúsdóttir (2008:41) writes, "The myth of the 'strong' Viking woman, as she is illustrated in the Icelandic sagas, has not been challenged with any intensity, in spite of the critical examination of the sagas in general." She notes that the sagas were written by powerful thirteenth-century men, who also wrote sagas about their own times in which women were portrayed in these texts with far less active roles. She argues that the actions these sagas' authors attributed to Viking Age women led more often to disaster than success, while the more muted portrayal of thirteenth-century women invests them with less ambiguity. Together, these differing visions of Viking Age and thirteenth-century Norse women, produced by the same authors, raise difficult questions about whether the accepted vision of "strong" women in the Viking Age is accurate or apocryphal, factual or fictive. However, historical research on women's contributions to the North Atlantic economy, especially textile production, suggests that women gained stronger roles in household and regional economic structures *after* the Viking Age—in the medieval period—and this has been confirmed by ongoing research on textiles (Bek-Pedersen 2007, 2009, 2011; Cartwright 2015; Gelsinger 1981; Guðjónsson 1994, 1998a; Hayeur Smith 2012, 2014a, 2014b, 2015, 2018; Hoffman 1974; Øye 2016; Róbertsdóttir 2008; Þórláksson 1988, 1991, 1999). Some of these more powerful roles appear to have come not only from producing cloth that was economically central but from the very nature of textile work, deeply held associations with concepts of life, death, birth, and fate, and men's seeming anxiety over this highly gendered activity (see Chapter 1; Bek-Pedersen 2007, 2008, 2011; Heide 2007; Milek 2012; Norrman 2008). Yet the continued focus on men and men's roles in the later medieval and post-medieval sources, whether law codes or literary works, and in much secondary scholarship leaves many questions about whether women's changing roles in economic activities merely increased their workloads or enhanced their positions. At the very least, the documentary-based vision of medieval women in the North Atlantic cannot be considered unproblematic, making archaeological perspectives essential in understanding women of the North Atlantic past.

A second strand of research on women in the North that relies almost exclusively on archaeological data has been spun from studies of mortuary sites and their representations of women in death. Many of these analyses, undertaken in mainland Scandinavia (Arwill-Nordbladh 1991; Dommasnes 1982; Gräslund 1995, 1999, 2001, 2003; Solberg 1985), may be only partially applicable to the North Atlantic setting. In 2003 and 2004, for example, I showed that the North Atlantic mortuary program for women's graves had its own logic, different from Viking Age mortuary traditions in mainland Scandinavia. These differences may perhaps be consonant with studies of mitochondrial DNA showing that Iceland's female population was drawn heavily from the British Isles, although the male population was drawn from Scandinavian gene pools (Helgason et al. 2001; Price and Gestsdóttir 2006). Yet while Gestsdóttir (1998) and Maher (2007) have reviewed the mortuary corpus, drawing attention to the need for separating biological sex from gender in mortuary analyses, we do not know who made decisions about how the dead were to be buried and whether the representation of women in death reflects their own wishes, those of their kinsmen, or some combination of the above. The mortuary record, like the literary record, is not unproblematic, and across the North Atlantic it becomes nearly silent after AD 1000, when these societies adopted Christianity and corpses went to their graves unadorned. Recent work at early Christian cemeteries, such as the eleventh-century graveyard at Keldudalur in northern Iceland (Zoëga 2009) and Greenland's Herjolfsnes cemetery (Østergård 2004), shows that men and women were buried in different parts of these cemeteries, suggesting that gender, more than marital status, age, or kinship relationships, defined the place of women in death and perhaps in life.

These important studies provide key insights into the ways women were viewed by others in literary and legal documents or in death, but few projects have focused directly on women's *lives* and women's *living* contributions to North Atlantic Norse society without the intermediacy of the book or the graveside ritual. Doing so requires approaching women archaeologically, by what they did and what they made.

Excavations at summer farms (*sel*, shielings) inhabited by women engaged in dairying provide an interesting approach to understanding engendered space (Arge et al. 2005; Kupiec and Milek 2015; Lárusdóttir 2011:236–247; Sveinbjarnardóttir et al. 2012). Still in their early stages, these investigations promise to provide new insights into women's contributions to the subsistence economy. And recently, the "Woman in Blue" project, of which I was a curatorial advisor and a main researcher and which is touched upon briefly in Chapter 2, used a multidisciplinary approach integrating artifact analyses, bioarchaeological analyses, isotopic analyses (C, N, O, Sr), aDNA, and accelerated mass spectrometry (AMS) dating to develop an integrated approach to understanding the life history, identity, and death of an early female settler in Iceland, with an exhibition at the National Museum of Iceland presenting these interdisciplinary approaches to the public (Hayeur Smith 2015b; Hayeur Smith et al. 2019).

However, another avenue to finding women, the focus of my research, is to assess changes through time and variation across space in one of the industries women controlled—textiles. Globally, textiles have been produced by both men and women (Weiner and Schneider 1989), yet textile production and the manufacture of clothing were overwhelmingly women's work in traditional European societies (Wayland Barber 1995; Larsson 2008). Medieval Icelandic and Danish colonial sources document that textile production in Iceland was in the hands of women (Róbertsdóttir 2008), even though the *total* process—from raising sheep to trading cloth or making clothing—was served by an engendered division of labor. Across the North Atlantic, until the mid-eighteenth century, the tasks of cleaning and combing wool, spinning, weaving, and producing clothes were women's work. In Viking Age burials, North Atlantic women were frequently interred with weaving and spinning implements. They also embroidered woolen textiles (Guðjónsson 1973; Hägg 1974), knitted by a single-needle method (*nálbinding*) (Guðjónsson 1964), and, during the sixteenth century, began knitting with two needles (Thirsk 2003).

Through the course of nine centuries (AD 870–1800), Icelandic women produced these textiles in their households, without specialized craftsmen or factories (Róbertsdóttir 2008). In Greenland, the Faroes, Norse Scotland, and rural Norway the situation was similar: weaving and textile production were female activities, undertaken on farms. From the mid-eighteenth century onward, however, these gendered relations of production changed. Under Danish and British colonial policies to "modernize" North Atlantic societies, men were trained to produce textiles in factories, using new technologies. Understanding the changing roles of women in North Atlantic societies is, therefore, in part a study of the different roles of cloth within these North Atlantic islands and the interrelationships these roles suggest about the local and transregional importance of domestic production.

Therefore, I have argued that by looking at textile production as *women's labor* (Hayes-Gilpin 2000), at the material culture of textile production, and at the processes of women's production as rich bodies of evidence for women's active decision making, we can begin to identify these women and the roles they played in shaping the societies of the North Atlantic.

In addition to decision making and the production of women's labor, cloth was about female expression. In a society where women were not equal to men and were not given equal voice, textiles provided a way for women to express themselves in terms of their opinions and solutions vis-à-vis the challenges that faced them (Norrman 2008). Norse society valued male verbal expression, the cultivation of poetic skills, and verbal prowess, but how did women commune in such an environment? As Norrman (2008) argued, the weaving of cloth and the embroidery of wall hangings and tapestries were visual mechanisms that women in Norse society used to express their messages. Berlo (1992:116) drew a similar parallel in Latin America, where women demonstrate a visual fluency and cultural knowledge in the *molas* they weave, constituting an alternate form of discourse. There too male expression has largely been focused on verbal skill.

Textiles are loaded with social messages; they assert personal identities as well as religious, economic, and cultural ones (Berlo 1992:115). For anthropologists and those interested in the cultural ramifications of cloth, textiles are "eloquent historical texts, encoding change, appropriation, oppression and endurance as well as personal and cultural aesthetic visions" (Berlo 1992:115).

The Collections and the Nature of North Atlantic Norse Societies

The textile collections from the North Atlantic are surprisingly rich, given that archaeological textiles do not usually, as organic remains, survive the effects of time. A few other areas globally offer a wealth of these precious organic remains, and in the North Atlantic the unique environmental conditions and the way textiles were deposited have all contributed to their preservation, largely in the middens of Norse farms.

The Greenlandic archaeological textile collection includes roughly 866–1000 fragments, while the Faroese material, a much smaller collection, comprises 142 fragments. The Icelandic corpus, on the other hand, which sparked my interest in textiles and laid the groundwork for all subsequent studies, possesses approximately 8,000–10,000 fragments and is still increasing. I also incorporated elements from the Scottish corpus when appropriate but found that apart from Viking Age material of the Northern Scottish Isles, it became unclear in subsequent centuries what derived from Norse versus local Scottish textile traditions. The Scottish collections from the later Middle Ages can hardly be described as Norse, since the Norse were less numerous than the local inhabitants of the British Isles and quickly assimilated, leaving few distinguishing cultural traits that could be identified in the textile corpus. As a result, the coverage of these collections in this book is minor. What broad conclusions can be derived from a collection of 142 fragments?

The numbers of textiles in these collections are not final because research is ongoing, and new material comes to light yearly. In some instances it was never my intention to do a complete sweep of a collection because analyzing 8,000 fragments of a 10,000-fragment corpus doesn't advance their interpretation, particularly from a sociocultural perspective; moreover, funds are not infinite, and my goal was not to provide textile catalogs but rather to synthesize and establish the overall trends of these textile traditions and to extract key social elements that fueled or curtailed production.

The islands of the North Atlantic serve as a unique laboratory setting because none of these places had local populations—excepting Scotland—before their Norse settlement. Iceland was, apart from a handful of Papar, or Irish monks, most of whom fled with the arrival of the Norse, settled in AD 874±. Greenland was settled later, in AD 985±, by a group of people fleeing western Iceland, where Eirik the Red, their leader, had been outlawed. Some indigenous inhabitants had been present in Greenland but did not enter the Norse-occupied southern areas—known as the Eastern and Western Settlements—until the fourteenth century, when climatic cooling from the Little Ice Age pushed the migrating Thule peoples into Norse settlement areas. The Faroe Islands were settled in AD 800±, but there, as in Iceland, no local inhabitants were present.

The remoteness and isolation of these North Atlantic societies from Western Europe provide a unique opportunity to observe archaeologically their evolution, far from their country of origin, each one dealing with its own social and environmental dynamics and evolving into completely different models of Norse culture. The settlers were largely from Scandinavia, but in each of these islands people from the British Isles and Ireland were brought over as slaves and concubines, creating societies that differed from the Scandinavian societies of the Viking Age.

Time Frame, Scope, and Material

The period under investigation is a long one, from the late ninth century to the beginning of the nineteenth century, because only over long periods of time can the changes in material culture really be documented. Textiles in traditional cultures rarely change and remain surprisingly conservative over centuries. When changes do occur in spin direction, weave type, or thread counts, these can signal important social, environmental, or cultural changes and manifestations taking place within societies (Minar 2001).

In Iceland, looking at textile traditions over a 900-year period has permitted me to track physical changes in cloth—a chronology of weaving that could be used as a relative dating method in conjunction with other absolute dating methods—as discussed in Chapter 2. In Norse Greenland (Chapters 4 and 5), the comparison of cloth from the early settlement to cloth from the end of the settlement facilitated the study of weft-dominant cloth, as cloth from the early settlement closely resembles that of Iceland. Analyzing thread counts in medieval Icelandic cloth suggests (in Chapter 3) that the use of cloth as currency did not end in the thirteenth century but that its standardization as a monetary entity in Iceland continued until the early seventeenth century.

This book largely focuses on homespun cloth, the everyday cloth used by the masses, not on the elaborate, fine textiles of the elite, though in these regions the elite wore clothes similar to those of everyone else, perhaps with minor additions of imported cloth (Chapters 6 and 7). This cloth was homespun, functional, and warm and was made from the wool from a group of breeds called the European Vari-colored Short-Tail or the Northern Short-Tail sheep (Walton Rogers in Østergård 2004), with its unique characteristic of two different fiber types incorporated into its fleece. The *tóg* was the outer coat, with long, coarse, outer guard hairs recognizable by the presence of a medulla, and the *þel* was a fine, fluffy undercoat without medullas, and soft as merino wool. In the early settlement of these islands, as well as in Viking Age Scandinavia, the wool was combed, and the coarse outer guard hairs were separated and used as warp yarns because they were strong, whereas the soft and fluffy inner coat was used as weft and felted naturally, making a type of cloth that was both semiwaterproof and warm. Eventually the Icelanders stopped combing the wool, to produce a product known to this day as *lopi*, incorporating both fibers.

All across the North Atlantic islands the main cloth types were largely twills (2/2, 2/1) and patterned twills and tabbies (plain weaves) woven with Z/S-spun yarns. Other weaves are also present, depending on the period. Some shaggy pile-woven cloth—known as *varafeldir* in modern Icelandic—has been recorded, though in minimal quantities. Knitting occurs late in the sequence, around the sixteenth century, and new textile technologies only make their appearance across the North Atlantic in the eighteenth century, as the result of Danish colonial rule (see Chapter 7).

The device these women used for 1,000 years was the warp-weighted loom, a Neolithic invention said to have been introduced to Scandinavia in the third century (Bender Jørgensen 1992). This simple upright loom was portable, easy to set up, and relatively straightforward to operate. Weaving often took place in a separate structure called a *dyngja*, a small pit house usually located outside the main hall (Bek-Pedersen 2007, 2009). It was only in the Middle Ages, after Christianization, that the *dyngja* was abolished and weaving was moved into the central *skáli* or longhouse (Milek 2012).

It was possible to weave cloth of great widths, up to 1,880 mm, on the warp-weighted loom based on finds from the west Greenlandic site of GUS (Østergård 2004:59). Because of the loom's upright position, loom weights—often just perforated stones—were suspended from the warp yarns, creating tension. Heddle rods placed horizontally could be added to create more complex weaves by moving certain warp yarns forward or backward, for yarns that were "knitted" to the heddle rods.

Yarns were initially spun using the drop spindle in the Viking Age, which was replaced over time by the high top whorl, whereby the spindle is set in motion by rolling it up or down one's leg (Østergård 2004:46–47). The drop spindle was often used with a distaff. Spindle whorls are common on Norse farms across the North Atlantic, mostly made of soapstone and of different diameters depending on the desired thickness of yarn (for tools in Viking Scandinavia, see Andersson Strand 2011).

But this study involves more than homespun; it also includes cloth imports in the medieval and early modern periods in the North Atlantic. This aspect of the research provided insights into trade and the export and import of woolen goods into and from the North Atlantic.

The chapters are arranged according to region and follow a temporal sequence, beginning with the Viking Age and progressing through the early medieval, late medieval, and early modern periods. Throughout these chapters I have attempted to bring women's lives into the discussion, to bring them to the forefront, as symbolized by the Valkyries, an embodiment of female mythical power, interweaving important themes: the ideological frameworks within Scandinavian societies that linked women's work on textiles to mythic themes involving the Valkyries and other female deities and spirits; to the prominence of *vaðmál*, the cloth that became currency in Iceland and a trade commodity across the North Atlantic; and the roles men played in transforming the textiles women wove into products of trade.

1

"Cold Are the Counsels of Women"

Bloodied Warps and Gilded Wefts

The Engendered Economy of Cloth in the North Atlantic

Blood rains
From the cloudy web
On the broad loom
Of Slaughter.
The web of man
Grey as armour
Is now being woven;
The Valkyries
Will cross it
With a crimson weft.

The warp is made
Of human entrails;
Human heads
Are used as weights;
The heddle rods
Are blood-wet spears;
The shafts are iron-bound,
And arrows are the shuttles.
With swords we will weave
This web of battle.

"Darraðarljóð," *Njáls Saga* (Magnusson and Pálsson 1969:349)

The poem "Darraðarljóð" provides a good starting point to discuss weaving in Norse society and perceptions held about textile work during the Viking Age in the North Atlantic and Scandinavia. Textiles and textile work appear to have generated considerable trepidation on the part of the men in this society. This chapter will explore these issues in Iceland, delving into the archaeological record and the sagas, documents written from the late twelfth through mid-fourteenth centuries but recounting events and attitudes from several centuries earlier, during Iceland's so-called settlement period (AD 870–1000). While they are not taken as accurate narratives of events from the Viking Age, they do present ethnographic information that is of value when analyzing cultural attitudes in the North Atlantic.

The Settlement of the North Atlantic

Iceland was settled in AD 874 by Scandinavian settlers—"Vikings"—best known for their marauding behavior, including pillaging, trading, and ultimately colonization, across the Western world. Iceland was discovered as Greenland was, accidentally, by storm-tossed sailors, though Iceland can boast of having three discoverers, the best known of them Flóki Vilgerðarson, also called Hrafna-Flóki (raven Flóki) for his use of ravens in seeking land. He named the country Iceland because during his first winter his livestock perished, and when he climbed a mountain to oversee his prospects for settlement, what stretched before him were the frozen landscapes of Árnafjöður (Jones 1986:274). He returned to Norway disenchanted with the place, and only a decade later, in AD 874, according to Ari the Wise, Iceland's earliest historian, Iceland's founding father, Ingólfur Arnarson, sailed back to establish a permanent settlement (see Grønlie 2006).

Scandinavian Vikings had settled the Faroe Islands a few decades earlier, whereas Greenland was settled from Iceland more than a century later by the outlaw Erik the Red, who had been banned from Norway for manslaughter and from Iceland for three years for the same reason, prompting him to sail westward looking for greener pastures (Jones 1986:290). Following the route of an earlier sailor, Gunnbjörn Ulfsson, Erik reached the southwestern coast of Greenland in AD 982 and encountered uninhabited rich farmland, not unlike what he had left behind in western Iceland. He returned to Iceland in 986, after his three years of outlawry, and gathered 25 ships of settlers to sail back to Greenland. Of these 25 ships, only 14 arrived safely. They settled in what came to be known as the Eastern Settlement, with a population of 1,120–4,800, 12 parish churches, and a cathedral at Garðar, now called Igaliku (Jones 1986:292–293; Koch Madsen 2014:16). Iceland's population at the time of the settlement—also

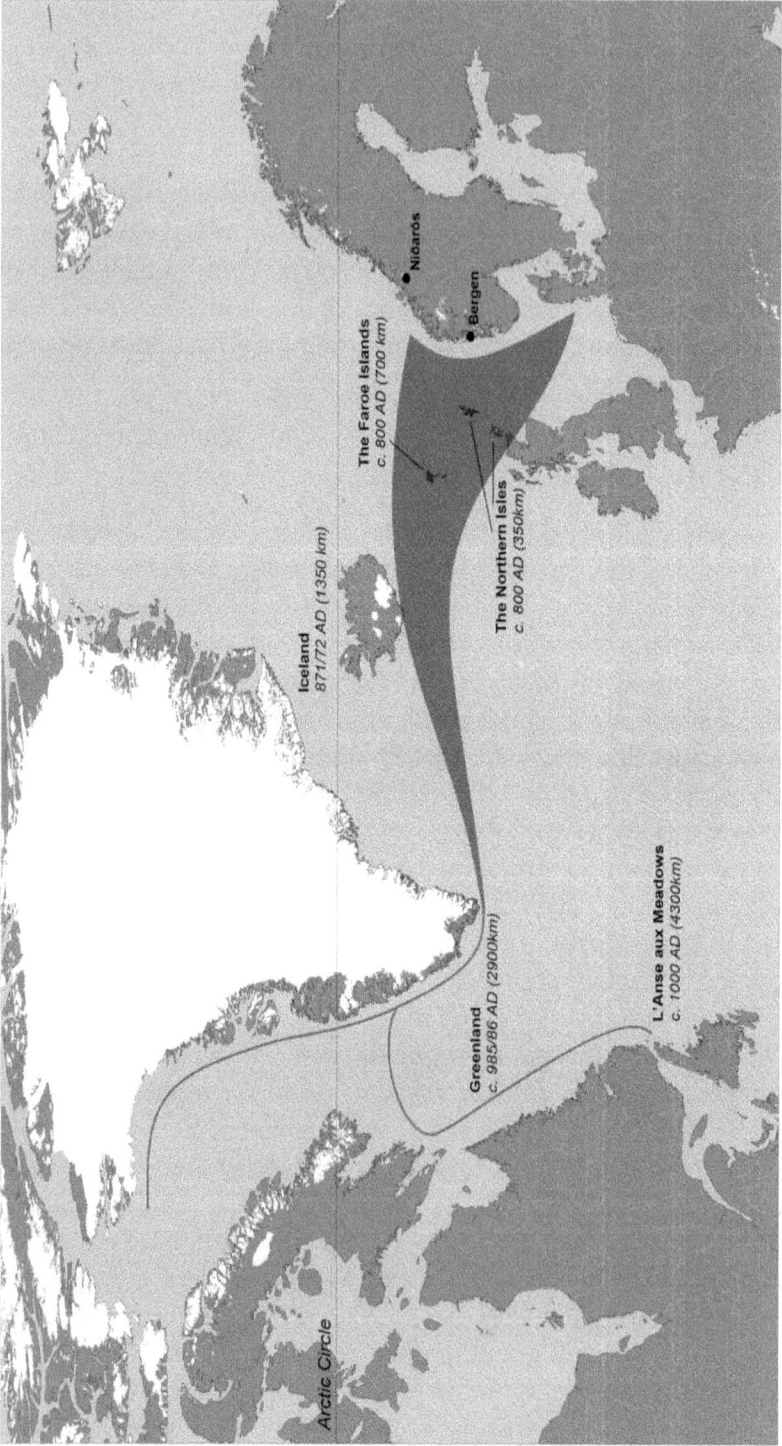

Figure 1.1. North Atlantic colonization routes taken by the Vikings in the ninth century. (Koch Madsen 2014:12.)

called the *landnám* period, the taking of land—was considerably larger, numbering between 40,000 and 70,000 (Koch Madsen 2014:16).

Certain parts of the British Isles were occupied by Norse settlers even earlier than the Faroe Islands, Iceland, or Greenland (circa AD 800). Ireland is considered the first area in the North Atlantic to have been colonized by the Norse, who founded the town of Dublin and exercised considerable control and power over local inhabitants (Ritchie 1993:11). Other Norse settlement areas in the British Isles included Orkney, Shetland, Caithness, the Hebrides, the Isle of Man, and much of northern England—from the Midlands to the Scottish marches—where the city of York became their regional center. From these areas, Norse settlers gleaned information on the North Atlantic isles farther west.

These Vikings who settled across the North Atlantic were not a cohesive invading army, nor were they culturally unified. They brought with them cultural practices and beliefs from Norway and the rest of mainland Scandinavia. Although their dominant cultural traditions were Scandinavian, from the ways they organized their economy to their animal husbandry practices and the legal systems that they established in their new colonies, many of these Scandinavians appear to have come from families who had already settled in the British Isles, where they had set down roots, married local women, and had many Irish or Hebridean slaves. Through the contacts these families had made and through the diverse traditions shared by their members, other cultural influences made their way to the more westerly North Atlantic settlements. Mitochondrial DNA studies on modern Icelanders, undertaken by Helgason and others (2001) as well as other researchers, have demonstrated a significant Celtic component among Iceland's female settlers. These different cultural influences are also visible in textiles and textile production in the western North Atlantic settlements. Two approaches to textile work, Norwegian and Insular, can be distinguished and are reviewed in detail in Chapter 2.

Women, Cloth, and Sagas: Text and Archaeology

The overall political and economic spheres of these North Atlantic Norse societies were dominated by men, yet textile production was a very gendered occupation, controlled by women, that intersected with all aspects of political, economic, and domestic life and gave rise to beliefs that connected textiles with women's lives, activities, and beliefs. Textiles wove their way into all aspects of human existence, from birth to death and, more importantly, in the determination of fate. Cloth and its production became symbolically gendered and associated with a women's world and with female power. Schneider and Weiner's (1989:21) characterization of associations between women and cloth rings true for the North Atlantic: "women not only make cloth but also preside over its allocation at major rituals of death and regeneration, marriage and the establishment of new families, investiture and the transmission of ancestral authority." Textiles had such varied utilitarian purposes as clothing, household accessories, sails for ships, and tents (Hayeur Smith 2014b:731). Their social roles changed over an 800-year period from being products of local household domestic weaving, frequently deposited in burial contexts, to elements of central importance within Iceland's economic system during the Middle Ages. Textiles were used as currency in a commodity-money system, legally regulated in medieval law codes, and based on legally negotiated exchange rates that established the value of different goods relative to other products (Hayeur Smith 2018). Textiles were used for paying taxes and tithes and for trade both local and overseas (see Chapter 3 and Hayeur Smith 2014b, 2018).

The Norse colonies in Iceland, Greenland, and the Faroe Islands were all rural societies without urban centers or industrial production. All textiles were produced on individual farms until the eighteenth century, when Danish colonial rule introduced industrialization and changed the nature of textile work. But this characterization of *where* women wove begs two essential questions: why did women weave, and why did men not?

For millennia, within the Norse world and well beyond it, women have woven textiles, made and repaired clothing, created the very items that have protected humans from the elements, and, through the products they made, actively taken part in visually crafting and projecting cultural identities and affiliations. This is particularly true in Europe and the Northern Hemisphere, including the areas of interest in the present study. But why is this the case? Not all cultures delegate textile production to women. In some societies (for example, in much of Africa), men are the weavers (Schneider and Weiner 1989:21), and in other cultures textile production has shifted over time from women's work to men's.

In Northern European Iron Age and early medieval societies, women sat together spinning and weaving for hours at a time, talking, singing, and co-ordinating their individual efforts to create cloth. Mythological sources and vignettes contained in the sagas suggest that their efforts and the work of producing cloth were viewed as somewhat spiritual activities, wrapped in mythological beliefs, that were either frowned upon or feared by men. Across Europe, the production of cloth was linked to female deities or other supernatural beings with whom women negotiated: from Athena and Arachne in ancient Greece to Rumpelstiltskin in Northern Europe (Ellis Davidson 1990; Norrman 2008; Schneider 1989).

Archaeological excavations have documented Viking Age women's burials equipped with implements associated with textile production and use, such as spindle whorls, wool combs, weaving swords, loom weights, needle cases and needles, distaffs, weaving tablets, and glass linen smoothers with whalebone plaques, possibly used as ironing boards. Literary sources, on the other hand, suggest that in the Scandinavian Viking Age powerful female deities oversaw textile work and that spinning itself may have been linked to the practice of *seiðr*—a form of ecstatic magic and divination connected with the goddess Freyja and practiced exclusively by women (Heide 2007; Price 2002). Some scholars have argued that the etymology of the word *seiðr* itself—meaning "cord," "snare," or "halter"—is compatible with *seiðr* as an ecstatic form of sorcery because in both cases there is a notion of sending forth: in the case of sorcery, the sorcerer's mind is sent to the spirit world, often in the shape of a thread or rope and regarded as something spun or the result of spinning (Heide 2007). Men never engaged in *seiðr*, fearing it would lead to allegations of homosexuality, and *seiðr* itself was linked to spinning, the production of thread, and therefore weaving, all distinctively female domestic chores (Heide 2007; Price 2002).

Norse mythology linked the concept of fate with spinning, a potent concept illustrated by the Norse myth that the three Nornir, elemental female beings, sat under the world tree Yggdrasil spinning the fates of gods and humans.[1] The Nornir, Urð, Verðandi, and Skuld, are generally interpreted as the present, past, and future and are credited with creating the destinies of humans before their births (Norrman 2008). These three Nornir were not the only ones, as Norse mythology describes additional good and bad Nornir. According to Snorri Sturlusson's *Edda*, bad lives were attributable to the evil Nornir, whereas good Nornir shaped the lives of the lucky. Wayland Barber (1995) suggests that the connections between thread, spinning, and fate, while not unique to the Norse world, stem from the action of women creating thread out of nowhere, just as babies are created from nowhere (Norrman 2008; Wayland Barber 1995). The connection between the creation of life and of thread is clear in English, and Norrman (2008) argues that even the term "lifespan" contains the word "spin," initially meaning to draw out, though no such equivalent was noted in Old Norse.

Connections between spinning and fate occur frequently in Northern European folklore. Heide (2007), for instance, described how the Sámi poem "The Son of the Sun" refers to a cord with three "wind-knots" containing the soul of an unborn child. A central theme of the poem involves untying the three wind-knots while at sea, resulting in the conception and birth of a baby.

The same connection is seen in an early Christian context, in the Book of James, which in describing the Annunciation depicts Mary spinning when the angel comes to her, implying that the making of thread was a symbol for the making of a child (Badalanova Geller 2006:223–234, in Bek-Pedersen 2009:180). A similar motif occurs in a Norse context; in *Orkneyinga Saga*, Earl Sigurðr of Orkney consults his mother about the outcome of an impending battle; she responds negatively, adding, "I would have kept you for a long time in my wool basket, if I knew that you would live forever, but it is fate which rules life and not where a man comes from; better to die with dignity than to live with shame" (Bek-Pedersen 2009:18). Keeping someone inside the "wool basket" suggests enduring life and protection from death and the basket as a symbolic womb with its unspun wool that has not yet been transformed into textile, symbolizing a person-to-be, or a person's fate (Bek-Pedersen 2009:179–180). This resonates with Terence Turner's (1993) labeling of textiles and dress as a "second skin," a social and cultural skin that we wear over our naked "biological bodies," where we can display and manipulate information about who we are and where we belong.

During the Viking Age, spinning was also deeply connected to witchcraft, and the idea that fate or the giving of life may come from a thread also implied that a life could be manipulated through spinning. An example from the sagas describes a woman who harms others through the act of spinning (and practicing sorcery). In the *Laxdaela Saga*, Bolli, who is married to Guðrún, returns after killing Kjártan (the man Guðrún truly loves, though he has married another woman), at which point Guðrún remarks that "morning tasks are often mixed: I have spun yarn for 12 ells of cloth and you have killed Kjártan" (Ellis Davidson 1990:101; Heide 2007; Magnusson and Pálsson 1969:176). While she did not kill her lover directly, many (Bek-Pedersen 2007, 2009; Ellis Davidson 1990; Heide 2007) have argued that Guðrún's spinning is similar to the spinning of the Nornir and that it was a magical act intended to influence the outcome of a fight between these two men.

Similar themes about the control of others' fates through textile work and the making of cloth come to the fore in the poem "Darraðarljóð" from *Njáls Saga*. In Caithness, Scotland, before the battle of Clontarf, Dörruðr, a young man, observes 12 female riders approaching a woman's hut and disappearing inside. He peers through the window and sees Valkyries weaving cloth on a warp-weighted loom made from the entrails of men fallen in battle (Figure 1.2).

This gruesome poem illustrates warrior women using their weapons and human body parts as components of the warp-weighted loom: the loom weights are human heads, the heddle rods their spears, the shuttle their arrows, and their swords the beaters. Some scholars feel that the Valkyries worked in a capacity similar to that of their sisters the Nornir in determining fate, since the Valkyries appeared on battlefields to collect the dead and convey them to Valhalla (Bek-

Pedersen 2007; Guðjonsson 1989). The poem is presented in the context of a dream foretelling the death of several men in an upcoming battle (Bek-Pedersen 2009; Norrman 2008). Here, in keeping with the spinning imagery, are depictions of weaving, textile work, and the weaving implements themselves linked to the body and body parts, to fate and the giving and taking of life. Each thread may symbolize the fate of a man about to die in battle, and interestingly, the heads suspended from loom weights are upside-down, like infants in the womb.

Toward the end of the poem, the cloth woven by the Valkyries is cut down and divided into 12 pieces, one for each to take with her. They leave the weaving hut the same way they arrived, after which dreadful things befall various Christian leaders and men across the North, not to mention the terrible outcome of the battle. The final verses seem to remind the reader of the strength of the old Norse religion, deep rooted, powerful, and capable through its magic of overcoming the

Figure 1.2. Rendition of the "Darraðarljóð". (Artwork by Greg Rebis, 2015.)

new Christian fate. The poem also suggests that powerful magic and the control of fate would be realized in these weaving huts through textile production.

The Archaeology

Archaeological evidence in both Scandinavia and Iceland has revealed the existence of such huts—generally semi-subterranean pit houses—with varying interpretations of their use and function. Some believe these huts were used for weaving, while others argue they were for private ritual and religious activity (Einarsson 2008; Milek 2012; Mortensen 1997; K. P. Smith, personal communication 2018). The literature on weaving huts and pit houses is vast. Milek (2012) discusses at length the uses and purposes of these huts in Iceland. While not all pit houses have evidence of textile production, the presence of textiles, spindle whorls, and loom weights in situ in the majority of these huts in Iceland and on the Scandinavian mainland indicates they were used for weaving and textile activities (Milek 2012; Mortensen 1997), which ties in with the imagery and actions depicted in the "Darraðarljóð".

The pit houses examined had an internal dimension of 5–16 m², suitable for a small number of people, and were generally rectangular or ovoid in shape, with wooden walls (a unique feature in Iceland, where wood is rare and the preferred construction material is turf). The absence of clear entranceways in most of these structures suggests they may have been entered through doors cut in the roofs or in the upper walls of their aboveground superstructures (Mortensen 1997:187; K. P. Smith, personal communication 2018). Mortensen (1997:187) described a Norwegian pit house with a maximum depth of 0.5 m, and Milek (2012:102) identified possible furnishings in 62% of Icelandic examples. She identified raised platforms at a maximum height of 0.3 m at Grelutóttir I, Stóraborg, Hvítárholt V and VII, Sveigakot MT2 and T1, and Vatnsfjörður 10. The interiors were equipped with small corner or side ovens, using a building technique that is not customary in longhouses. Others in Scandinavia contained four hearths, with one located in the southwest corner of the pit and made of three standing slabs (Mortensen 1997). Milek (2012) argues that this type of side oven was suitable for keeping houses warm, while reducing the risk of sparks that could have inflicted serious damage on cloth being woven.

The largest category of artifacts in Icelandic pit houses relates to textile work: loom weights were found in 76% of the pit houses and spindle whorls in 43% (Milek 2012). Additionally, these pit houses contained what Milek (2012:105) called "pinholes," or perforations in the floors, 1–3 cm in diameter and filled with charcoal-rich floor sediment. They are present in 72% of the floors of excavated

Icelandic pit houses and have been tentatively associated with iron distaffs, particularly the symbolic ones frequently found in burial contexts and associated with spinning and magical practices involved in *seiðr* (Milek 2012; Price 2011). All these elements of Icelandic pit houses point toward long-standing cultural traditions from mainland Scandinavia, and toward the possible associations described above relating to textile work, magic, and *seiðr*.

The Icelandic saga literature is also informative about the function and use of the houses called *dyngja*. Bek-Pedersen (2009) and Milek (2012) have argued that because the warp-weighted loom requires a more permanent installation, all weaving took place inside the *dyngja* where these looms were set up, and that this was a strictly female space from which men were excluded. Two scenes, one from *Njáls Saga* and the other from *Gisla Saga Súrssonar*, recount two incidents where men overhear conversations inside a *dyngja*, and in both cases, the men cannot help acting upon the information overheard, resulting in fatal consequences and suggesting that otherworldly happenings occur in the *dyngja* (Bek-Pedersen 2009). Otherworldly events also occur in the poem "Darraðarljóð", and in a passage from *Jómsvíkinga Saga*, a woman called Ingibjörg dreams that while she is weaving linen inside the *dyngja*, a loom weight falls off the loom and turns out to be a man's head.

Bek-Pedersen (2009) argues that these various examples indicate the connection of activities inside the *dyngja* to death and fate and point to it as a place where decisions about life and death are made. By analogy, the production of textiles is almost akin to the making of a human being, with the *dyngja* constituting a type of womb-like space. This womb-like element is further supported by the lack of a clear doorway, making it completely enclosed.

As mentioned above, spindle whorls are frequently found inside the *dyngja*, but they are more commonly recovered from burials. The most common items placed in women's burials from Viking Age Iceland are shears and spindle whorls (Janis Mitchell, personal communication 2018). This is true across Scandinavia as well: textile tools occur predominantly in female burials, attesting to the gendered nature of this activity (Hedenstierna-Jonson and Kjellström 2014:187). Some spindle whorls in Iceland bear runic inscriptions that either point directly to magical practice or are marks of ownership such as one from Stóraborg, "Anna owns me" (Mjöll Snæsdóttir, personal communication 2018), or "Þórunn owns me" from Alþingisreitur in Reykjavik (Garðarsdottir 2010). Many inscriptions, however, are more cryptic, with a sequence of repeated runes suggesting magico-religious formulas (Flowers 2010). A spindle whorl from the site of Urriðakót, a shieling (or women's summer farm) in western Iceland, bore a runic inscription dated to the twelfth century; however, because the spindle whorl was badly worn and the runes quite faded, it remains unclear whether the spindle bore the owner's name or the runic alphabet as a magical formula (Traustadóttir 2015:322). Overall, artifacts decorated with runes are uncommon in Iceland, yet among these are 11 spindle whorls dating from the eleventh to fourteenth centuries. From Stóramörk in Rangárvallasýsla, a spindle whorl was found with the inscription *mariafuþork-hniastbmly*. As mentioned above, the use of the runic alphabet (*fuþorkhniastbmly*) was thought in itself to serve as a magical formula (Flowers 2010).

Weaving implements with runic magical formulas are more common in Scandinavia, though a whalebone weaving sword from Kornsá in Vestur-Húna-vatnssýsla, Iceland, does have an X rune very faintly carved on its blade (see Eldjárn and Friðriksson 2000:400). From Lund, Sweden, comes an example of a more deliberate runic formula, specifically a curse, carved on a bone weaving tablet: "Ingmar, Sigvor's son (or Sigvor's Ingmar), shall have my weeping (or my misfortune), aallaati" (Moltke 1985:358). This straightforward example of a curse is aided by the incomprehensible string of runes at the end, *aallaati* (Moltke 1985). These particular weaving items with carved magical runic formulas mirror some of the stories, myths, and beliefs discussed above.

By the twelfth century, the weaving huts in Iceland were abandoned, though some of the tools retained their magical properties (Milek 2012:120). According to Milek, the weaving space was moved into the central house, with little change in its overall layout. For Milek, this shift and the disuse of the pit houses reserved for textile work must represent some wider social and economic changes in Icelandic society, possibly the conversion to Christianity, as the *dyngja* encoded pre-Christian beliefs.[2] Milek also noted that several pit houses had been almost ritually sealed or transformed into middens and rubbish dumps. The "moving" of textile production into a central space in the main dwelling may also correlate with an increase in textiles used as currency in medieval Iceland (on currency, see Chapter 3 and Hayeur Smith 2014b, 2015a, 2018). Perhaps because textiles had become economically viable, men saw this as a way to oversee production and the creation of wealth. While this may have been the intent, men avoided textile work until the eighteenth century, when the Danish colonial authorities established the first weaving workshops run by men, in Reykjavik (Hayeur Smith 2015a, 2018; Róbertsdóttir 2008).

Men, Women, and the Fear of Cloth

Gender studies acknowledge that gender entails not only the social and cultural aspects of sex but also the male versus female dichotomy (Hays-Gilpin and Whitley 1998; Mygland 2015). The traditional roles of Viking Age women have been touched upon by many scholars (Gräslund 2001, 2003; Gräslund and Quast 2011; Hedenstierna-Jonson and Kjellström 2014; Jesch 2005; Jochens 1995; Sawyer 1991, 1992, 2004). Viking Age Scandinavian societies were male centered; women were not considered equals and were not granted the same rights, though they had more rights than their European contemporaries (Hayeur Smith 2004; Jochens 1995; Norrman 2008). However, scholars consider the more extensive rights of women in Scandinavia to constitute a unique situation in which women did enjoy greater power, possibly because men's extensive traveling forced women to assume more central roles as farmers and traders (Hedenstierna-Jonson and Kjellström 2014:184). Icelandic and North Atlantic society was nonetheless male-dominated and heavily centered around the family and extended, bilaterally reckoned family units in which individuals traced their kin groups and lineages back through both male and female ancestors (Boyer 1992:198; Miller 1996).

Historical research on women's contributions to the North Atlantic economy, especially textile production, suggests that women gained stronger roles in household and regional economic structures in the medieval period confirmed by research on textiles (Bek-Pedersen 2007, 2009, 2013; Cartwright 2015; Gelsinger 1981; Guðjónsson 1994, 1998a; Hayeur Smith 2012, 2014a, 2014b, 2015, 2018; Hoffman 1974; Øye 2016; Róbertsdóttir 2008; Þórláksson 1988, 1991, 1999). Some of these more powerful roles appear to have arisen not only from producing cloth that was vital to the medieval economy but from the very nature of textile work and the deeply held beliefs that cloth was intrinsically linked to concepts of life, death, birth, and fate and to men's seeming anxiety toward this highly gendered activity (Bek-Pedersen 2007, 2009, 2013; Hayeur Smith 2018; Heide 2007; Milek 2012; Norrman 2008).

Mythological and archaeological evidence supports these cultural beliefs vis-à-vis textiles, to the point that such beliefs extended to the physicality of the space where textile work took place: the *dyngja*, or weaving hut. During the medieval period, when weaving activities moved into the central longhouse, the continued lack of male involvement in textile production suggests that male avoidance and anxiety regarding textile work had not completely disappeared. Textile production was clearly something that women did and men did not, and perhaps no one could remember exactly why.

Fear of Textiles Was a Fear of Women

Goldwater (1998) argued that men's fear of women is ancient and stems from women's ability to bring new life. The male perception that women are able to control male sexuality, whether for procreation or other purposes, is at the root of this fear, and it is unconscious (Goldwater 1998:211, 216): "Men's other great fear is very ancient. But it continues to crop up whenever men think about women. . . . It is the fear of women as *witch*. What women lack in might, they sometimes make up for in magic." This second point is relevant to the Norse context under discussion here, as the fear of women and textile work was also linked to a fear of women's magic. The Norse worldview regarded the strange and inexplicable as magic, so that what transpired inside weaving huts became linked with the control of the supernatural (Jakobsson 2008).

Kimmel (2012:86) further elaborates that men in general not only learn to define themselves by reinforcing culturally accepted masculine social norms involving power and control but also learn to renounce the feminine, starting with the negation of their own mothers. Masculine identity is thus born in the renunciation of the feminine, not simply in the direct affirmation of the masculine.

But what did it mean to be male in the Viking Age, and what did men perceive as proper gender-specific traits to uphold? Which aspects of female identity were threatening to this male ideal, enough to keep them away from generating wealth (i.e., textiles) and participating directly in the control of the Icelandic economy during the Middle Ages?

Viking Age Male Ideals, Honor, and Homophobia

As mentioned, men were the dominant players in Norse society, and central to all life was the family unit. This family included not only blood relatives but also fictive kin resulting from fostering or blood-brotherhoods (Miller 1996:166). As a result, protecting and avenging members of the family unit were of primal importance, resulting in long-lasting feuds and fights (see Miller 1996). Behind the feuding and at the root of all social and cultural ideals was the issue of honor and of preserving, avenging, and saving one's honor. The honor of one's family was a central theme in the early Icelandic law codes (Byock 1982).

All other traits appear to have revolved around this central issue of honor and the desired masculine ideal to which men aspired. Many of these are expressed literally in the law codes such as Grágás and other medieval texts: for example, the right to carry weapons, dressing in proper male attire (involving the growing of beards), participation in political and legal life (attending the Althing), land ownership, property rights, and inheritance (Dennis et al. 1980, 2002). From these sources it is possible to deduce that most free men, or *bændur*, felt that knowledge of the law, defense, protection of one's family, land and livestock ownership, bravery and stoicism, poetic abilities, wit, knowledge, and potency and procreation (and particularly, having valiant sons) were are all key compo-

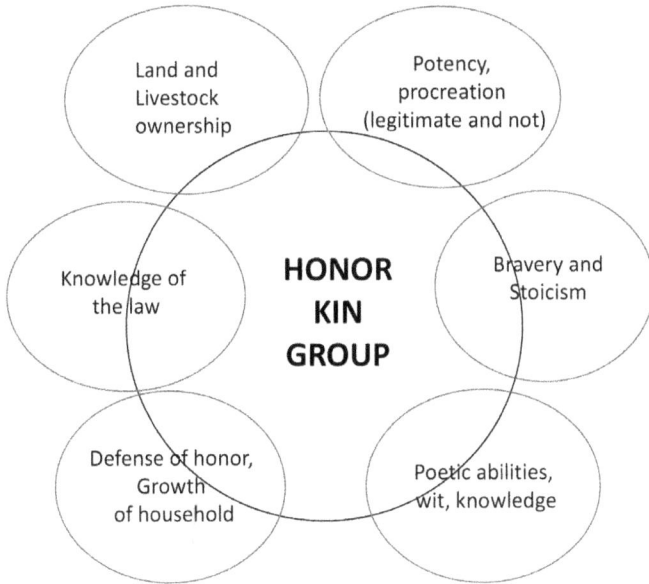

Figure 1.3. Concept of masculinity in the Viking Age.

nents of the male model, with honor at its center (see Figure 1.3). Women, by contrast, appear to have had another set of ideals, some of which were framed in opposition to those of men. Unlike men, women could not participate to the same degree in legal and political life, could rarely own land and livestock, and could only inherit from their deceased children, but they frequently instigated fights and feuds to assure that family honor was avenged. To this effect, it is worth pointing out a contradiction in Norse cultural perceptions of gender. Recent research from the site of Birka has demonstrated that the well-known "male" warrior grave of Bj. 581 actually contained a women based on recent aDNA research (Hedenstierna-Jonson 2015; Price et al. 2019), suggesting that the presence of female warriors and of women assuming public roles of men and masculinity was not unknown. It is possible that these females were not the norm and could have held both the role of actual warrior or war chief or that of a "spiritual warrior" on par with Valkyries and other mythical war-related beings. Further osteological analysis might determine if this woman bore skeletal traces of handling heavy weapons. The behavior of instigating fights, described as "goading," included harassing or nagging male kinsmen or performing witchcraft. All of these are common themes in the saga literature (Miller 1983:181). From *Njáls Saga*, Hildigunn and Flosi provide an example of this type of female goading and of women seeking revenge for a killing to restore family honor:

She [Hildigunn] took out the cloak which Flosi had given Höskuld and which he was wearing when he had been killed. She had preserved all his blood in it. She returned to the hall with the cloak and quietly went up to Flosi. Flosi had eaten and the food had been cleared from the table. Hildigunn flung it over Flosi and the blood clots showered all over him. Then she said: "You gave this cloak to Höskuld, Flosi, and now I am giving it back to you. He was killed in it. I call God and all good men to witness that I charge you by all the powers of your Christ and your manhood and bravery to avenge the wounds he had on his body when he was killed or else be called a nithing, and contemptible creature, by all men." (*Njáls Saga* in Miller 1983:181)

Not only does this passage illustrate the importance of family honor; it also demonstrates the intimate relationships between women and textiles, as well as the power that textiles had as a symbol of human skin, in this example symbolizing the body and essence of the deceased person and his identity. It also reveals how women were perceived as having control over the destiny and fate of other humans, and the types of allegations that were incompatible with perceived male ideals of the time. Of particular importance is Hildigunn's threat that Flosi will be killed or called a *nithing* if Höskuld is not avenged.

The term *nithing* (Old Norse *niðingr*) is cognate with *nið*. The concept of *nið*, as a form of curse, is specific to the male Norse conceptual universe as it engages the antithesis of the masculine ideal described above. By accusing Flosi of being a *nithing*, Hildigunn is questioning his masculinity; to be cursed with a *nið* was in essence to be accused of homosexuality and of being unmanly (Meulengracht Sørensen 1983:17). Being accused of homosexuality was punishable by outlawry in the Icelandic and Norwegian law codes. According to Price (2002:211), *nið* could be communicated in more than one way, either verbally, as described above, or with a *tréníð*, that is, a wooden *nið*, when runes were carved in a wooden sculpture depicting men engaged in sexual acts. Occasionally in the saga literature one will find descriptions of *nið* poles, where the head of a mare was placed on top of a pole and pointed in the direction of the accused. To accuse a man of *niðingr* was the most powerful insult in Viking Age warrior ideology (Price 2002:212), and linked to it was the concept of *ergi*, more closely connected with witchcraft.

The noun *ergi* is the basis for the adjective *argar* and the metathesis *regi/ragr* (Meulengracht Sørensen 1983:18). *Ergi* is thought to have had many meanings in thirteenth- and fourteenth-century Iceland and was rarely used in reference to women, except to describe uninhibited lust and sexuality. It was also used to refer to two men engaging in sexual relations with one other, which was thought to detract from their "manhood," as well as to describe something that would lead men to become effeminate, "something that men cannot do without losing manliness." Additionally, *ergi* was used to describe a lack of courage, again believed to be the result of unmanliness, since cowardly men were thought to have switched genders. Lastly, it was used to describe something that was done or that occurred during the performance of magic (Jakobsson 2008:55). According to Meulengracht Sørensen (1983:19), the term relates more specifically to "perversity in sexual matters," along with being "versed in witchcraft." The practice of witchcraft and sorcery included, according to Douglas (1966), sexual activities and taboo breaking and, of course, men appearing as women and vice versa: basically the disruption of social norms and desired social behaviors. In *Heimskringla* and *Ynglinga Saga*, when Óðinn practices sorcery he breaks all rules in ways that only a god could because "when sorcery takes place it is accompanied by so much *ergi* that men could not be associated with it without disgrace and this is why this pertains to the goddesses" (Meulengracht Sørensen 1983:19). Witchcraft and magic, particularly the kinds associated with textile work and spinning, such as *seiðr*, contained a lot of *ergi* and belonged to the goddess Freyja (Price 2002:108), though Óðinn performed female witchcraft as well. Freyja was also the goddess associated with textile work and carried the epithet *hörn*, meaning "flax." It is also thought that "Friday" is named after her, as it was the day when flax was sown (Ellis Davidson 1990; Näström 2003). *Seiðr* is not compatible with manliness, yet Óðinn, while involved with *seiðr*, does not lose his manliness in the process because he is a god, though many see him as androgynous (Solli 2002). Further, the Norse religion is often perceived by scholars as a shamanistic religion. I would argue that in shamanistic religions, gender is frequently fluid, particularly during shamanistic trance.

Associations between *ergi*, *seiðr*, witchcraft, and homosexuality are present in *Egils Saga* and *Gunnars Saga Keldugnúpsfífls*. *Seiðr* was said to make a victim fidget. Almqvist (2000:258, in Heide 2007) interpreted this as making "their bottoms itch," as *seiðr* attacking the backside, in keeping with the homosexual associations of *ergi* and with potential penetration by another man. In *Þorleifs Saga Þáttr Jarlsskálds*, verbal *nið* makes the earl's bottom itch so much that he has two men pull a coarse woolen cloth, with three knots, between his buttocks, again linking textiles and textile production with witchcraft and allegations of unmanliness (Heide 2007).

This homophobia or fear of perceived sexual deviance in Norse society was at odds with ideals of manhood. Successful manhood was a requisite proof of social success. To achieve it, men defined themselves in contradiction to the other and by the exclusion of the other, in this case women and forms of women's work that had clearly become demonized or feared because of their *ergi* (Kimmel 2012). Homophobia, according to Kimmel (2012:87), comes from the scrutiny of other men and is more than the fear of being perceived as gay; rather, it is a matter of men's watching and ranking each other for esteem in the realm of manhood. Applied to the Norse context, the written sources do suggest that men feared being perceived as inadequate, unmanly, or humiliated by other men. Yet according to Mary Douglas (1966:96), danger also lies in transitional states because transition is neither one state nor the next and is undefinable. Underlying the anxiety of appearing "unmanly," not only is a man perceived as inadequate but he is put into a transitional state, a dangerous position at variance with and marginal to accepted norms of manliness. Additionally, Douglas (1966:99) suggests that when people hold ambiguous roles, they become dangerous and are associated with uncontrolled, dangerous, disapproved powers such as witchcraft.

To recapitulate what has been described so far on the nature of textile work and the seeming fear of it by male society, men feared textile work not because of the textiles themselves but for what they symbolized: a women's world, the control of fate through textile production—and by analogy the female goddesses associated with women's magic, *seiðr*, which in turn is filled with *ergi*, unmanliness, and deviant sexuality where men are not men but potentially women—and the blurring of socially accepted gender boundaries. Moreover, the concept of *ergi* reflects a strong homophobic tendency in Norse society, where the fear of homosexuality is equated with a fear of being judged by other men and of being humiliated, losing the honor of oneself and one's family.

Women may have played on these fears to achieve some level of control and power. When the sagas describe women harassing and nagging men to avenge family honor, they become active participants in the propagation of this fear, as in the case of Hildigunn playing on Flosi's fear of unmanliness in the eyes of other men. In essence, women were helping to solidify these beliefs by acting out and playing on men's fears. They may have strengthened the beliefs surrounding and stressed the fear of textile work, as Hildigunn did by throwing a blood-soaked garment possessing the essence and honor of a dead man. Through this action, Hildigunn probably also conveyed the messages that she was the keeper of the cloth, that she controlled the making of cloth, and by the same token was versed in witchcraft, manipulating life, birth, death, and fate. Through her symbolic actions she controlled the outcome and the fate of these men, not unlike the Valkyries weaving cloth inside the weaving hut before battle.

The fear of textile production, of the space where textiles were made, and the avoidance of textile production by men in general during the Viking Age suggest that this was an activity where men were uninvited, a place where women could be together, free from spousal obligations. In the medieval period, when weaving was moved into the *stófa* of the *skáli* (the central longhouse), they kept these fears alive in a newly Christianized society that had stripped them further of their rights. The propagation of fear around a product that was so important to the Icelandic economy may have provided women with a sense of power and an active role in the economy of their society.

Weaving textiles has been compared to composing text, an art form used by women to express themselves in societies where their voices remained otherwise unheard (Berlo 1992; Norrman 2008). Men spoke while women wove, and in Iceland, great emphasis and prestige were placed on men's ability to perform verbally through poetry and oratory. To quote Berlo (1992:116), "men's arts are oral while women's are literally material; men speak, women make cloth." In medieval Iceland, women, through *vaðmál*, wove the verbal messages that men and society required of them, but at the same time women may have been active participants in the propagation of a mythology about gender and weaving, keeping it secret and shrouded in fear to provide themselves with one mode of expression and power that was uniquely their own. Cloth currency or *vaðmál* was not the only type of cloth they created; in their finer decorative textiles and tapestries, which are unfortunately rarely preserved, some of this unique power of expression may have been more apparent.

At the same time, the importance of *vaðmál* may have profited from this secrecy and this fear, as we shall see in subsequent chapters. Spinning and textile work were so deeply entrenched within women's lore that even beyond the Viking and early medieval periods, men dared not engage in it for fear of being accused of practicing *seiðr* and of possessing *ergi* (Bek-Pedersen 2009:174; Price 2002). These mythological associations may have valorized cloth currency further, filling it with supernatural power. As a result, men may have been quite satisfied and convinced to leave this part of textile production to women, since cloth as material culture had become imbued with female power, symbolizing the concepts of fate, birth, and female reproductive power that in turn conferred additional value upon the cloth itself. By the same token, women who seemed so complacent working alongside men in this economic system may have maintained age-old beliefs that provided them with a voice and power in what was a strongly patriarchal society that did not consider women as equals.

2

Weaving in the Viking Age

Iceland and the North Atlantic Expansion

Textiles are often overlooked as a category of artifacts, in part because they do not preserve as well as other finds or because they appear uninteresting, lacking in visual appeal. Further, their study has more often than not proceeded along highly technical lines, without considering the society that produced them, and has been largely inaccessible or uninviting to archaeologists unacquainted with the technical details of weaving, wool, or textile production. Some studies have attempted to bridge the gap between technical and social analyses, but mostly in anthropology (Eicher 2000, 2001; Eicher and Roach-Higgins 1992; Moore et al. 1966; Niessen and Eicher 1998; Roach-Higgins and Eicher 1992; Schneider 1989; Schneider and Weiner 1989; Tranberg Hansen 2004).

Textiles from the North Atlantic and Scandinavia have been the topic of numerous scholarly works, including Andersson Strand (2003, 2007, 2011), Bender Jørgensen (1986, 1992), Christensen and Nockert (2006), Hägg (1974, 1984a, 1984b, 1986, 1991), Hagen (1994), Kjellberg (1979), Kjellberg and Hoffman (1991), Vedeler (2004, 2007, 2010, 2014), and many more in regard to Scandinavia. Icelandic textiles have been addressed by Damsholt (1984), Guðjonsson (1962, 1965, 1970, 1973, 1980, 1989, 1990, 1992, 1994, 1998), and more recently, Hayeur Smith (2012, 2013, 2014a, 2014b, 2015a, 2018) and Róbertsdóttir (2008), whereas Greenlandic textiles have been discussed by Walton Rogers (1998, 2012), Nørlund (1925, 2017), Østergård (1989, 2004, 2005), and more recently, Hayeur Smith (2014a) and Hayeur Smith and others (2016).

As explained in the Introduction, I have tried to center my approach on the social use of textiles, treating them like any other artifact category as a manifestation of the societies that created them and, in the case of the North Atlantic, as a way to access half of the population, namely women. By linking textiles to sites, women to textiles, and textiles to both environmental and social issues, I have attempted to reposition women within our understanding of the North Atlantic culture's social, ecological, and economic realms and to reaffirm the role of material culture in understanding these past societies.

One Thousand Years of Cloth

In the North Atlantic, the remains of textiles vary in number from region to region; in Iceland, their numbers surpass those of any other collections in the North Atlantic: 8,000–10,000 fragments of cloth from the settlement or *land-nám* (settlement) period to the nineteenth century.[1] This is largely attributable to preservation issues, as woolen textiles (animal protein), which make up 90% of the corpus, tend to favor acidic environments, while cellulose-based fibers prefer alkaline soils. As a result, linens and silks are poorly represented.

Textiles in Iceland are frequently recovered in midden contexts that render soil acidic and are found sandwiched between layers of turf. Greenland's textile collections are less abundant than Iceland's (866–1,000± fragments), and there is nothing from the Viking Age, as the colony was founded after the settlement period in Iceland. The Faroe Islands have far fewer textiles (142± fragments), with most from the early modern period and very few from the Viking Age. Scotland is a bit more difficult to assess: from the Viking Age, there are, according to Gabra-Sanders (1998), 130 burials containing 274 fragments, most of which are mineralized. For later periods, the material becomes difficult to distinguish from local Scottish medieval or early modern textiles, as many of the Norse settlement areas no longer defined themselves as Norse—with the exceptions of Orkney and Shetland—and had amalgamated into mainstream Scottish society.

Viking Age textiles across the North Atlantic are far less numerous than later material and are for the most part recovered in burials, not in middens. As a result, preservation is less than adequate because the textiles are exposed to erosion. Many of the textiles subjected to analysis are no longer organic remains but have become mineralized with other objects.[2]

In Iceland, due to the elevated numbers of textiles over such a long time span, they can be divided into temporal categories with specific physical characteristics. Some of these characteristics do not apply to other regions of the North Atlantic such as Greenland and will be discussed in subsequent chapters, as the dynamics of the Greenlandic settlement are quite distinct. If traditional dating were not available, the categorization of Icelandic textiles could almost be used as a relative dating method. The table presented here provides some basic guidelines for dating textiles in Iceland, based on physical characteristics of the cloth.

Table 2.1. Chronology of weaving over a 1,000-year period

Period AD	Find context	Weave type	Spin direction	Presence of visible dyes or exotic fibers (silk, linens, metals)	Surface treatment	Combing of fibers separating *tóg* from *þell*
874–1050	Burial Farm (rare)	Diverse, 2/2 twills, plain, panama, patterned twills, tablet weaving, *nahlbindung*	Z/Z, some Z/S*	Yes, all of the above	No	Yes
1100–1500	Middens	2/2 twill, plain weave, other weaves are rare	Z/S—few Z2S in warps in 1400s—S/S, Z/Z suggest imports	Rare but does occur	No, except imports that are generally S/S or Z/Z-spun. By 1400 some fulling is observed on homespun cloth.	Yes on homespun, early on, but by 1400 this occurs less often.
1500–1700	Middens	2/2 twills; increase in imports, introduction of knitting in Iceland	Z2S in the warp of homespun on most sites	Yes, mostly on imports	Yes	Not on homespun
1700–1800	Middens and farms	2/2 twills Decrease in plain weave	Z2S in the warp and sometimes weft of most homespun	Yes on imports and industrial production from Reykjavik's wool workshops	Yes	Not on homespun

Notes: Based on the analysis of archaeological textiles from these projects.
    For details about Z- and S-spinning, see pages 37–38.

In Iceland the most elaborate textiles date to the Viking Age, with more variety in weave types, colors, and the incorporation of exotic fibers such as silk (though none have been found in Iceland yet) and metal. This very much mirrors Scandinavian textiles of the same period. They tend to be spun Z/Z and are found in burial settings.[3] By the end of the Viking Age and the emergence of the early Middle Ages, textiles become less conspicuous and more restrained, with fewer weave types and an overall tendency toward standardization, which is reflective of the role of textiles in the Icelandic economy at that time (see Chapter 3). Textiles from roughly AD 1100 become a standardized form of currency and are ubiquitous across the island, on all farms. This economic use of cloth is not as obvious in other North Atlantic colonies, except perhaps for Shetland, where documentary records hint at the economic use of cloth (Smith 2013), in Iceland this may have contributed to the large numbers of textile finds on Icelandic sites. Cloth currency appears to persevere until the sixteenth century, when the internal structure of homespun textiles changed from Z/S-spun yarns to incorporate plied-warp yarn (Z2S)/S. This is followed by the introduction of knitted products and an increasing number of imported textiles making their way onto the island. The imports in general are easily distinguished from Icelandic homespun because they are spun differently and often exhibit more elaborate finishes and dyes. The number of textile imports increases steadily into the seventeenth century and decreases again in the mid-eighteenth century, when industrialized workshops are established in Reykjavik under Danish colonial authority (Róbertsdóttir 2008). The main points of this thumbnail sketch of Icelandic textiles over 1,000 years are discussed in greater depth in Chapters 3, 6, and 7.

The variety of sheep's wool used in textile production constitutes an important aspect of all North Atlantic woolen items. As discussed in the Introduction, the North Atlantic sheep is called the Northern Short-Tail (Østergård 2005:81; Ryder 1982:224; Walton Rogers 1998, 2001) and is characterized by its dual coat. To reiterate, in Iceland the outer coat is called the *tóg* and the fibers are coarse and possess internal medullas, while the inner, softer coat is called the *þel* and has the appearance of soft merino wool with an absence of medullas (Figure 2.1).

Figure 2.1. Note the presence of a medulla or channel on the larger fibers (*tóg*). Scanning electron microscopy. (Photo by M. Ordoñez.)

During the Viking Age and much of the medieval period, these two fibers were combed and separated and used for different purposes. This feature is unique to the Norse textile tradition and is first noted in Viking Age Norway, according to Bender Jørgensen (1986, 1992), and may have been adapted to the structure of the warp-weighted loom and the need for strong and coarse fibers able to withstand the tension created from the loom weights suspended on the warp yarns. The inner, softer coat was used for weft yarns and, due to its softness, naturally felted and created a barrier to the cold.

Viking Age Textiles: Iceland

A look at Viking Age burial practices reveals that before AD 1000, when Iceland became Christian, the inclusion of grave goods was an important aspect of pre-Christian burial ritual, as was a belief in the afterlife. Because death involved the passage of the deceased person's spirit into the otherworld, the deceased were often accompanied on their voyage by various implements placed in the grave. Men were frequently buried with weaponry, jewelry, horses, and dogs; women with textile production implements, cooking utensils, jewelry, and animals. With a significant number of metal artifacts, mineralized textiles occur quite frequently and are usually found on swords, brooches, knives, axes, and other objects placed in close proximity to the body and the person's clothing. These mineralized textiles (which in some cases, when completely transformed into metal, are referred to as pseudomorphs) provide information that would otherwise be lost.

The textile corpus for Viking Age Iceland is smaller than from later periods. The total number of fragments from the Viking Age amounts to 123; most of these are from burials and include mineralized, pseudomorphic, and non-mineralized textiles. Once again, as with all these collections, these numbers are subject to change with the ongoing discovery of new finds.

Despite their relative paucity, Viking textiles are quite diverse, with plain weaves, panama weaves, simple and patterned twills, tablet weaves, and pile weaves all represented, along with evidence for colorful patterning, dyeing, or decorative additions. Actual (non-mineralized) textiles account for 59 objects, 23 of which tested positive for indigotin, implying they were dyed blue, with the majority of these from female burials. This use of the color blue is mirrored in Scandinavia, and Icelandic sagas suggest that blue was associated with death (Walton 1988:19; Wolf 2007:71).

Thread counts reflect how finely or coarsely a textile is woven and are useful archaeologically for tracking changes in textile production strategies, as-

Table 2.2. Approximate number of Viking textiles from Iceland

Site Name	Site Type	County and Region	Periods	Number
Alþingisreitur	Harbor site	Reykjavik (SW)	Late Viking–1600	161 (1 Viking Age)
Bessastaðir	Elite residence	Gullbringusýsla (SW)	Viking Age–1900	102 (1 Viking Age)
Þórisá, Eyrartigur	Burial	Múlasýsla (S)	Viking Age	17
Ketilsstaðir	Burial	Múlasýsla (N)	Viking Age	16
Reykjasel	Burial	Múlasýsla (N)	Viking Age	12
Hofstadir	Farm site	Mývatnssveit (N)	Viking Age and 18th century	17
Kaldarhöfði	Burial	Árnessýsla (S)	Viking Age	9
Granagil	Burial	Skaftafellssýsla (W)	Viking Age	8
Dalvík Brimnes	Burial	Eyjafjarðarsýsla (N)	Viking Age	8
Vestdalur	Burial	Seyðisfjörður	Viking Age	5
Daðastaðir	Burial	Þingeyjarsýsla (N)	Viking Age	3
Syðri Hofdalir	Burial	Skagafjarðarsýsla (N)	Viking Age	2
Silastaðir	Burial	Eyjafjarðarsýsla (N)	Viking Age	2
Selfos	Burial	Árnessýsla (S)	Viking Age	2
Hrísar	Burial	Eyjafjarðarsýsla (N)	Viking Age	2
Gamla Berjanes	Burial	Rangárvallasýsla (S)	Viking Age	2
Snæhvammur	Burial	Múlasýsla (N)	Viking Age	1
Berufjörður	Burial	Barðastrandarsýsla (NW)	Viking Age	1
Austarihóll	Burial	Skagafjarðarsýsla (N)	Viking Age	1
Glumbær	Burial	Þingeyjarsýsla (S)	Viking Age	1
Heynes	Farm site	Borgarfjarðarsýsla (W)	Viking Age	1
Kalastaðir	Burial	Borgarfjarðarsýsla (W)	Viking Age	1
Skógar í Flokadal	Burial	Borgarfjarðarsýsla (W)	Viking Age	1
Litlu Nupar	Burial	Þingeyjarsýsla (S)	Viking Age	1
Hrisheimar	Burial	Mývatnssveit (N)	Viking Age	1
Hábaer	Burial	Rangárvallasýsla (S)	Viking Age	1
Dysnes	Burial		Viking Age	2
Landssimareitur	Unknown		Viking Age	4

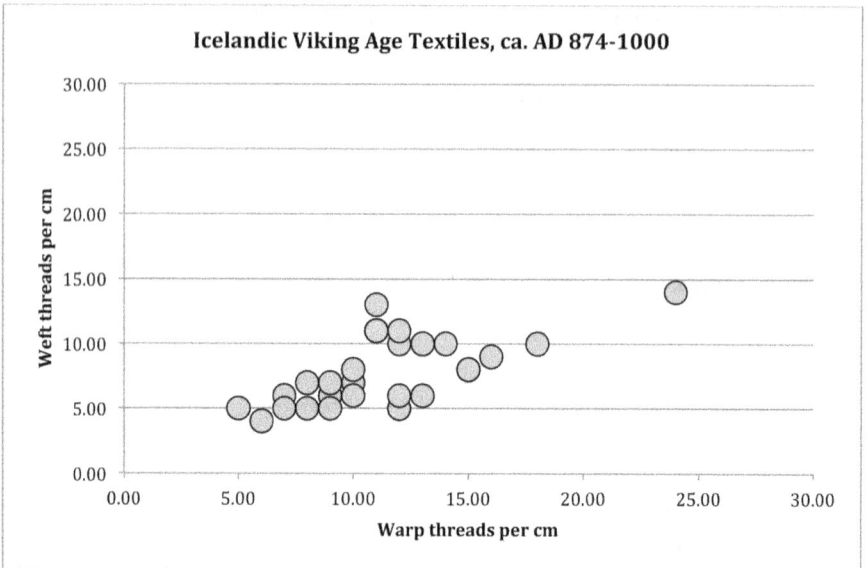

Figure 2.2. Thread counts for Viking Age textiles from Iceland. (Courtesy Oxford University Press.)

semblage variability, cloth standardization, industrialization, and more (Hayeur Smith 2012, 2014b, 2018); this is particularly true in Iceland, where the abundance of cloth allows for quantitative analysis and the mapping of its production over time.[4] Viking thread counts suggest that warp threads range over a broad span of 4–25 per centimeter, while weft thread counts range from 4–15 per centimeter (Figure 2.2). The presence of multiple, loose clusters within this distribution, as well as the breadth of the distribution itself, suggests that a wide range of cloth types, differing in quality, coarseness, and probably use, was produced at the household level to meet farms' needs for clothing, storage and transport media, and so on.

An interesting and defining characteristic of Viking Age textiles in Norway and in the Viking Age settlements of the North Atlantic is the spin direction. Some scholars, such as Minar (2001), view spin direction as a marker of cultural affiliation rather than the result of some technological necessity. Minar conducted a large-scale study (including spin experimentation with modern spinners) on the prehistoric cord-marked pottery of North Central Florida, where spin direction appeared to remain constant over broad geographic regions, as did decisions to use counterclockwise spun or clockwise spun yarns for warp or weft. She concluded that spin patterns and the distribution of final twist direction had more to do with the learning process in communities of practice over

Figure 2.3. S or Z twist.

time and space than anything else (Minar 2001:386). This is a somewhat novel idea in textile research, and many textile analysts disagree, arguing that the reason for consistency in spin is technological, that certain fibers "work better" when spun in one direction over the other, or that certain tools "just produce this type of spin," or that handedness had something to do with final spin direction. Minar's experiments, using a group of modern spinners, found that fiber type and handedness had no impact on determining final twist direction, though most of her spinners did customarily spin in one direction. When asked why, they replied that it was the "traditional" way to spin, and the only reason to spin in the opposite direction might be to obtain some desired effect (Minar 2001:388–389). In some instances, they felt a reluctance to spin in the opposite direction because of beliefs regarding "widdershins," or counterclockwise direction, which was thought to be related to witchcraft.

Therefore, the decision to spin yarn either clockwise (Z-spun) or counterclockwise (S-spun) is technologically neutral: either direction will produce usable yarn. The geographic consistencies noted above, which are also prevalent in other parts of the world, such as Northern Europe, suggest that such choices and decisions are elements of daily production passed down from experienced to inexperienced makers of cloth as part of their education (Minar 2001:384). As a result, spin direction and the combinations in which differently spun threads are used are nonrandom, culturally informative attributes of textile assemblages. Conversely, major changes in regional patterns of spinning and weaving are also socially informative acts.

From the late ninth to early eleventh centuries, Icelandic Viking Age cloth was largely Z/Z-spun, using single yarns, but with occasional pieces of cloth spun Z/S. Z/Z-spun cloth also appears to have been the norm in Scandinavia from AD 200 onward, where the shift to Z/Z spinning in Roman Iron Age Scandinavia has been linked to the adoption of the warp-weighted loom along with the weaving of 2/2 twills (Bender Jørgensen 1992:126).

By the Viking Age, Z/S-spun fibers are noted at some Scandinavian sites, though Norwegian and Gotlandic traditions remained more conservative, with a persistent use of older spinning methods and the continued production of Z/Z-spun twills (Bender Jørgensen 1992:39, 2007:137). In the Icelandic case, Z/Z textiles produced in ways similar to contemporary Norwegian textiles dominated at the time of settlement and are found in burials. Z/S-spun textiles are also minimally present but came to replace Z/Z textiles in the eleventh and twelfth centuries in Icelandic assemblages. By the twelfth century, twills and tabbies woven with Z/S-spun yarns became the norm, and this pattern persisted homogeneously and uninterrupted until the introduction of the flat loom (Figure 2.4).

As revealed in the analysis by Minar (2001), it is unlikely that the shift or desire to spin Z or S had much to do with technological concerns, since spin-

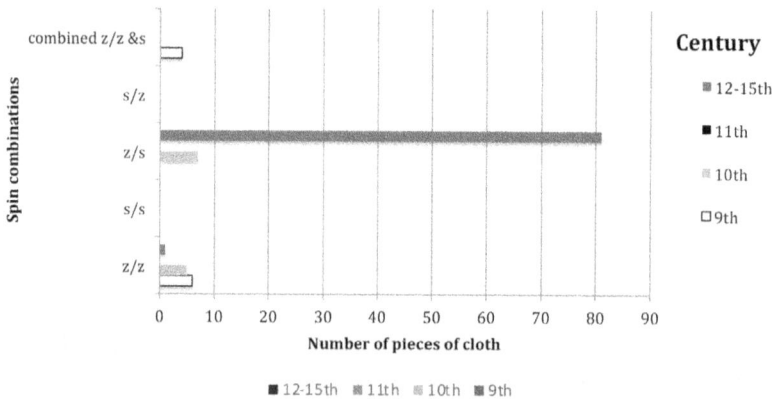

Centuries	z/s	z/z	Combined z/z & s	s/s	s/z
12th-15th	98.8%	1.2%	0	0	0
10th	58.3%	41.7%	0	0	0
9th	40%	60%	0	0	0

Figure 2.4. Percentage of Z/Z and S/Z-spun textiles in Iceland from the Viking Age to the fifteenth century. (Courtesy Oxbow.)

ners and weavers used the same tools in Northern Europe as of AD 200 to spin equally well in one direction or the other (Bender Jørgensen 1992:122). Two explanations most likely account for this shift in Icelandic spin direction: the ethnic origins of the spinners who were producing the yarn and bringing different textile traditions into Iceland, or trade and pressure from international markets that encouraged Icelanders to modify their textile technology to meet European market needs.

As discussed in Chapter 1, modern Icelanders share the DNA of both Scandinavians and people from the British Isles (Helgason et al. 2001:733), and the shift in spin direction may be indicative of non-Norse spinning techniques brought to Iceland by this culturally diverse group of settlers. Women from the British Isles may have introduced Z/S-spun cloth (which appears to be have been common in non-Norse areas of the British Isles) and integrated it into the Z/Z spinning traditions of the Norwegian settlers. In fact, Bender Jørgensen (1992) and Walton Rogers (1989) noted that textiles from the ninth to tenth centuries at urban sites across the British Isles were generally Z/S-spun, quite unlike the textiles from Viking burial contexts in Scotland, Ireland, and the Isle of Man. The deceased were presumably of Norwegian descent: the spinners of their communities were producing Z/Z-spun textiles as in Norway (Bender Jørgensen 1992:40; Walton Rogers 1989:334). While this does not explain why everyone in Iceland eventually adopted Z/S spinning for the production of all cloth, it suggests that ethnic origin may have had some influence. Both authors concluded that textile finds from ninth- and tenth-century urban settlements in the British Isles are different from those in Viking burial contexts. They argued that urban cloth types should be more closely compared to similar find groups from continental Europe, where Z/S cloth is more prevalent (Bender Jørgensen 1992:41).

The pattern in the British Isles is therefore not dissimilar to that in Iceland (Figure 2.5). Finds from burials dating to the *landnám* period show significant numbers of Z/Z-spun textiles, whereas contemporary settlement sites such as Hofstaðir (Lucas 2009:318–320) and Bessastaðir suggest an equal if not greater proportion of Z/S-spun textiles, and by the eleventh century, all textiles are spun Z/S. This may also reflect particular attitudes about the dead by burying with them either old, discarded cloth or unique cloth that was associated with their Norwegian heritage. In the next section, I present material from an Icelandic burial where the mix of Scandinavian and Insular cultural traditions is very clear. Textiles and burial goods from Ketilsstaðir offer striking insights into the nature of early Icelandic society of the Viking Age within the North Atlantic sphere. The Ketilsstaðir burial, featured as an exhibit at the National Museum of

Figure 2.5. Distribution of spin directions in Northern Europe, Scotland, and Iceland. (Map by Hayeur Smith 2016a. Courtesy Oxbow.)

Iceland in 2015, was called Blaeklaedda Konan, "The Lady in Blue." The results of the textiles and dress analysis were published in a coauthored paper with Kevin P. Smith and Karin M. Frei in *Medieval Archaeology* in 2019.

The Ketilsstaðir Burial

In the early tenth century, a young woman was buried in northeastern Iceland, 300 m north of the abandoned farm of Litlu-Ketilsstaðir, and 2.5 km north of Ketilsstaðir (Friðriksson 2013:500). The site was accidentally discovered in 1938 by road builders. Road workers and their equipment frequently hit components within burials, a skeleton, a brooch or the like, and in this case uncovered the partial remains of a youngish woman in full Norse-style clothing and regalia. For many years, her cultural identity was assumed Scandinavian, based on her typical Norse-style jewelry and material culture, indicating she was a wealthy Norse woman. Her burial is considered among the wealthiest due to its abundant grave goods: textiles; two oval brooches of the P52 style common in Scandinavia and also found in Scotland; a trefoil (three-tongued) brooch adorned with an acanthus motif that was formerly classified as a P91 according to the Pedersen typology (Eldjárn and Friðriksson 2000); 50 whole and fragmented beads; a piece of blue chalcedony; a soapstone spindle whorl; a whetstone and touchstone; two carved bone plates thought to be the remains of a knife handle; and several fragments of iron, suggesting that some grave goods had been placed in a wooden box (Einarsdóttir 2015; Eldjárn 1956; Eldjárn and Friðriksson 2000).[5] Two unpublished reports from 1978 and 1982 were identified following the research done on the textiles for the exhibit, indicating that preliminary analysis had taken place at the Bryggens Museum in Bergen, Norway. The 1982 report was carried out by Inger Raknes Pedersen, conservator at the Bryggens Museum. The jewelry from Ketilsstaðir was analyzed by Eldjárn (1956), Eldjárn and Friðriksson (2000), and Hayeur Smith (2004).

Later, in 2014, in the collections repository of the National Museum of Iceland, a jar was identified containing formaldehyde and the soft tissue and skeletal remains of a female's partial face and cheek from the Ketilsstaðir burial. There were more grave goods than osteological remains, but those grave goods provided the opportunity for in-depth analyses. The bronze brooches were in direct contact with the face of the buried woman, and this not only preserved her textiles and bones but preserved the soft tissue of the left side of her face. When discovered, the soft tissue of her left cheek was present as was her left eye, her maxilla or lower jaw, and teeth (Einarsdóttir 2015:17). Þórðarsson had placed this unusual find in a jar of formalin solution, and in 2014 the jar was retrieved from the museum's storage area (though the eye had disappeared), prompting the establishment of a multidisciplinary research team focusing on different aspects of the find. A full-scale international project was undertaken between 2014 and 2015, looking at all the preserved remains to reconstruct the life, death, and identity of this early settler (Hayeur Smith et al. 2019).[6]

At least four and possibly five different textile types were identified in the Ketilsstaðir burial, along with the finds listed above. These textile analyses included on-site visual inspection using digital microscopy; McCrone Associates (Chicago) were commissioned to perform fiber analyses; the University of

Figure 2.6. Woman from Ketilsstaðir and the position in which she was found. (Illustration by Greg Rebis, Hayeur Smith et al. 2019. Reprinted by permission of Taylor & Francis Ltd., http://www.tandfonline.com.)

Rhode Island's Department of Textiles undertook both fiber identification and dye analysis; the National Museum of Denmark oversaw the analysis of strontium in two samples of the woolen textiles; and Beta Analytic (Miami) provided radiocarbon dating of the textiles. The textiles consisted of a linen plain weave, a woolen diamond twill fragment, a tablet-woven band, a 2/2 twill, and a possible herringbone twill.

Like most Viking women from mainland Scandinavia, the woman from Ketilsstaðir wore a long undershirt or gown known in Scandinavian languages as a *serk*. This garment was sometimes made of pleated linen fastened at the neck with a brooch (Hägg 1991:108). This long undergarment is thought to be reflected in the partly mineralized plain weave textile stuck to a woven woolen fragment. The plain weave pseudomorph is also visible adhering to the oval brooches' copper alloy shells and to the corroded iron pins that held the *serk* in place (Figure 2.7). Fragments from this mineralized piece (12438–2) were analyzed by McCrone Associates, and it was concluded that three of these fiber fragments were made of cellulose. These fibers suggest that the long undergarment was probably made of linen, as was customary in Scandinavia (Ewing 2006:28). The cloth was a plain weave with Z-spun warp yarns and Z-spun wefts. A full thread count was not possible for these textile fragments because the pieces were too fragile and small, though it was possible to determine a thread count of 18 in one system, suggesting a finely woven fabric.

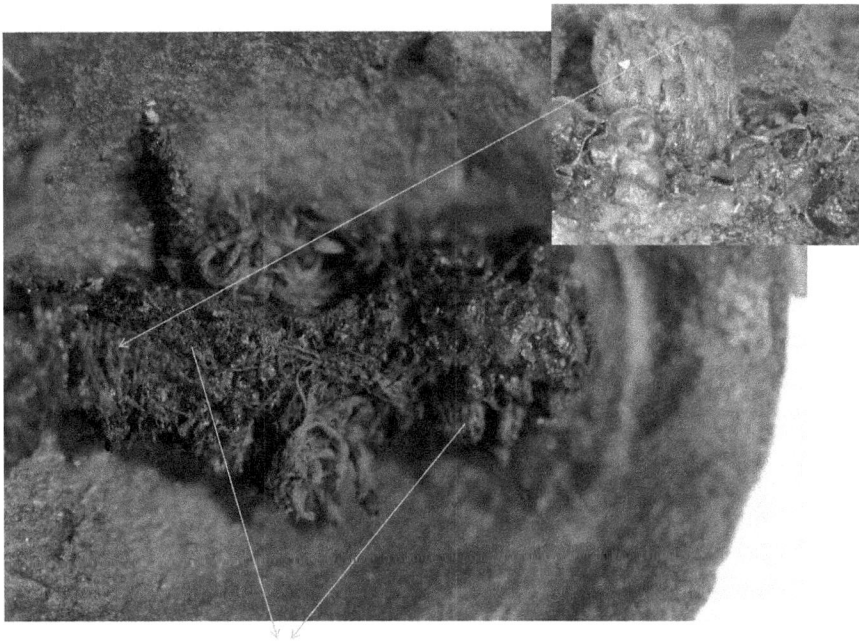

Linen fibers from the undergarment

Figure 2.7. View of fiber on the underside of the oval brooch from Ketilsstaðir, National Museum of Iceland. (Photo by Hayeur Smith, Hayeur Smith et al. 2019. Reprinted by permission of Taylor & Francis Ltd., http://www.tandfonline.com.)

Over this long shift the woman at Ketilsstaðir wore an apron (*smokker*) or the typical pinafore noted by Geijer (1938) and Hägg (1991), fastened in place by oval brooches (Figure 2.7). The tailoring of these aprons remains unclear: they may have been constructed in two panels with open sides, or made of one piece of cloth and open to one side, or constructed and sewn like a short tube (Ewing 2006:27). Alternately, some have suggested they opened in the front, revealing embellished undergarments, or as proposed by Geijer (1938), they comprised one or two rectangles wrapped around the body with loops through which the straps and brooches could be fastened (Ewing 2006:27; Geijer 1938). Between the brooches, a string of beads or a pendant was frequently hung, along with other useful implements: knives, scissors, and sometimes keys (Hägg 1991).

The apron from Ketilsstaðir was made of wool, according to fiber analysis by the McCrone Associates, and had been decorated at the top by a tablet-woven (also known as card-weaving) band.[7] The apron itself, represented by fragment 12438–4a, is a woolen diamond twill that was not immediately recognizable. In fact, due to the corrosion products on some of the pieces, the distinction between different twills was difficult to assess. This patterned twill was Z/Z-spun with a thread count of 9/5. An additional piece 12438–1 was thought to belong to the same *smokker* and was located under the shell of the left oval brooch, retaining the shape of the dome of the inside of the brooch. Given its placement, it seemed obvious that this piece was connected in some way to 12438–4a. Further analysis suggests that while 12438–4a is definitely part of the *smokker* made of a diamond twill, this other piece may also be a part of the *smokker* and is more than likely a herringbone twill, Z/Z-spun, with a thread count of 11/11. This suggests that the Ketilsstaðir *smokker* may have been made in two parts, possibly with two different panels with two different twills. Alternatively, this herringbone twill may have been the remnant of a shawl often worn by Viking women (Marled Madder, personal communication 2019). For the purposes of burial, dress practices in Iceland may have been more an exercise in bricolage and piecing together what was available, in addition to any social messages the survivors were trying to convey.

Diamond and patterned twills are rare in Icelandic Viking Age material. Two other diamond twills are known, from Snæhvammur and Gamla Berjanes: the latter is mineralized to the pin of an oval brooch, and both are diamond twills. Patterned twills are found in Scottish Viking Age material, though largely as textile imprints on the inside shells of oval brooches, and are the result of metalworking techniques rather than fragments of garments (Bender Jørgensen 1986).

According to Bender Jørgensen (1986:358), the full diamond twill is also called the "Birka type" and is a worsted twill of extremely fine craftsmanship encountered in the Baltic areas of Scandinavia and in western Norway. This type is also abundant at Birka (hence the name) and at other trade centers such as Hedeby in Schleswig, and Kaupang in Norway (Bender Jørgensen, in Welander et al. 1989:167). She also suggested it was woven in western Norway, where every third grave with Merovingian and Viking period textiles contains this type of weave (Bender Jørgensen 1992:138). She identified three qualities of the Birka type in the west Norwegian examples: cloth with up to 30 warp threads per centimeter, cloth with 30–40 warp threads per centimeter, and finely woven cloth with more than 40 warp threads per centimeter . These categories represent medium, fine, and very fine qualities of cloth, with an overarching standard of uniform production and appearance (Bender Jørgensen 1986:360). Her study complemented that of Agnes Geijer (1938) and her own analysis of the Birka type from the site of Birka in Sweden. Bender Jørgensen (1986) argued that while various qualities of this textile type were found in western Norway, only the very fine versions made their way to Birka, and that the very high quality and uniformity of the Birka type could only have originated in what she defines as "a more advanced type of society, possibly even something comparable to a weavers' guild" (Bender Jørgensen 1986). Clearly the material from Ketilsstaðir represents the lowest quality, but the western Norwegian connection is interesting, given that this is also the area from which the settlers of Iceland were likely to have emigrated.

Additional information obtained from strontium isotope analyses by Karin Frei, a first of their kind in the context of Icelandic textiles, suggests that the Icelandic diamond twill from Ketilsstaðir was made with wool locally obtained in Iceland. Two samples were taken from the Ketilsstaðir burial (one from the *smokker* and the other from the 2/2 twill; for details of the analysis, see Hayeur Smith et al. 2019) and tested for strontium isotopes. Both wool samples proved to be of local origin, made of wool from sheep that grazed on Icelandic soils.

This contradicts Bender Jørgensen's (1986) contention that diamond twills were produced in more sophisticated urban settings of continental Scandinavia. Fragment 12438–4a suggests that this type of weaving was done in Iceland, utilizing knowledge that had come with the Icelandic settlers from western Norway, though it is nowhere near the quality of the diamond twills encountered in Norway or Birka.

The presence of Z/Z-spun yarns noted in the linen undergarment and the twill (12438–2) suggests a Norwegian origin for these garments. As mentioned above, from the late ninth to early eleventh centuries, Icelandic Viking Age cloth found in burials was largely Z/Z-spun, using single yarns but with occasional pieces of cloth spun Z/S.

Fibers from the apron tested positive for indigotin, implying it had once been dyed blue with woad (*Isatis tinctoria*). The presence of blue clothing at Ketilsstaðir reiterates a common theme in female Viking burials in both Scandinavia and Iceland.

The tablet-woven band—weft faced, with both warp and weft plied Z2S that decorated the apron's upper margin had a light cream-colored central band flanked by two bands on either side (K12438–4b). Tablet-woven bands were common features of Viking Age dress, and those added to the garments of wealthy men and women could be quite ornate. However, the tablet-woven band from Ketilsstaðir was not overtly decorated except for a faint wave-like motif, one of the simpler patterns that can be produced with card weaving. In Iceland, as in other parts of the North Atlantic, tablet-woven bands were frequently used as starting borders for fabric woven on the warp-weighted loom. The ubiquity of this approach as a way of starting woven panels has in fact often been cited in textile analyses as proof that this type of loom was used (Hoffman 1974). The tablet-woven band from Ketilsstaðir has one selvaged edge, as is normal for tablet-woven bands used as starting borders. If it were a decorative band sewn to the garment, it would have had two (horizontal) selvaged edges delineating the band and displayed stitching holes where it had been sewn to the garment. This suggests that the apron was woven and integrated into the band during its production. Unlike the apron, however, the band did not test positive for indigotin, so it would have stood out against the blue of the apron's body.

An additional textile fragment was identified among the remains from Ketilsstaðir (12438–3). Two sides of the piece had been folded under, suggesting it was one of the straps holding up the apron described above, and the imprint of the oval brooch was indented into the fabric. Such straps were threaded through loops attached to the back of the apron, then wrapped over the shoulder and through comparable loops on the apron's front. Fragments of such straps are commonly found preserved on the inside of oval brooches and are occasionally wrapped around the pin, as was the case with this one, where its coarser twill was mineralized along with the linen plain weave.

This strap was a 2/2 woolen twill made with Z/S-spun yarns and an unbalanced thread count of 9/7, woven in the style that became associated with medieval Icelandic *vaðmál* a century or two later (Hayeur Smith 2014b:13, 2018). This piece tested positive for indigotin, supporting its identification as one of the straps holding up the apron. Furthermore, it too underwent strontium isotope analysis and, like the apron, proved to be of local Icelandic wool (Hayeur Smith et al. 2019).

As part of the study, the textiles from Ketilsstaðir were also dated using accelerated mass spectrometry. One textile sample (K12438–3) was taken from the strap; the second (K12438–4a) came from the apron. Frei's strontium isotope analyses of two of the woman's textiles indicate they were woven from the wool of locally kept Icelandic sheep. Assuming that settlers arrived with sheep in eastern Iceland no earlier than circa AD 880 (the earliest settlement is estimated at AD 874), the two consistent AMS dates from this woman's clothing suggest they were woven from wool shorn in the interval of AD 880–895. The AMS date from the woman's tooth, on the other hand, suggests that she was most likely born around AD 930 (see Hayeur Smith et al. 2019). If she arrived in Iceland as a young girl and died around the middle of the tenth century, aged 17–25 (see Walser 2015), it is possible that the clothes she was buried in were heirlooms woven in Iceland by early colonists who had settled there and woven these garments from locally raised sheep decades before she was born. However, the calibrated range of the date from her tooth also implies that she could have been born as early as the last quarter of the ninth century and that the clothes she was buried in might have been 10–20 years old at the time of her death, woven when she was a young girl from the wool of sheep her family raised in Iceland.

The woman from Ketilsstaðir was not native to Iceland (Walser 2015:53). Whatever her cultural origins, she died in Iceland, where she was buried in Scandinavian style with a mixture of objects reflecting Hiberno-Norse culture. She was wearing textiles made with wool from sheep that grazed in Iceland, reflecting textile traditions from Norway (diamond twill and Z/Z-spun yarns). We know that her straps reflect a non-Norwegian tradition from the British Isles and were also made of local Icelandic sheep. Her jewelry, as discussed in Hayeur Smith and others (2019), reflects a similar mixture, as well as connections with the world beyond.

When cultures come into contact through colonization or trade, dress codes steeped in tradition can become potent symbols of cultural identity, at times generating symbolic amalgamations as each group adopts or rejects symbols of the other. Chris Gosden and Chantal Knowles (2001:5) suggest that this occurs at three levels: "acculturation," resulting in a form of cultural loss; the maintenance of tradition; or through hybridity. Through the process of bricolage, older items of dress can be replaced by newer versions made, in some cases, with different materials (Berlo 1992:116; Rovine 2009:44). In dress theory, and specifically applied to textiles, Erekosima and Eicher (1981) refer to "cultural authentication" (Eicher 2004; Vollmer 2010). This term was initially coined by Erekosima (1979) to describe cloth from the Kalabari inhabiting the southern tip of the Federal Republic of Nigeria, who imported cloth from India and "authenticated" it into their own cultural context by physically modifying the cloth. Thus, the term refers to material culture that is borrowed from another culture, transformed, and fully integrated into a new cultural system (Eicher 2004). This was done through 1) a process of selection, 2) of giving the item a name, and making it "visible," 3) of incorporating the item into a meaningful aspect of cultural life, and 4) transforming the item from its original state (Eicher 2004; Erekosima and Eicher 1981; Vollmer 2010). According to Vollmer (2010:74), "All processes of authenticating dress are forms of invention based on an aspect of unfamiliar dress that another culture selects as something that can be tried on and freely adapted to new uses or purposes. Through integration the garment is made "authentic" to the adoptive cultures." The outfit of the woman from Ketilsstaðir presents an interesting amalgamation of northern dress styles and traditions, reflecting hybridity as a mix and amalgamation of two cultural traditions, resulting in cultural authentication of the textiles, and the creation of something completely different. This cultural mix is often referred to as "Hiberno-Norse" in Scottish/Norse or Irish/Norse cultural settings but clearly extends to Iceland and the North Atlantic.

In this case an overall appearance of dress is different from Scandinavian styles but still heavily reliant on them. The Ketilsstaðir outfit highlights the cultural reality of this region and of the Viking Age as a whole. This was a period of vast expansion and exchanges of people, ideas, technologies, and materials, indicating a globalized Viking culture stretching from the Mediterranean to the Frankish kingdoms and Great Britain. In death all of these interconnections across the Western world are on display, reaffirming the global lifestyle of the Viking Age in which these people lived, grew, and died.

Viking Age Textiles: Scotland

Not all settlement areas in the North Atlantic have yielded collections of Viking Age textile material. Greenland was settled at the end of the Viking Age, and the Faroe Islands have one or two items from this period. Only Scotland and Iceland allow for comparisons between regions, as both have comparable numbers of textile finds for this period. In Scotland all material comes from burial contexts; 130 burials have been reported, not all of which had been studied for textile remains by Gabra-Sanders before her untimely death. Before her efforts to compile all of the Viking textile material, Lise Bender Jørgensen had covered much of the Scottish textile data for her publication *Northern European Textiles* (1992). Gabra-Sanders took over where Bender Jørgensen left off and examined 49 burials. Thirty-one of these contained textile remains (Gabra-Sanders 1998), for a total number of 274 textile fragments. My work follows from her analysis and listing, and unfortunately I did not have the opportunity to consult the full collection beyond the confines of the National Museum of Scotland, as Viking artifacts are scattered in other museums and repositories across Scotland and the UK.

Like Icelandic examples, Scottish Viking textiles are very similar in their weave types and how the textiles are made. They are dominated by mineralized pieces stuck to swords, axes, and brooches or even used on the inside of brooches as part of the casting process. Cloth impressions on the inside of copper alloy artifacts occur when a piece of cloth is inserted into a two-part mold. When hot metal is poured into the mold, the cloth burns up, adding carbon to the inside of the mold and preventing a buildup of unwanted oxygen; the cloth also provides a gauge of the desired thickness of the brooch (Hayeur Smith 2005:87). It is known that nonferrous metal workers, while melting bronze, will add boric acid to the melt and the crushed charcoal to prevent oxygen from being introduced. Too much oxygen will result in a flawed cast, with air bubbles or obstruction of the shape (Hayeur Smith 2005:87–88). In this case, rather than adding boric acid, the textile piece in the mold assumes the same function. This occurs consistently on the insides of oval brooches and was a part of the fabrication process.

Twenty-nine of the Scottish mineralized textiles have impressions on the inside of oval brooches, and two were identified on belt buckles, while Iceland has four examples. The weaves of the Icelandic textile impressions did not seem of particular importance until I analyzed the Scottish material and realized that while spin direction and thread counts are almost impossible to see, all manner of weaves were used in this process, including 20 examples of tabby weaves, 1 herringbone twill, 4 diamond twills, 1 possible sprang, and 1 twill undefined. In Iceland, the presence of patterned twills used in this context during this period is extremely rare, and tabbies are most commonly used during the fabrication process.

Table 2.3 enumerates the total amounts of textiles found in each location, how many of these are actual organic textiles, and how many are now mineralized. It is curious that more organic textiles have survived in Iceland than in Scotland where most textiles are mineralized, which could be due to overall preservation conditions in Iceland, even though erosion presents serious problems for the overall condition of pre-Christian burials. Without mineralization, the study of Viking textiles would be impossible.

A look at the main weave types from Scotland compared with the Icelandic material shows an interesting distribution of textile types. While the tabby weave is very popular in Viking Age settlements in Scotland, appearing as mineralized fragments stuck to objects, in Iceland 2/2 twills are more popu-

Table 2.3. Number of mineralized textiles in Scotland and Iceland

Viking Age textiles	Full collection	Mineralized, pseudomorphs, and imprints
Iceland	123	56
Scotland	274	271

Note: Without these mineralized textiles, information on cloth and dress for the Viking Age in this region would be incomplete.

lar. It remains unclear why this would be the case. Bender Jørgensen's (1992) analysis indicated that Viking Age tabbies in the whole of the British Isles made up 77.1% of textiles, whereas twills comprised only 6.2%. These findings were similar to those in Denmark, where 77% of textiles from the ninth century and 75% in the tenth century were tabbies (Bender Jørgensen 1992:38). By contrast, in Norway 42.6% of all textiles were tabbies, and 29.6% were twills, while in Sweden 52.5% were tabbies, and 33.3% were twills. Iceland, where 28.6% were tabbies and 51.8% were twills, differs from all of these and seems more similar to Gotland, where all textiles were said to be twills, according to Bender Jørgensen. The mechanism responsible for these textile preferences remains unknown: local taste or fashion? In the Icelandic context, these preferences may or may not have something to do with local non-Norse textile traditions and the strong presence of Irish and Hebridean slaves and settlers who brought with them different textile traditions, or it may be that textiles were used as currency (*vaðmál*, a 2/2 twill) far earlier than previously believed (Hayeur Smith 2014b). Tabby weaves in Iceland appear to be more common as casting imprints; no patterned twills have been identified. In Scotland, tabby weaves were also used in the casting process, though other textile types were as well (Bender Jørgensen 1992; Gabra-Sanders 1998).

Another peculiarity of Scottish textiles involves the use of other materials uncommon in Iceland. Fragments of hair or haired skins were identified on six swords, two knives, a pair of tweezers, and three boat nails. This suggests that scabbards were fur-lined during the Viking Age, something that is not widely recorded. Feathers also made their way into mineralized form on bronze and iron objects and were probably associated with furnishings inside the grave. In 1991 a richly furnished grave was found in Balnakeil, Scotland. It belonged to a 12-year-old boy, and among his grave goods was a full-sized sword that during conservation was found to be covered with feathers (Gabra-Sanders 1998).

Thread counts from Scotland (Figure 2.8), while similar to those of Iceland,

Table 2.4. Types of weaves encountered in Viking Age Iceland and Scotland

Weave ICELAND (N = 122)	Percent of "real" or mineralized cloth (N = 122)	Casting imprints
Tabby weave	28.6%	0.01%
2/2 twill	51.8%	0.0%
Full basket weave (panama weave)	0.9%	0.0%
Half basket weave	0.9%	0.0%
Diamond twill	4.5%	0.0%
Cordage/threads	2.7%	0.0%
Pile weave	0.9%	0.0%
Tablet-woven band	1.8%	0.0%
Unknown	8.0%	0.0%
Weave SCOTLAND (N = 259)	**Percentage of "real cloth" or mineralized cloth (N = 232)**	**Casting imprint (N = 27)**
Tabby weave	56.5%	74.1%
2/2 twill/ 2/1 twill	5.2%	3.7%
Diamond/herringbone twill	0.0%	18.5%
Pile weave (tabby)	0.4%	0.0%
Sprang	0.0%	3.7%
Spin patterned tabby (with floats)	0.4%	0.0%
Unknown	37.5%	0.0%

show a greater range of high thread counts, with warp yarns above 12 warp threads per centimeter. This suggests the Scottish textiles are finer, perhaps produced in more sophisticated contexts or in specialized trade centers. Icelandic textiles from the Viking Age and later rarely exceed 18 warp threads per centimeter, while Scottish textiles often contain 30 warp threads per centimeter.

Bender Jørgensen, who carried out an extensive comparison of Norse textiles across the British Isles and Scandinavia, argued that Viking Scottish textiles resemble those from Viking Age Denmark rather than Norway or Sweden, not

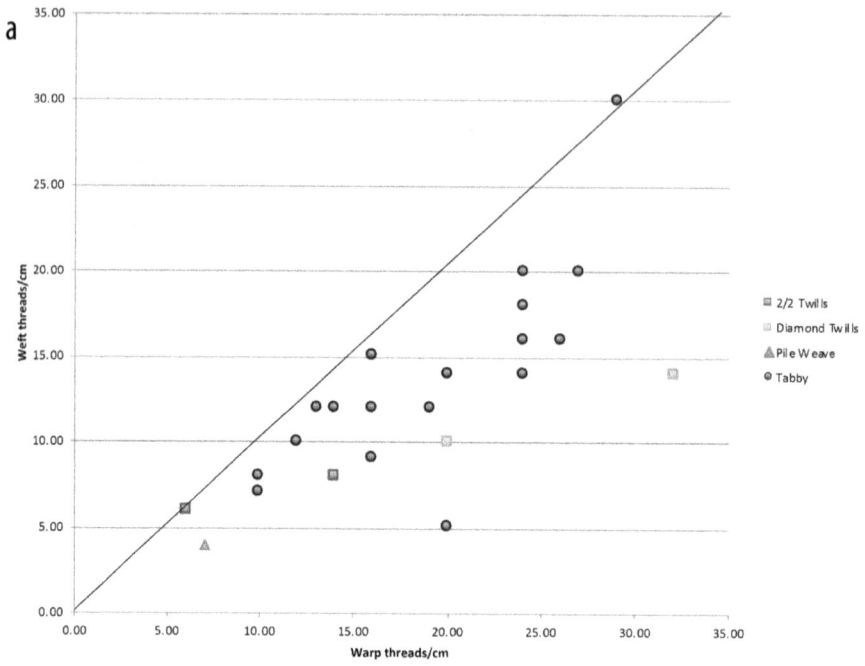

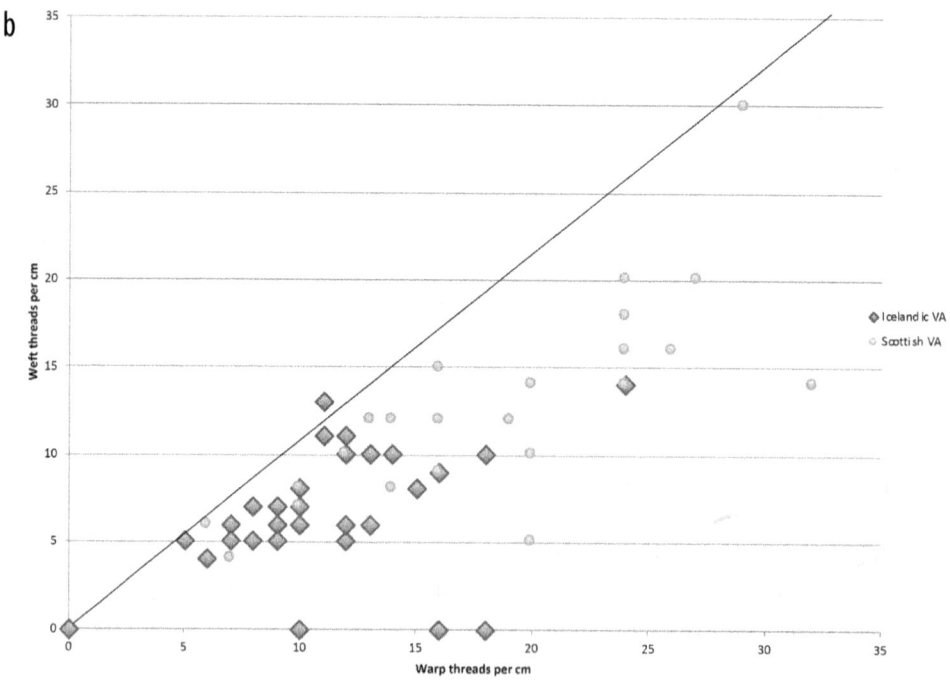

Figure 2.8. (*a*) Scottish Viking Age thread counts and (*b*) Scottish and Icelandic thread counts.

only in this respect, but in the range of cloth types and the use of the Z/Z spin (Bender Jørgensen 1992:41). Spin direction in Scottish Viking textiles suggests that out of 274 examples, 103 are Z/Z-spun, an additional 18 are Z-warp and unknown in the weft, and 7 are Z/S-spun. The remaining textiles were single yarns or plied yarns or allowed for no spin identification due to high levels of corrosion.

Based on this overview of Scottish and Icelandic Viking Age textiles, it is difficult to assess what social processes were at work in both these colonies from the textiles alone. Was Scotland slightly more prosperous than Iceland with its finely woven textiles, perhaps because of its proximity to Scandinavia? It was also settled earlier than Iceland and may have had access to a more continuous flow of goods from Scandinavia, in addition to silver bullion, which was the currency of choice in use during the Viking Age. Scotland's Viking settlements also show a preference for the production of Z/Z Norwegian textiles over Z/S, despite the intermarriage of Norse and local populations that took place in the Hebrides, Ireland, the Isle of Man, Orkney, and Shetland. Perhaps the Norse were more intent on stressing Norwegian cultural ties and power as the conquerors in Scotland and, by the time they settled Iceland, were faced with different challenges and embraced more easily the material culture of the other. Iceland was remote and the silver supplies brought over during the settlement period quickly ran out, leaving the Icelanders with little choice but to use wool—which they had in abundance—as the new currency, a cultural practice borrowed from Norway (Hayeur Smith 2018).

In both locations, it is clear that colonists were referencing a textile tradition from Norway and elsewhere in Scandinavia, where they originated. The presence of women from the British Isles in Iceland may have also favored the prevalence of Z/S-spun 2/2 twills that eventually took over the textile corpus in the Middle Ages. This trend may have begun slowly in the Viking Age and culminated in the cloth currency that was legally regulated, distributed, and used to purchase all manner of goods within Iceland.

3

Textiles, Weaving, and Currency in Iceland during the Middle Ages

Late in the tenth century, according to the thirteenth-century *Ljósvetninga Saga*, a Norwegian merchant named Helgi struck a bargain with a farmer named Thorir Akraskegg in northern Iceland's Eyjafjörður district. Thorir agreed to pay for the merchant's goods with woven cloaks, which he brought to the ship, but in Helgi's haste to depart, he did not immediately have them examined. At sea, Helgi examined the cloaks and found them full of holes, upon which he exclaimed, "This is a great fraud, and it's going to turn out badly for him" (Andersson and Miller 1989:170). Thorir—a troublesome individual—was ultimately outlawed because of this bad bargain.

Helgi's accusation and its consequences reflect the manner in which medieval Icelandic laws closely governed and protected transactions in cloth. From its settlement (AD 870–930) until the late thirteenth century, Iceland's powerful chieftains held much of the island's wealth and controlled its distribution, and as silver supplies dwindled after the Viking Age, cloth became Iceland's dominant currency (Gelsinger 1981). Legal standards and exchange values for cloth currency were established after the Althing or National Assembly was founded in AD 930. This assembly created laws (codified in writing after AD 1117) governing relationships between chieftains and their followers, the organization of the legal system itself, methods of punishment and retribution, and standards for economic, social, ritual, and personal conduct. Within this system, cloth was used for all legal transactions, to pay tithes and taxes or settle fines, for internal trade, and for export as well as home consumption (e.g., clothing, tents, sails, farm items; Gelsinger 1981; Hayeur Smith 2012, 2014, 2018; Ingstad 1982; Þórlaksson 1991). Standards for the production and trade of cloth were legally defined in successive medieval law codes: Grágás (AD 1117–1271; Dennis et al. 1980, 2002), Járnsíða (AD 1271–1281), Jónsbók (after AD 1281), and Búalög (twelfth–nineteenth centuries).

The Origins of Icelandic Cloth Currency in Norway

Hoffman (1974:195, 218–219), Gelsinger (1981), and Þorláksson (personal communication 2010) have all argued that the use of cloth as currency in Iceland had its roots in Norway. This is not surprising. Notwithstanding settlers from the British Isles who were brought to Iceland as slaves, wives, or concubines, most settlers were of Norwegian descent and brought with them Norse cultural traditions. Among these Norse cultural traits was textile production, along with the concomitant tools (Hoffman 1974).

In the settlement period (AD 870–930), the value of goods was measured against silver, of which considerable amounts are thought to have circulated in Iceland during the tenth century, the result of Viking raids and trading (Gelsinger 1981:34; Graham-Campbell 2011). Eventually, however, these raids ceased, and population increased along with exchange and trade. Gelsinger (1981) argued that at this point, Icelandic silver supplies were no longer adequate to support local needs, and silver was mixed with foreign coins and alloys, creating a new currency called *bleikt silfir* worth half the value of pure silver. Silver coinage was never produced within Iceland, but *vaðmál* (cloth currency) was valued in terms of silver and was used as a parallel currency (Hayeur Smith 2018). Gelsinger (1981:35) argued that its production was "the most important industry during the Icelandic Commonwealth period (AD 930–1262) and possibly during the settlement as well."

Silver and coins were critically important within the Norwegian economic system of the Viking Age. However, as in Iceland, this was an economy based not solely on coinage but rather on a more complex system, including various commodities used as media of payment, equated with silver (Skre 2011:74). According to Skre, economic transactions could involve weights of silver or other items, such as cows, cloth, butter, or grain, whose values in silver were known and agreed upon, such that all were interchangeable at established rates in Viking Age Norwegian transactions. By the medieval period, when the law codes were written down, this, too, was true of Iceland. Similar values were ascribed to the weights of silver, whether pure or impure, and parallel units of measure were established following the Norwegian model. In Iceland, the unit of weight and value with the highest mass was a *vætt*, followed by the *fjórðung, mörk, eyrir/aurar, örtugar*, and *penningar* (Gelsinger 1981:33). The Icelandic *mörk* was equal to 217 grams, comparable to the Norwegian *mark* of 214 grams (Skre 2011:73). In both systems, values were comparable: in Iceland, 1 *eyrir* of silver was equivalent to 3 *örtugar*, while in Norway, 1 *ora* was equivalent to 3 *ertogs*. In both places, 1 *eyrir/ora* of silver was equal in value to 6 ells of *vaðmál* during the late Viking Age and early medieval periods (1 legal ell = 49.2 cm) (Dennis et al. 2002:155; Hayeur Smith 2018; Larson 2008:421–422).

In establishing *vaðmál* as a regulated currency, Iceland's legal system mirrored that of Norway. According to the thirteenth-century Íslendingabók, a Norwegian settler named Úlfjótur was sent from Iceland back to Norway to draft a law code modeled on the legal system of the Gulathing, the legislative assembly of a province on the west coast, north of Bergen (Dennis et al. 1980). The Gulathing law contains some of Norway's earliest recorded laws and in its current form is thought to date to AD 1150, roughly contemporary with Grágás, its Icelandic equivalent (AD 1117–1271) (Dennis et al. 1980, 2002; Larson 2008:26). Both of these documents are assumed to contain legal provisions that considerably predate the times when the former orally transmitted laws were written down. The Gulathing law provides several instances in which cloth is mentioned as a form of payment, e.g., for shipbuilding or the consecration of a church, or for legal compensation, such as for killing the king's bailiff at the Thing (Larson 2008:333). *Vaðmál* does not dominate the Gulathing law code, as it does the Grágás, and appears less frequently than silver or cows as a form of payment; however, it has clear legal standing, importance, and value as a form of commodity currency. In the Gulathing law, no distinctions are made between the values of linen and *vaðmál*, as opposed to Grágás, where 1 ell of linen was worth 4 ells of Icelandic *vaðmál* (Gelsinger 1981). Instead, cloth in all its forms possessed the legal equivalent of 1 *ora* in silver to 6 ells of cloth. The specific guidelines that regulated the ell (öln, ölnir) as a unit of measure for cloth will be discussed in more depth in this chapter, but for the moment it is clear that the Icelandic model was heavily based on the Norwegian one and that cloth currency in Norway was important enough that its roles and values were described in law books.

Background: *Vaðmál* in the Legal Documents

As discussed, the Icelandic commodity-money system, as understood through medieval and post-medieval Icelandic law codes (Bernharðsson et al. 2005; Dennis et al. 1980, 2002; Jónsson 2004; Schulman 2010), was based on stable, legally negotiated exchange rates for the value of different goods relative to other products. Thus, values for commodities such as cattle, butter, sheep, foodstuffs, and manufactured goods, including cloth, as well as hack-silver and coins, were established through exchange rates initially based upon standardized weights of refined silver. Skre (2011) and Gullbekk (2011) described the structure and details of the Norwegian commodity system through reference to both linguistic and legal sources. This Norwegian commodity-money system reveals sufficient similarities to that of Iceland that there can be little doubt of their close developmental relationships (Hayeur Smith 2014b, 2018).

However, toward the end of the Viking Age, the commodity-money systems of Iceland and Norway evolved and diverged. In Iceland, cloth gained tremendous importance within its own currency system, possibly due to a combination of population increase, stabilization of the Icelandic pastoral economy, and declining access to sources of silver (Gelsinger 1981:34; Hayeur Smith 2014). While regulated barter still formed the basis for this economic system, it is clear from the legal texts that formalized and standardized units of cloth emerged and gained such importance that homespun woolen fabric became a legal form of currency throughout the medieval period. Although its value was still measured, in theory, against silver, this cloth (*vaðmál* or *vöruvaðmál*) came to be legally regulated as an exchange good in and of itself. The name of this cloth currency, *vaðmál*, integrates the Old Norse root words *váð* (stuff/cloth) and *mál* (a measure) to mean "cloth measured to a standard" (Cleasby et al. 1957:673, 683; Hayeur Smith 2014b, 2018). It is ubiquitous as a measure and medium of exchange in Icelandic legal texts, sales accounts, church inventories, and farm registers into the seventeenth century (e.g., Lárusson 1967; Hayeur Smith 2014b:731).

For use as legal currency, cloth had to be woven in a particular manner and in specific lengths and widths, as evaluated by regional authorities. The law codes provide extremely useful information about the periods when each code was applied. The earliest regulations addressing Icelandic cloth currency are found in Grágás. Its oldest portions were written in AD 1117 and remained in force until 1271 (Dennis et al. 1980, 2002). According to Grágás, *vaðmál*, two ells in width and six ells in length, was considered legal as currency. This unit, the *eyrir* (pl. *aurar*) is equivalent to one ounce of silver and became the basic unit of measurement for all types of exchange in Iceland (Dennis et al. 1980; Hayeur Smith 2018).

Changes in the lengths and widths required for *vaðmal* as legal currency are recorded in successive law codes and narratives (Hayeur Smith 2018). For example, Búalög stipulates that *vaðmál* was to be woven in panels of 3.5 ells in width, or roughly 1.5 m (Østergård 2004). The ell also changed in length: around AD 1100, the long ell was set at 56 cm, replacing an earlier 46-cm ell, and was eventually replaced by a 49.2-cm ell (Dennis et al. 1980; Gelsinger 1981; Hayeur Smith 2014b). Gelsinger (1981) used these changes to infer periods of inflation and economic stress in Iceland but argued that some of these fluctuations were the results of trade with the British Isles (Hayeur Smith 2014b, 2015a). English demand for Icelandic cloth grew after changes in the woolen industry allowed the English to sell most of their own fine wool, but they needed the cheaper Icelandic material to clothe their urban poor (Gelsinger 1981). English custom records from 1303 have several mentions of "wadmol" testifying to this trade (Gras 1918). Gelsinger (1981) notes that fluctuations in the Icelandic ell directly mirrored changes in the legal length of the English ell, suggesting close trade links between these countries.

The quality of woven cloth was critical for its use as currency. Grágás describes methods for evaluating cloth currency or legal cloth (*vaðmál*) in a 20-ell piece:

> A new law. Homespun shall not be so slack at the selvage that it makes a difference of more than one ell in a twenty-ell piece. If the difference is greater, it is to be measured along the middle. Homespun is to be double the forearm broad and it is lawfully offered if the breadth amounts to that, measured with fingers extended and it is of good quality. The parties to a deal shall take two lawful viewers to view trade goods offered as payment should it be slack in the selvage or narrow. (Dennis et al. 2002:350)

The 20-ell unit is mentioned in another passage of Grágás under the heading "lawful measures," which describes using the *stika* to measure legal cloth. This was a measuring tool 1/10 of the 20-ell length marked on the wall of the church at Þingvöllr, where the Althing met, around AD 1200, to standardize units of cloth measure (Dennis et al. 2002; Gelsinger 1981; Hayeur Smith 2014b, 2018). Although women presumably wove *vaðmál* in various lengths, the range of laws regulating the ways cloth was to be measured and evaluated underscores its significance in legal and commercial transactions.

As Thorir's case exemplifies, penalties existed for those who produced inadequate *vaðmál* or cloth (it would seem that Thorir was trading in pile-woven cloaks esteemed at a higher value than *vaðmál*) who attempted to cheat by trading in false ells, or who skimped in the quality of the cloth traded. Helgi was legally entitled to prosecute Thorir, and Thorir was outlawed for his deception. This and similar legal cases eventually led to the creation of standardized portable devices for measuring ells, notably rods of wood (*stikur*) of the appropriate length and stones in churchyards that were used for measuring ells and resolving disagreements (Andersson and Miller 1989; Hayeur Smith 2014b).

Information on the quality required of cloth to be legally traded is less clear in medieval sources, yet regulations apparently dealt with widths, warp counts, cloth weight, and the prices of specific types of cloth termed *gjaldavoð* (*vaðmál* suitable for legal payments), *klæðavoð* (cloth for clothing), *vöruvoð* (marketable cloth or common *vaðmál*), and *smávoð* (finer quality cloth). Although Hoffman (1974) felt these guidelines were frequently inconsistent, she concluded that legal cloth had 4–14 warp threads per centimeter. Þorláksson (1991) identified legal guidelines from circa AD 1300 and AD 1613–1640 stating that *gjaldavoð* was to have 9–10 warp threads per centimeter, *klæðavoð* 11 warp threads per centimeter, and *smávoð* 11–14 warp threads per centimeter (Hayeur Smith 2014b, 2018; Þorláksson 1991). The finest of these, *smávoð* and *þragðarvoð*, had the highest thread counts and, although never used in domestic trade, could be used to pay tithes to the church (Østergård 2004).

Identifying *Vaðmál* in Iceland's Archaeological Record

Shifting our attention from medieval law codes to the archaeological record, how does one identify an artifact as legal cloth (i.e., cloth used as currency)? Documenting exchange systems based on the production and circulation of organic products can be difficult archaeologically due to poor preservation (Gullbekk 2011:102) and the potential transformation of these commodities into other products before being discarded (Skre 2011). In Iceland, for example, many pieces of cloth from midden deposits show evidence of stitching, repatching, and wear, suggesting a high degree of recycling and the importance of cloth as a household commodity. Therefore, trying to compare textile lengths and widths in the archaeological specimens with those described for cloth currency in medieval law codes is impossible because of the fragmentary nature of the cloth. However, the standardized nature of their production suggests most were initially intended to serve as currency before they were transformed into useful products.

One way of locating cloth currency in archaeological textiles involves the observation of patterns in the data that are suggestive of standardization, a required trait in all currency. Therefore, in an assemblage of roughly 1,250 fragments of medieval cloth, such patterns emerge by painstaking analysis and by graphically plotting the data. Thread counts are useful for tracking changes in textile production strategies (Hayeur Smith 2012, 2014b, 2018). This is especially the case in Iceland, where close parallels exist between the physical cloth and the technical descriptions and regulations of cloth currency provided in historic texts.

Assemblages of late Viking and medieval (ca. AD 900–1500) textiles come from various farm sites, for example, Kúabot, Reykjavik (Alþingisreitur), and Bessastaðir, as well as the northern harbor site of Gásir and an adjacent elite site, Möðruvellir, that may have exerted jurisdiction over the harbor (Harrison et al. 2008) (Figure 3.1).

Figure 3.1. Map of Icelandic sites with substantial textile collections.

Textile assemblages from these sites include woolen tabbies, twills of vary-ing structure and density, felts, and processed wool. Thread counts were un-dertaken on all textile fragments to help define the overall quality and pro-duction patterns of these textiles. At Gásir and Möðruvellir—two sites with clear links to mercantile trade—the textile assemblages are dominated by 2/2 twills with tightly constrained, overlapping thread count distributions: 6–12 threads per centimeter on the warp and 4–8 threads per centimeter on the weft (Figure 3.2). Given these sites' roles in commercial activity and tithe/tribute consolidation, legal cloth currency would be expected to dominate their assemblages.

Other non-mercantile sites, as depicted in Figure 3.3, present the same pat-terning observed at Gásir and Möðruvellir, with overlapping thread counts of 6–12 threads per centimeter on the warp, and 4–8 threads per centimeter on the weft. I argue that the thread count boundaries at these sites provide contextually reasonable archaeological signatures for vaðmál, and although these signatures are generated independently from medieval historical sources, they are consis-tent with information from Hoffman (1974) and Þorláksson (1991) on vaðmál thread counts, based on later medieval and post-medieval texts.

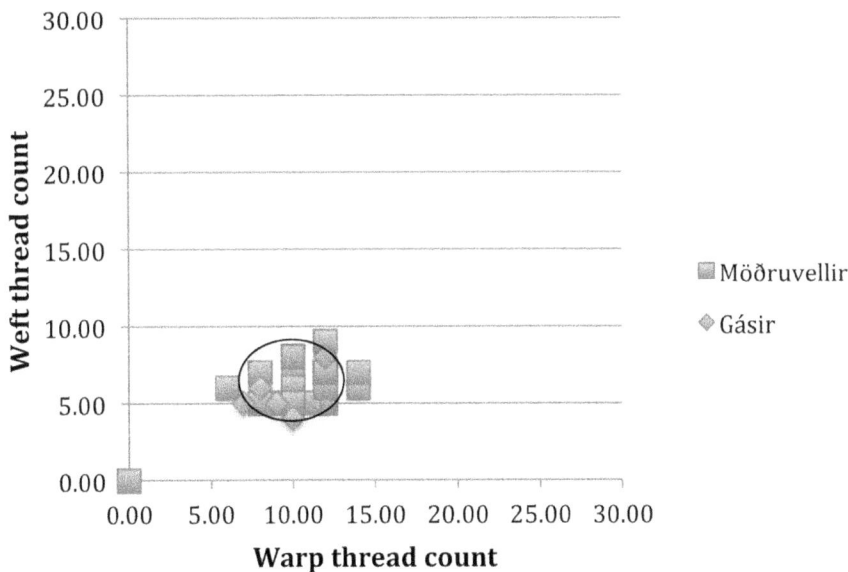

Figure 3.2. Thread counts for the sites of Möðruvellir and Gásir, two sites with links to mercantile trade (Hayeur Smith 2013. Courtesy *World Archaeology*.)

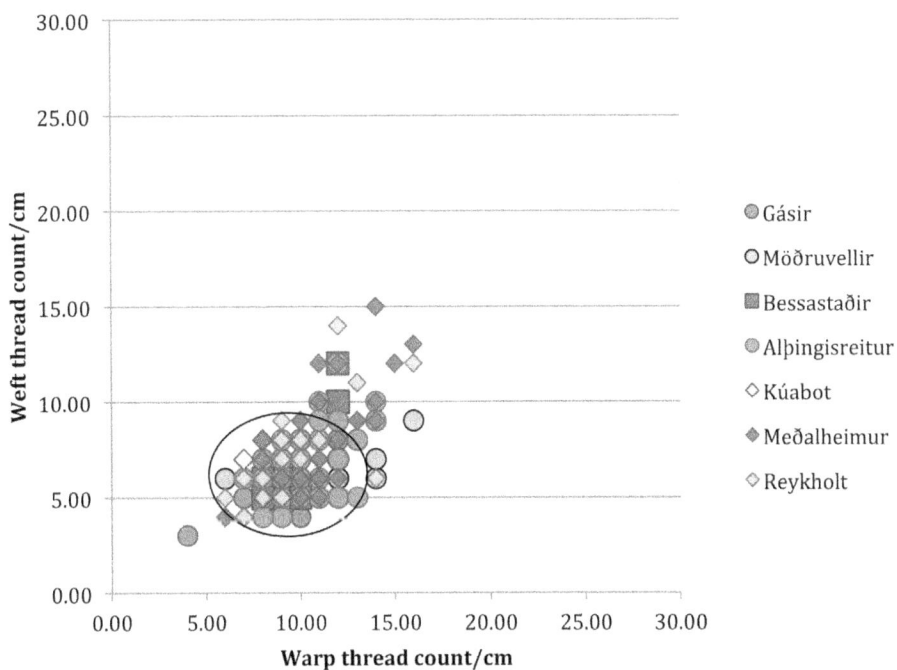

Figure 3.3. Thread counts from non-mercantile Icelandic sites. (Hayeur Smith 2014b, 2018. Courtesy Oxford University Press.)

A further attribute of *vaðmál* as legal cloth is its spin direction. In Chapter 2, I addressed the issue of spin direction in the Icelandic textile record and noted that in the Viking Age, textiles were made with yarns that had been spun Z/Z and that at some point during the tenth century, Z/S yarns appear alongside them. By the eleventh century, Z/S yarns comprise the dominant spin for all locally made textiles, especially *vaðmál* (see Figure 2.4). The adoption of a uniform spin direction and thread count ranges across Iceland suggests standardization, a characteristic apparent in other monetary systems (Gullbekk 2011; Maurer 2006).

How ubiquitous and significant was *vaðmál* production in medieval Iceland? At every medieval site analyzed, 2/2 twills outnumbered all other textiles, and the vast majority of these mirrored the narrow thread count distributions recorded at Gásir and Möðruvellir (Figure 3.2). The constrained nature of these distributions is especially evident when compared with textile assemblages from earlier Viking Age sites, where thread counts ranged from 6–25 warp threads per centimeter. Similarly, later post-medieval assemblages (Figure 3.4) regularly exhibit a broader range of thread counts (4–24 warp and weft threads per centimeter). These broader ranges in thread counts from assemblages both predat-

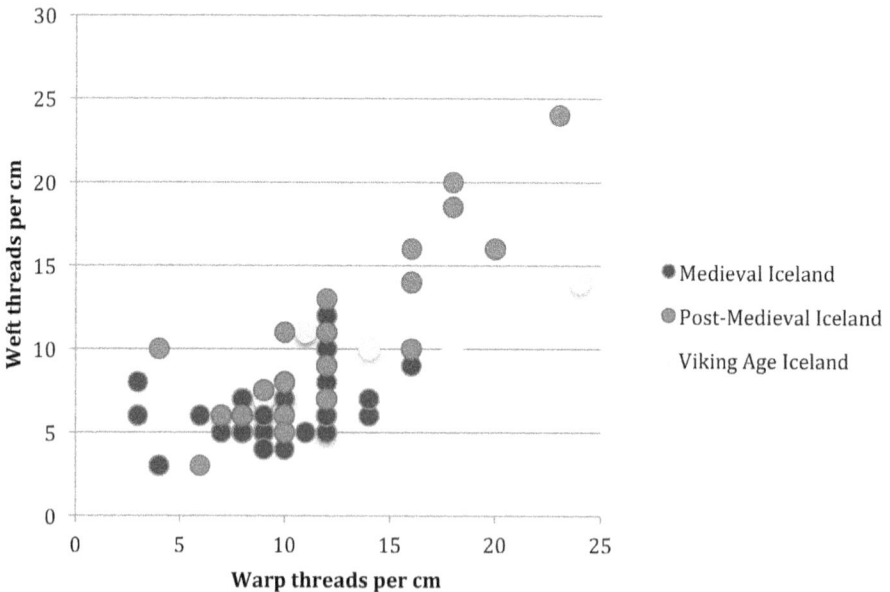

Figure 3.4. Post-medieval Icelandic cloth exhibits a broader range of thread counts. (Hayeur Smith 2014b. Courtesy Oxford University Press.)

ing and postdating the medieval period would be expected of production for domestic or household use, where the range signals the production and consumption of a diverse assemblage of cloth, including coarser and finer textiles employed in a similarly broad range of uses. In contrast, in the medieval period, textile production appears to have been remarkably constrained and standardized (Figure 3.3).

Standardization is a key factor in the emergence of any currency beyond the barter system, providing a "universal yardstick" by which to evaluate goods (Mauer 2006), while currency itself comes to symbolize and measure the social value of other objects (Harris 1995; Saul 2004). In Iceland, the reduction of variability in the range of textile types found on sites across the island during the medieval period and the marked standardization in their production at this time strongly suggest a significant shift in household production strategies to near-industrial levels of cottage industry focused on the production of legal or trade cloth. In essence, it appears that during the medieval period, Icelandic women were weaving money in abundance.

Early Medieval Icelandic Cloth: From Commodity to Legal Currency

During the medieval period (AD 1050–1550), changes in spin direction, weave types, and thread counts provide a clear indication that cloth in Iceland had become more than just a basic material for producing other objects. Instead, it functioned as a standardized legal unit of currency produced on a quasi-industrial scale.

In Scandinavia as elsewhere, the standardization of currencies (silver or otherwise) developed as interregional trade intensified and conflicts or confusion over exchange rates increased (Skre 2011). In Iceland, the emergence of this standardized pattern of textile production correlates with both legal and literary evidence for intensified trade with mainland Europe through Scandinavia and the British Isles (Gelsinger 1981). The impact of this trade on the Icelandic economy can be gauged, in part, from these standardized assemblages' ubiquity. Not only does standardized *vaðmál* dominate textile assemblages from every medieval site examined so far, but evidence for the production of cloth has also been recovered at virtually every site of this period (Hayeur Smith 2014b, 2018). This implies, based on the full range of site types of this production, that it was not only decentralized but also household based.

There are no indications in historical, archaeological, or ethnographic sources that specialist tools were required to produce *vaðmál*, as distinct from other types of cloth. Moreover, the tools of cloth production have been found on virtually every medieval farm excavated in Iceland: loom weights and spindle whorls, supplemented, where organic preservation is good, by examples of roving (unspun combed bundles of wool prepared for spinning), spun threads, tablet-woven starting-border scraps, and off-cuts of cloth from warp-weighted looms. At farms of this period that yielded both organic and inorganic evidence of textile production, standardized 2/2 twills with the characteristics of *vaðmál* are the only or the dominant type of textile recovered. In sum, the evidence for textile production on farms is widespread, and the type of cloth found on these farms, where preserved, is *vaðmál*. Interestingly, this appears to characterize farms at all socioeconomic levels, from elite sites such as Reykholt (Sveinbjarnadóttir 2012) to smaller sites such as Meiðalheimur (Steinberg et al. 2009), suggesting that the production of cloth currency was not a prerogative of elite farms alone. Historical records and sagas similarly record the payment of debts in cloth by smaller farms and its use in legal and commercial transactions by farms at all levels within the hierarchy, supporting the archaeological evidence that *vaðmál* was produced in the home on nearly all farms with sufficient labor (women) and resources (wool).

The adoption of uniform and tightly constrained thread count ranges, the reduction in variability of spin directions at sites across Iceland at the end of the Viking Age, and the reduction in weave types suggest standardization, whereas the dominance of *vaðmál* in medieval textile assemblages from the full range of site types implies that its production was decentralized and household-based.

At what point in Icelandic history did this cloth currency become so standardized that nearly all other types of weave disappeared? Dating this transition archaeologically is complicated by the limited number of excavated Icelandic sites with organic preservation from the period AD 1050–1200. Nevertheless, direct AMS dates on *vaðmál* from the sites described here suggest a clear temporal sequence. While twills do occur in the Viking Age, such as at the site of Hofstaðir in northeastern Iceland (Lucas 2009), most of them do not have thread counts that fall consistently within the ranges discussed. Furthermore, within these sites, twills are present as minor elements within a far more variable and evenly divided textile assemblage that implies production for diverse uses rather than a focus on making standardized products for exchange. For example, only one fragment from Hofstaðir and one from Ketilsstaðir fit the criteria of later legal cloth. The former is a Z/S-spun, 2/2 twill with a thread count of 12 warp yarns to 7 wefts, though no AMS dates have been determined for this piece. The Ketilsstaðir fragment discussed in Chapter 2 would also fall within the legal guidelines of cloth currency. This object (12438-3), part of the apron's strap (Z/S, 2/2 twill), produced a calibrated age (through AMS dating of a fragment) at two standard deviations (95.4% probability) of calAD 716–940 (Beta-380903; 1200 ± 30 ybp), with an 87.8% internal probability that the age of this sample falls within the interval calAD 765–895. This is a very early date for Iceland and would, in the absence of other evidence on cloth production, imply a very early date for the emergence of standardized legal-currency cloth. However, this fragment and a small number of others of similar type represent just a small percentage within the full range of Viking Age weaves.

Although these examples are infrequent, they suggest that the type of cloth that became legally regulated *vaðmál* originated in the Viking Age and was being produced before it dominated the textile assemblages of the medieval period. The earliest known example of *vaðmál* that fully exhibits all of the characteristics listed above for legal cloth comes from a deeply buried wet site (Alþingisreitur) in the center of Reykjavik (Garðarsdóttir 2010). This fragment (ATR 2008-32-715) produced a calibrated AMS date of calAD 1020–1160 (Beta-339967, 2 sigma) with intercepts at AD 1040, 1110, and 1120 and highest internal probabilities at calAD 1082–1125. Eight further dates for cloth with the characteristics of *vaðmál* and from assemblages dominated by this form of cloth were obtained from the sites of Vík, Reykjavik (Alþingisreitur), Stóraborg, Kúabot, Bergþórshvoll, Bessastaðir, and Gilsbakki. These dates document *vaðmál*'s production through the sixteenth century and suggest that while woolen cloth may have declined as an item of international trade by AD 1300, as some have suggested (e.g., Gelsinger 1981), to be replaced by dried fish or *skreið*, it continued to be used within Iceland and circulated as a medium of exchange until the sixteenth century (Hayeur Smith 2014b, 2018). This is evident in the consistent mention of *vaðmál* in various harbor records from the fourteenth century, and its likely presence noted in Norwegian harbor sites such as Trondheim, Bryggen, and Borgund Kaupang (Hayeur Smith, forthcoming).

Although more samples from the eleventh and twelfth centuries will need to undergo dating and analysis to establish precisely when Z/S-spun 2/2 twills became legal cloth, the degree of standardization seen within the data from medieval Iceland suggests that during the late eleventh or early twelfth century, this 2/2 twill with 4–15 warp threads and 4–8 weft threads was promoted for use both as legal currency and as a commercial product. This twill dominates all Icelandic site assemblages after circa AD 1100, and, given the date from Alþingisreitur, combined with the age at which the earliest portions of Grágás (the earliest medieval law book) containing references to *vaðmál* as legal cloth were written (ca. AD 1117; Dennis et al. 1980:9–13), one may reasonably conclude that this currency acquired its official standardized status roughly between AD

1080–1150, and from then on was produced on farms of all types across Iceland until the late sixteenth century or even later (Hoffman 1974; Þórlaksson 1991).

Legal Cloth as Currency and Gender Relationships

The study of medieval legal documents, together with anthropological studies of textile work in ancient communities, suggests that cloth was often produced by women (Hayeur Smith 2014b, 2015b; Róbertsdóttir 2008). As discussed in Chapter 1, strong sexual taboos surrounded textile work in both Viking Age Scandinavia and Iceland (Bek-Pedersen 2007, 2009; Milek 2012). Legal texts quite explicitly state that women were not considered legally equal to men or always permitted a public voice (Hayeur Smith 2004; Jochens 1995; Norrman 2008). Women in Scandinavia, including Iceland, were the keepers of the home, whereas men were normally more active participants in the world outside (Norrman 2008). Yet women had critical economic roles. Among these, women produced *vaðmál* and other textiles from wool that they gathered, carded, washed, and spun (Meulengracht Sørensen 1983). While men were responsible for other aspects of textile production pertaining to sheep husbandry, establishing trade relationships, and setting legal guidelines, women made cloth that conformed to legal regulations and established standards. How did relations between the sexes play out regarding the production and distribution of cloth currency in a society without urban centers and in which cloth was quite likely produced on every farm for both household and legal use?

As we have seen, weaving provided a means of expression that was uniquely female and perhaps associated with strong female deities linked to concepts of birth, life, and death (Bek-Pedersen 2007, 2009; Hayeur Smith 2012, 2014; Heide 2007). The silence of historical sources on women's roles in the regulation and distribution of cloth currency obscures their involvement in this important activity, but an illustration in Heynesbók, a fifteenth-century manuscript of the Jónsbók law code (GKS 3269b 4to.), suggests that women in Iceland were not excluded from its public distribution. In this image, a woman is depicted conversing with a man who carries a measuring stick to verify the dimensions of the *vaðmál* she is presenting to him. She asks, "Ert þú konungs umboðsmaður?" ("Are you the King's steward?"), to which he answers, "Já, já" ("Yes, yes") (Figure 3.5). It is unclear whether she is assisting him or if the illustration indicates the necessity of identifying who had the king's authority to validate goods in exchange after Iceland became a colonial dependency. In either case, the artist's choice of a woman as a participant in a legal action is significant. Iceland's medieval sources provide little evidence of women's resistance to male domination of economic interac-

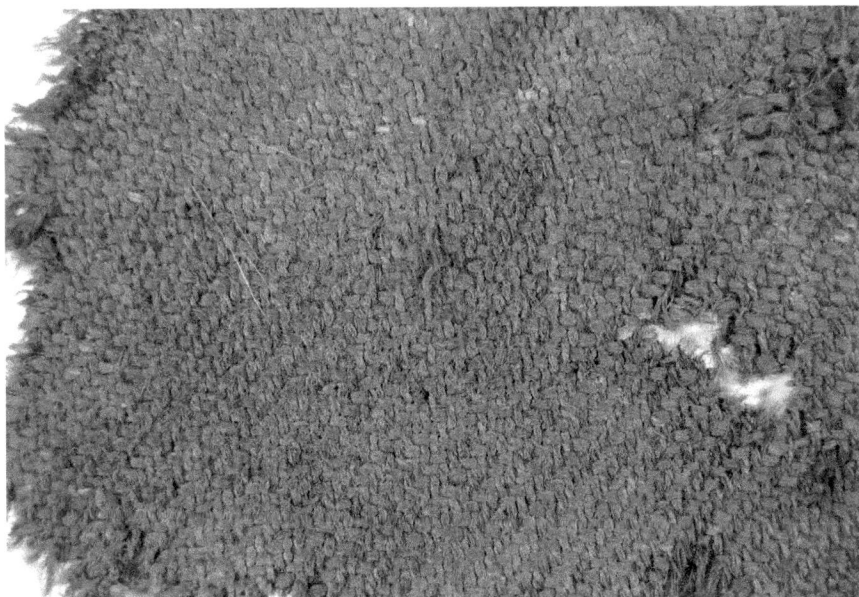

Figure 3.5. (a) Measuring *vaðmál*. (© The Árni Magnússon Institute, Reykjavik [Ref.: Jónsbók, GKS 3269b 4to.], fifteenth-century photo by Jóhanna Ólafsdóttir.) (b) A photo of the cloth *vaðmál*, National Museum of Iceland. (Photo by Hayeur Smith.)

tions that set values for cloth currency. Each gender appears to have understood its complementary role in this economic system.

At the same time, making *vaðmál* was making money, and this may have provided women with a source of power that was socially understood, as the weavers knew best the differences between good and poor quality *vaðmál*. This seeming symbiosis may stem from the small size of the Icelandic colony, the harsh nature of the North Atlantic environment, and the need for collaboration between the sexes to guarantee survival. This is not to say that resistance did not exist, but it may have been subtle and reflected in the values and symbolic associations connected to the making of cloth, as discussed in Chapter 1 (Hayeur Smith 2012, 2014b, 2018).

The Importance Cloth

The discussion of cloth currency in Iceland brings us to the final question: why cloth? As we have seen, legal sources and archaeological data indicate that cloth was used in Norway and Iceland as a means of exchange, but why was it chosen as a form of commodity money in the first place, and what lay behind its value and worth?

Skre (2011:70) argues that commodities that are accorded the value of currency also have utilitarian value. This differentiates a commodity-money system from a purely monetary system based on abstract representations of value. In Viking Age Scandinavia, coinage and silver were introduced and used as methods of payment alongside other commodities for nearly one millennium. In this system, different commodity-money media functioned not only as units of account and means of payment but also as commodities with inherent utilitarian value (Skre 2011:71).

In late Viking Age and early medieval Iceland, textiles served all these functions: they could be kept and stored for future use; used to pay taxes, tithes, and other financial obligations; or consumed and transformed into household items. Cloth was transportable and malleable and catered to basic human needs for shelter and protection (Schneider and Weiner 1989:2). When transformed into clothing, textiles also provided information about the "social self": social rank, status, gender, and cultural affiliation (Eicher and Roach-Higgins 1992:12; Turner 1993:15). Through these diverse concepts and the predominant roles women upheld in cloth production in many cultures, textiles and textile work have frequently become associated with life-giving, life-taking, and destiny (Schneider and Weiner 1989:21).

One may wonder what this has to do with cloth used as a commodity for exchange. I argue that these concepts reflect deeply ingrained understandings about cloth in the Viking Age that may have contributed to its valuation by endowing it with more than utilitarian value, as a product that evoked a symbolic system firmly rooted in mythology and belief, in female agency and power. Schneider and Weiner (1989:3) suggest that in many cultural contexts, textiles became metaphors for society itself and social relations; they also argue that textiles can provide a convincing analog for the regenerative and degenerative processes.

In Viking Age Iceland and Norway, textiles acquired value not only for their practical uses but also from many deeply rooted metaphors. Regardless of their symbolic or metaphoric representations, however, textiles in both Iceland and Norway gained sufficient importance to be assigned a formalized and legal value on a par with silver. When it came to actual economic transactions, did everyone in Iceland routinely pay their debts in cloth from the eleventh century onward? Probably not, as the commodity-money system was as fluid as it was in Norway and gave people opportunities to choose from diverse media, depending on what was available. Yet legal obligations and the standard exchange values of those diverse commodities used ells of *vaðmál* as the official unit of measure. Grágás frequently lists *vaðmál* as the official unit of measure and provides equivalents for its worth in relation to silver and other commodities. In 1281, when Jónsbók was handed down from the Norwegian crown as Iceland's new law of the land in a novel colonial context, *vaðmál* was not as frequently mentioned by name as a commodity, but the standard unit of measure remained the "one-ounce unit" that was still equivalent to six ells of *vaðmál*.

The two legal codes differ, in that the compilers of Grágás seemed to find it important to reiterate that cloth was acceptable as a medium of exchange and also provided legal guidance on assessing its qualities. However, by the time Jónsbók was written, it appears that the transition from silver to cloth as the basic unit of account had been formalized and naturalized to the degree that I argue it was no longer necessary to justify its value or describe its appearance anymore, since cloth had become a universally understood means to economic ends (Hayeur Smith 2018).

4

Textiles in Greenland during the Medieval Period

While women were producing cloth currency in Iceland from the eleventh century onward, a different North Atlantic society was developing farther west in Greenland. The Norse had settled Greenland during the tenth century, from areas in western Iceland that had already converted to Christianity. Greenlanders, as expatriate Icelanders, brought with them Norse cultural traditions, including weaving and textile technologies. But did the Norse Greenlanders bring with them an economy based on using cloth as a form of currency in a commodity-money system? The data suggest that they did not and that cloth, in Greenland, served different roles.

The Eastern Settlement of Greenland is located at the island's southern extremity (Figure 4.6), where the landscape resembles that of Iceland with green pastures, valleys, and fjords; the Western Settlement is located farther north along the west coast in the area of Greenland's present capital, Nuuk. As in Iceland, settlements consisted of small and large farms. Their pastoral economy based on grazing sheep, goats, and cattle operated well until roughly AD 1300, when the climate began cooling dramatically with the onset of the Little Ice Age. The Greenlanders' responses to climatic deterioration included an increased hunting of wild animals and a decrease in animal husbandry on some farms, as well as a shift in emphasis regarding what animals to breed (Arneborg et al. 2008; Dugmore et al. 2007; McGovern 1991, 1980; McGovern et al. 2014; Nelson et al. 2012; Smiarowski 2012). The use of woolen cloth was also affected, as people adapted their clothing needs to suit the new climatic conditions.

In the next two chapters, I will address what makes Greenlandic cloth unique in the North Atlantic corpus, along with certain particularities I have noted in the data. I will also address the issues of recycling cloth and admixtures of Arctic species that the Norse may have added to their cloth. I will further extend the analysis to examine some suggested Norse textiles found in Canada's Eastern Arctic and confirm or dispel assumptions about their origins.

Greenlandic Cloth Compared to That of Other North Atlantic Settlements

What defines Greenlandic cloth in the North Atlantic assemblage? Archaeological research in Greenland has produced far less cloth than is known from Iceland.[1] It remains unclear whether this lower number of preserved samples is a reflection of the smaller size of Greenland's farms and its smaller population or whether the preservation of cloth on Greenlandic sites is not as consistent as in Iceland. As in Iceland, textiles have been found in both Greenlandic burial contexts and farm middens as the presence of permafrost in Greenland may have had beneficial effects on the survival of these organic artifacts.

Greenland's Norse population was never as large as Iceland's. In the thirteenth century, according to recent archaeological research, the population of the Eastern and Western Settlements combined amounted to no more than 1,400–6,000 people, compared to 40,000–70,000 for Iceland (Koch Madsen 2014, based on Karlsson 2000; Keller 1986; and Lynnerup 1998). However, these vast differences in population size do not appear to be sufficient to explain the smaller size of Greenland's archaeological textile assemblage. Social factors affecting the use and production of textiles are also apparent.

In Iceland every farm appears to have been engaged in the production of cloth during the early medieval period. In fact, evidence of cloth production is so uniform and ubiquitous there that one has the impression of a significant cultural phenomenon taking place, with production exceeding the needs of personal consumption at the farm level. In Greenland, large assemblages of cloth from individual sites are absent, but even more striking is that evidence for the standardization of cloth, a hallmark of its production as currency, is also missing. Whereas Icelandic assemblages are marked by vast amounts of identically produced cloth with tight clusters of thread counts suggesting extreme standardization, in Greenland the impression is that cloth was woven in many different weaves on individual farms, reflecting their needs for cloth to be put into domestic daily use, and that people prioritized exploring new ways to extend their limited supplies or to create cloth that was warmer in an increasingly colder environment.

Cloth Recycling: The "Burgundian Hat" from Herjolfsnes and Other Patched Garments from Greenland

In some parts of Greenland, the preservation of cloth is amazing. Excavations in 1921 at the medieval cemetery of Ikigaat (Herjolfsnes), near Greenland's southern tip, produced an astonishing assemblage of complete garments (Lynnerup 1998:20; Nørlund 2010:59). The soil conditions at this site were complex: some burials were in areas of deep permafrost, and others were near the surface or in areas of past melting, and while many textiles remained, few bones did (Østergård 2004:27). In total, 23 intact "outfits" were recovered, 3 of which are children's garments, with 16 hoods, 4 caps, and 1 pair of stockings as well as 4 single stockings (Østergård 2004:26). This major excavation was undertaken in 1921 by Poul Nørlund, whose goal at the time was to establish the nature of the Norse farm and church within the Eastern Settlement. Constant erosion was occurring on the site, and over the course of approximately 100 years before Nørlund's excavations, items of clothing, coffins, and a funeral stone with runic inscriptions had eroded out of the site (Lynnerup 1998:19). Nørlund (2010) himself was able to excavate 110–120 burials, and more were identified in the survey area.

Some of Nørlund's collections from Ikigaat/Herjolfsnes are now housed at the National Museum of Denmark, while other garments have been returned to Greenland, where they are curated at the Greenland Museum and Archives in Nuuk. This amazing assemblage of preserved garments is the largest of its kind from medieval Europe and provides unique opportunities for examining not only the kinds of garments the medieval Greenlandic Norse wore, but also the kinds of cloth they made, the ways they used and recycled it, and whether they acquired cloth or garments from abroad.

In 2015, when I visited the National Museum of Denmark, Jette Arneborg, the curator of these Greenlandic collections, mentioned to me that the material from Ikigaat (Herjolfsnes) included a particular hat—the "Burgundian tall hat"—that had come to symbolize the demise of the Greenland colony around AD 1450 (Figure 4.1). Arneborg suggested we sample the hat, which was made up of multiple patches (like many garments from the site), and submit these samples for AMS dating to acquire an accurate age for the hat and potentially gain insights into the use and recycling of cloth among the Greenland Norse. Cloth recycling was a practice I had already noted in the North Atlantic islands of Iceland and Scotland, but it seemed particularly prevalent in Greenland. In most places, however, patches and scraps were found discarded or attached to other scraps in middens or floor deposits. At Ikigaat, however, they were present on complete garments, providing insights into the ways that women and men in Norse Greenland maintained, managed, and recycled their resources. The Burgundian hat in particular offered an opportunity to examine how a complete garment was made and patched and how old the cloth was that had been used to repair it. The results of this study were published in 2016 in the *Danish Journal of Archaeology* in a paper I coauthored with Jette Arneborg and Kevin P. Smith; those results are summarized here.

In 2004 Else Østergård performed an in-depth reanalysis of all the textile finds from Greenland, with a focus on the Herjolfsnes material. Among those pieces was the famous Burgundian hat, unique within the corpus of Greenlandic textiles, and thus named after its discovery by Nørlund not only because of its specific shape but also because of the custom of wearing a hood over a cap that he noted in another of the Herjolfsnes burials. Nørlund drew parallels between the hat from Herjolfsnes (DNM D10608) and the "weepers" on the sarcophagus of the Duke of Burgundy (1425), where one character is depicted wearing a small cap and another is shown with a hood over the cap (Hayeur Smith et al. 2016; Østergård 2004:134).

Nørlund (2010:182) himself saw the hat as somewhat iconic and stated in 1924 that "it will then be one of the specimens serving to give the latest date for the find and the interruption of the intercourse with Europe" (Hayeur Smith et al. 2016). Over time, this hat came to symbolize the end of the Greenland colony, the end of contact with the European mainland, and the latest date for the burials in the churchyard (Arneborg 1996; Østergård 2004). In particular, a major implication of Nørlund's interpretation was that the Greenlanders, despite their marginality, remained tightly connected to continental European culture and constructed their identities in reference to the latest trends in Western European fashion, right up to the point at which the Greenland colony disappeared (Hayeur Smith et al. 2016). This view of fashionable Greenlanders in contact with continental traders until the very end added to the "mystery" of the Greenland colonies' disappearance. Why, if they were that successful and well connected, had their society collapsed?

After Nørlund's thorough analysis, the hat took on a life of its own and became known in the literature as the Burgundian tall hat. It was described as such by McGovern (1985), Martensen-Larsen (1987), and McGhee (2003), who used it to reference Greenland's contacts with the external world (Hayeur Smith et al. 2016). In 1996 Seaver mentioned the Burgundian hat in reference to merchants traveling to Greenland to sell their wares, arguing that such a hat would have been impractical at sea but that its height might have served to impress local inhabitants (Seaver 1996:230–231). Despite such long-lasting academic interest in this hat and its meanings, there was no certainty that the hat was actually made under Burgundian influence, nor was there evidence to support its role as an element of a man's or a woman's attire, since Nørlund was unable to associate it with a specific skeleton, and the hat itself had never been directly dated (Hayeur Smith et al. 2016).

This hat's role as symbol of the end of the Greenland colony was eventually debunked when Arneborg (1996:83) published ^{14}C dates from Herjolfsnes. Dating of the hat suggested it was made at least a century earlier than assumed and probably had no correlation with southern Europe, having perhaps more in common with Icelandic and Nordic clothing traditions (Hayeur Smith et al. 2016).

Archaeological Context of the Hat

At double the height of any of the other hats from Herjolfsnes, the Burgundian or tall brimless hat stood out among the five caps recovered during Nørlund's excavations (Nørlund 2010:12; Østergård 2004:221). It was found in the southwestern part of the churchyard, resting upon another piece of cloth that Nørlund thought was part of the same headdress. Inside this second piece were teeth that disintegrated during conservation (Nørlund 2010:180; Østergård 2004:133). Compared to all the other caps from Herjolfsnes, the tall hat was the only one lacking in clues about its absolute age (Nørlund 2010:182), presumably because Nørlund was having difficulties identifying parallels in Europe. Although another tall hat was found on the site, it was in such a poor state of preservation that it was discarded.

Construction of the Hat

The hat (Nørlund no. 87, DNM D10612) was made using both a tabby weave and a 2/2 twill (Østergård 2004:221). Its body was constructed with a wide lower portion measuring 190 mm, with an additional gusset of 130 mm × 130 mm, giving a flare to the bottom half. A separate 70-mm-wide band of tabby was sewn to the top of the main portion, while two pieces sewn together—a piece of tabby and a 2/2 twill—formed the crown (Figure 4.1).

Østergård remarked that the hat originally had a color arrangement of black and dark brown warp threads crossed by white or light tan wefts. Furthermore, the warps on the main body of the hat ran crosswise and were possibly spun with goat hair, while the wefts were made from the undercoat of the Northern

Short-tailed sheep (Østergård 2004:221). This would have produced an interesting striped effect that Østergård noted in three places: on the bottom portion of the main section, on the top narrow band, and on the crown of the hat. The hat today is very worn and decayed, but beyond that, its textiles were unevenly woven, in areas displaying warp threads in pairs. The thread counts measured on different parts of the hat ranged from 6/9–13 for the tabby weave sections, whereas the 2/2 twill that made up half of the crown piece was 8/9, suggesting that the cloth was slightly weft dominant (Hayeur Smith et al. 2016).

Stylistic Dating of the Hat

Nørlund dated the hat according to typological similarities with headdresses documented in paintings and sculptures from other parts of Western Europe. His main impression was that this hat, like the other caps recovered at Herjolfsnes, belonged to a male. To support this assertion, he provided examples from European art of the fifteenth and sixteenth centuries, such as Hans Memling's *Portrait of a Man* (1480) and details taken from the altarpiece of the Broby church (ca. 1500) in Funen, where a man is depicted wearing a hat similar to the Greenlandic examples. Norlund stated: "Its impressive height and broad back part point to the middle and the latter half of the fifteenth century and most probably it is a man's though the women of that period wore similar erections usually covered with a veil of lawn" (Nørlund 2010:182). However, Nørlund also mentioned its possible similarity to the Icelandic woman's faldur of the sixteenth century: a tall, conical headdress that underwent a series of transformations and variations, and is today worn as part of the national costume of Iceland (Guðjónsson 1978; Hayeur Smith et al. 2016; Helgadóttir 2013; Østergård 2004:133). Based on a review of Nordic dress by Falk (1918), Arneborg (1996:79) argued that Icelandic women's tall hats were also mentioned in the sagas of the thirteenth and fourteenth centuries (Arneborg 1996:83), and an image published by Sigurjónsdóttir (1985) supports its Icelandic origins.[2]

AMS Dating of the Hat and Other Greenlandic Garments

Most of Nørlund's dating of the clothing from Herjolfsnes was based on style and typology; despite a lack of access to absolute methods, he was relatively accurate for several pieces, but off by 100 years for the tall hat (Hayeur Smith et al. 2016). Nørlund thought it belonged to the late 1400s, whereas Arneborg's AMS dating (AAR-2201; 685 ± 50 bp) produced a two-sigma calibrated date of calAD 1250–1410. Based on the calibration curve used at the time of her

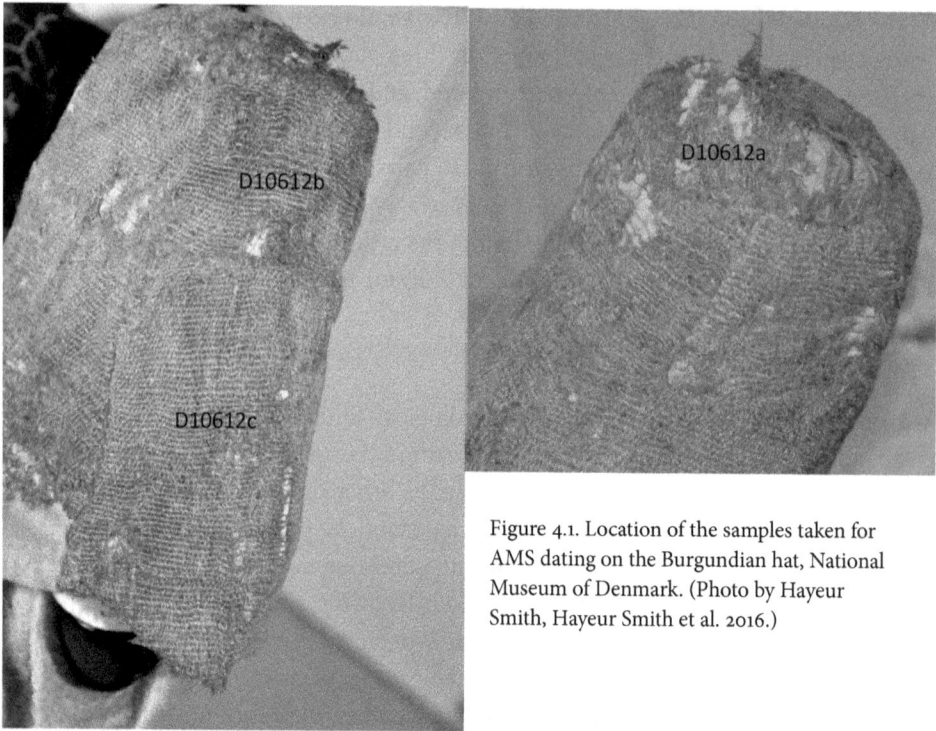

Figure 4.1. Location of the samples taken for AMS dating on the Burgundian hat, National Museum of Denmark. (Photo by Hayeur Smith, Hayeur Smith et al. 2016.)

publication, this date had a nearly even bimodal probability distribution at one-sigma, with a 37.3% probability that its actual age was calAD 1270–1320, and a 30.9% probability that the wool was sheared during a later range of calAD 1350–1390 (Hayeur Smith et al. 2016). Favoring the two-sigma range, Arneborg (1996:81) and Østergård (2004:33) placed its age generally between 1300 and 1400.[3] Their sample came from the main body of the hat, and while both authors mentioned the recycling of cloth in its construction (Arneborg 1996:79, 81; Østergård 2004:135), the possibility that different sections of the hat might produce different dates was not explored at that time (Hayeur Smith et al. 2016).

Therefore, during my visit to the National Museum of Denmark in 2015, we ran a series of new AMS dates to see if we could confirm Arneborg's date and verify whether the entire hat dated from AD 1300–1400 or demonstrate that Nørlund had it right. One sample was collected from the larger lower portion of the hat, a second was obtained from the narrower top band, and a third was taken from the most heavily worn part of the crown—the tabby weave section (Figure 4.1). All three samples were submitted for AMS dating at Beta Analytic in Miami, Florida.

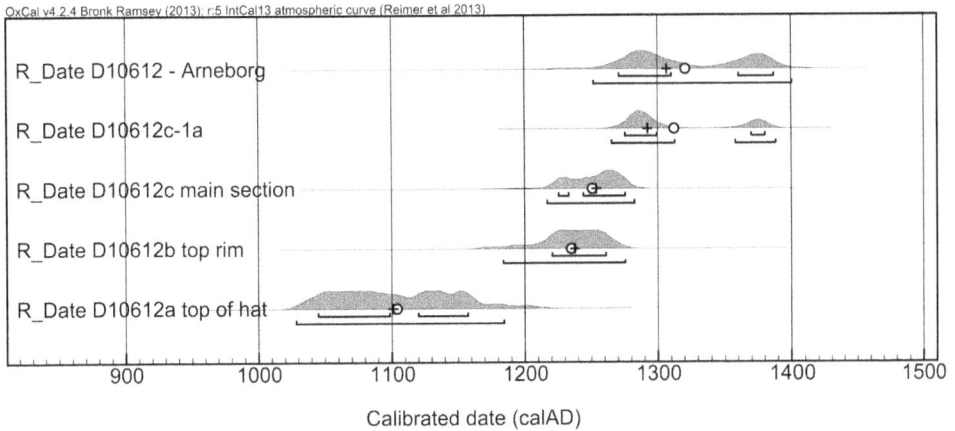

Figure 4.2. AMS date results for the Greenlandic tall hat. (Hayeur Smith et al. 2016.)

The dates for different parts of the hat were considerably different from one another. Two were essentially contemporary with, and one was earlier than, the single date reported by Arneborg (1996). Importantly, however, all were earlier than Nørlund's estimated age for the hat by at least 200 years (Hayeur Smith et al. 2016).

Before the 1980s, petrochemicals were frequently used to clean archaeological textiles. These chemicals can affect the overall results from AMS dating; for this reason, one sample (DNM D16012c) was rerun with a separate solvent extraction pretreatment process, designed to remove any residual chemicals, at Beta Analytic. Figure 4.2 shows the four new AMS dates, as well as the previous one by Arneborg (1996). All are now calibrated using OxCal version 4.2.3 (Bronk Ramsey et al. 2013) and the r:5 IntCal13 atmospheric curve (Reimer et al. 2013), under the assumption that the sheep from which the wool was gathered had a terrestrial diet (for a full discussion of the dates, see Hayeur Smith et al. 2016).

The solvent extraction pretreatment suggested that the three new calibrated AMS dates may be circa 40 years too old, due to residues from past conservation treatment. Adjusting for that offset, our new median date estimates for these samples are AD 1277–1294 for the body of the hat (DNM 16012b, c), and AD 1101 for the hat's crown (Hayeur Smith et al. 2016). The two new dates for the body of the hat clearly overlap and are consistent with the earlier half of Arneborg's previously run date. Together, these dates suggest that the main body of the hat was made from wool shorn and spun in the last half, and most likely the last quarter, of the thirteenth century. The age estimate obtained for the crown of the hat, however, is clearly much different, suggesting that this wool was gathered in the early twelfth century, approximately 150 years before the hat itself was assembled (Hayeur Smith et al. 2016).

While the new dates confirming Arneborg's previous one have finally put the question of the hat's origins to rest (it was too early to be of Burgundian origin), the dating of this piece provides important information on the use of cloth in the Greenland Norse colony. The different dates obtained from separate sections of the hat suggest culturally specific behavior regarding cloth use in Greenland that has also been noted in Iceland. Given that the fabric used to patch the crown of the hat dates to the early twelfth century and is much earlier than the other samples from the hat's body, it is possible that cloth was such an important commodity that it was preserved for centuries and reused in garment construction over and over again. Therefore, the frequently deteriorated conditions of these textiles may not be solely post-depositional, resulting from decay over time, but may instead be related to intense recycling. And, if the cloth used to patch the hat had been around, and perhaps in use as part of another garment, for such a long period of time, this also raises questions about how long the hat may have been in use after its thirteenth-century creation.

Additional garments and cloth fragments with intensive cloth recycling have been found in the Greenlandic corpus. Following the example of the tall hat, I performed similar analyses on other garments from Norse Greenland, including AMS dating of one of the complete gusseted robes (D10585) from the same site, Ikigaat (Herjolfsnes), and on another from Gården under Sandet.

This long-sleeved gusseted robe from Herjolfsnes is missing one of its sleeves and is made of a 2/2 twill. The front of the garment has four visible patches. I dated three of these, along with the main body of the garment. All the textiles in this garment are of the weft-dominant type or Greenlandic *vaðmál*, as classified by Østergård (2004) (Table 4.1, Figure 4.3). Originally this piece had a gray warp and a light gray weft (Østergård 2004:174). It was very worn, and the patches are a clear indication of efforts to maintain it in working condition.

The results of AMS dating suggest that the dates from the patches on the Herjolfsnes gown are effectively identical in age with the age of the gown itself. This implies that it was patched with cloth that was woven around the same time that the gown was made. While these results do not show that old cloth was used to patch newer garments, they do suggest that patching was important in fourteenth-century Greenland, just as it was during the thirteenth century, when the hat was made and worn.

The site known as Gården under Sandet was a relatively moderate-sized farm. No church or cemetery is known from the site, suggesting that it was the home of an economically and politically less powerful household than Herjolf-

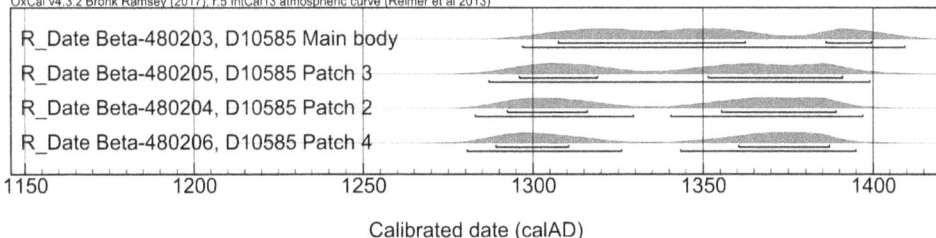

OxCal v4.3.2 Bronk Ramsey (2017); r:5 IntCal13 atmospheric curve (Reimer et al 2013)

Figure 4.3. AMS dates run on the gusseted gown D10585 from Herjolfsnes.

Table 4.1. AMS dates run on the gusseted gown D10585 from Herjolfsnes

	Location	Thread counts	AMS date (calAD)
D10585, main body of dress	Front	9/11	1307–1399 (1s*)
			1307–1362 (55.0%)
			1386–1399 (13.2%)
			1297–1409 (2s)
D10585, patch 2	Patch placed on frontal gusset	9/15	1292–1389 (1s)
			1292–1316 (27.5%)
			1355–1389 (40.7%)
			1283–1397 (2s)
D10585, patch 3	Patch placed on side gusset front, right side	8/12	1296–1391 (1s)
			1296–1319 (25.4%)
			1351–1391 (42.8%)
			1287–1399 (2s)
D10585, patch 4	Patch placed on right sleeve	8/15	1289–1387 (1s)
			1289–1310 (29.6%)
			1360–1387 (38.6%)
			1280–1395 (2s)
			1280–1326 (43.5%)
			1343–1395 (51.9%)

Notes: 1s = 1 standard deviation (68.2%); 2s = 2 standard deviation (95.4%).

snes's farm. Excavations at GUS yielded a significant number of textiles (174 finds). The site is located in the Western Settlement and was excavated between 1991 and 1996. Its designation is appropriate, as it was hidden under 150 cm of sand, with its cultural layer locked in permafrost (Berglund 1998:8). As a result, preservation on the site was excellent. Excavations revealed several buildings that show their development through sequential chronological phases that span the entire duration of the Western Settlement.

The textile-related finds at GUS included many from a weaving room—or *dyngja*—as discussed in Chapter 1 (Østergård 1998:58). This weaving room contained a bone needle case, a spindle whorl, 115 loom weights, an almost complete top beam from a warp-weighted loom (1. 88 m long) that would have allowed cloth to be woven (without preserved selvages) 940 mm wide (Arneborg 1993:167; Østergård 1998:65, Figure 3), and a fragment of a fixed shed rod.

One of the textile fragments from the weaving room (1950 x1337) was made up of seven different pieces of cloth patched together to create one piece (Table 4.2). The overall appearance of x1337 is enigmatic, and it could have been part of a sleeve made entirely of patches. Interestingly, all of the pieces are either tabby weave or 2/2 twills, all are spun Z/S, and are weft dominant except for C, which is warp dominant like textiles from Iceland from the same period.

Patches G (on the underside) C, B, and F (Figure 4.5) were sampled and dated to determine their ages, and all proved to be roughly contemporaneous, though the construction of C is more akin to early Greenlandic textiles of the tenth and eleventh centuries. Clearly, these examples indicate that in most cases, people were reusing every fragment of cloth to repair or salvage garments or to create new garments from the fragments available. This suggests that resources were scarce, or else that textiles in the North Atlantic were so important that people coveted and used them in ways to convey their own social messages.

A similar degree of cloth recycling is common in the Icelandic corpus, where approximately 70% of textiles show some kind of reuse. My analyses of textiles from the site of Bergþórshvoll in southern Iceland resulted in the discovery of a box of previously unknown textiles that had escaped conservation since their archaeological recovery some 90 years ago (Eldjárn and Gestsson 1952). After the textiles were cleaned, the box was found to include many heavily patched garments and fragments, including a footless stocking or garter (worn over trousers and shoes and said to be common among fishermen) and a possible hood.

The hood resembles several of the Herjolfsnes hoods, such as D10604 (Nørlund, No. 74), but with a very short liripipe extension at the back of the head rather than the long ones more commonly found at Herjolfsnes. The

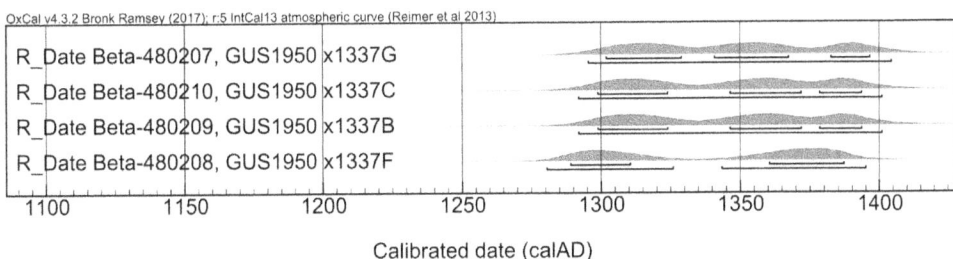

OxCal v4.3.2 Bronk Ramsey (2017); r:5 IntCal13 atmospheric curve (Reimer et al 2013)

R_Date Beta-480207, GUS1950 x1337G	
R_Date Beta-480210, GUS1950 x1337C	
R_Date Beta-480209, GUS1950 x1337B	
R_Date Beta-480208, GUS1950 x1337F	

Calibrated date (calAD)

Figure 4.4. AMS dates run on the garment fragment GUS 1950 x1337 from Gården under Sandet.

Table 4.2. AMS dates run on the garment fragment 1950 x1337 from Gården under Sandet

Patches on 1950 x1337	Thread count	Weave type	AMS date
A	7/5–7?	Z/S, tabby weave	-
B	10/16	Z/S, 2/2 twill	1299–1393 (1s) 1299–1324 (26.6%) 1346–1372 (26.5%) 1378–1393 (15.0%) 1292–1401 (2s)
C	8/6	Z/S, 2/2 twill	1299–1393 (1s) 1299–1324 (26.6%) 1346–1372 (26.5%) 1378–1393 (15.0%) 1292–1401 (2s)
D	7/9	Z/S, 2/2 twill	-
E	8/12	Z/S, 2/2 twill	-
F	7/7	Z/S, 2/2 twill	1289–1387 (1s) 1289–1310 (29.6%) 1360–1387 (38.6%) 1280–1395 (2s) 1280–1326 (43.5%) 1343–1395 (51.9%)
G	6/6	Z/S, tabby weave?	1302–1396 (1s) 1302–1329 (27.5%) 1341–1367 (27.0%) 1382–1396 (13.7%) 1295–1404 (2s)

Note: 1s=1 standard deviation; 2s=2 standard deviation

Figure 4.5. Garment fragment GUS 1950 x1337, Greenland Museum and Archives. (Photo by Hayeur Smith. Courtesy Greenland Museum and Archives.)

Bergþórshvoll example appears to lack the long liripipe familiar from the Herjolfsnes example but has a very short one at the back of the head (Østergård 2004). It has not been dated, but is similarly made up of 12 patches. The stocking was a nearly complete piece put together from many patches that included different types of *vaðmál* and knits. Like the Herjolfsnes tall hat, the stocking was sampled and two different portions were dated; both produced calibrated dates in the range calAD 1451–1513. A knitted patch was also present on the stocking. While this piece was not dated, it is well documented that knitting appeared in Iceland during the 1500s (Róbertsdóttir 2008).

Cloth Recycling and Cloth Reuse

Three approaches to cloth recycling are represented within the Greenland corpus: the tall hat and its use of very old textiles; the gown from Herjolfsnes, where repair seems to have been the main concern, as the patches are not vastly different in age from one another or from the garment that was repaired; and GUS, where contemporary textile fragments were assembled in a patchwork to create something new. This type of behavior can be coined either "reuse" or "recycling" of cloth, and the underlying motives are interesting and not always uniform.

Clothing in its cultural setting matters differently in different parts of the world (Tranberg Hansen 2004:387), but in all cultures, the dressed body allows the exploration of both individual and collective identities. The body is lacking in distinguishing features and is an ideal canvas for projecting social norms outward to the world (Tranberg Hansen 2004:372; Turner 1993).

The recycling and reuse of any form of material culture can be associated with heirlooms: objects that are reused serve to objectify memories and histories and remind the living of their ancestral antecedents, according to Lillios (1999). The patch on the crown of the Herjolfsnes tall hat could be such an item. The hat itself is unique within the textile corpus of Herjolfsnes; although a similar hat was found during Nørlund's excavation, it was discarded due to poor preservation. To possess such a hat may have conveyed a certain awe that the owner had means enough to acquire it or specific cultural links to Iceland where similar hats were found. Clearly this hat was important enough to its owner to use cloth on the crown that was significantly older than the rest. It may have served as a private reminder of his or her past heritage (Hingley 1996; Lillios 1999) and as a message to others of this person's position within society.

The social implications of this hat are all the more revealing when one considers its position within the burial context. It was said to be found at head level, whereas many hoods, hats, and gowns from Herjolfsnes were used in nonconventional ways as full-body burial shrouds or to wrap the feet. Østergård (2004) described the normal find context for textiles at Herjolfsnes as one in which the deceased was buried either in a wooden coffin or simply in shrouds made of clothing, stockings, and hoods or complete garments (Østergård 2004:24). This suggests that some or many of these garments were being discarded and used in lieu of coffins, as wood in Greenland was a rarer commodity, and the garments were not necessarily new. The contrast with this hat, found in its worn position, is therefore potentially important.

The clothing from the site of Herjolfsnes has been considered by many scholars to be the most complete collection of medieval European secular clothing in existence and a reflection of contemporary garments worn in Europe. Many of the gowns, such as D10585, whose patches were dated and discussed in this chapter, have been labeled as "gored gowns" similar to the "close-bodied" garments worn in fourteenth- and fifteenth-century Europe. However, Netherton

(2008) convincingly demonstrated that the Greenlandic gored gowns are differently made from close-bodied garments, as they possess no opening at the back to make them tight-fitting, and are too loose, with the waist situated too high. Netherton felt that while inserting gores and gussets may suggest skill and sophistication, it was also a simple mechanism to prevent waste and make use of recycled cloth in garments. Such a mechanism fits well in this discussion of cloth reuse and repair. Not all textile patches on garments were as old as those on the tall hat; the patches of D10585 may have been only slightly older than the gown itself and were clearly used to extend the life of the garment for as long as possible. They may also have conveyed messages about cultural affiliation. For the wearer, these patches may not have been eyesores but aids in emphasizing cultural origins and group cohesion.

In discussing the social mechanisms behind recycled clothing, Karen Tranberg Hansen (2004) invites readers to think differently about how the incorporation of secondhand clothing helps cultures reconstruct themselves through dress. Greenland was not impacted by imports of secondhand clothing; all garments were locally made, and who is to say that old clothing and patched, repaired garments were necessarily perceived as dilapidated or proof of extreme poverty, as a modern sensibility might conclude? By repairing or integrating old cloth into new garments, as may have been the case at GUS or with the patched garments of Herjolfsnes, the wearers may have been building upon personal and community identities and reinforcing their adherence to cultural norms, possibly even in contrast with the indigenous communities they came into contact with.

In this regard, McGovern (1980:265) argued that the Norse never adopted the efficient skin clothing the Inuit designed for an Arctic environment but continued to dress in the latest European fashions with ill-adapted woolen gowns, and yet the latest fashions they were not. By the thirteenth and fourteenth centuries, Greenlanders' contact with the European mainland was on the decline, with the last documented trading ship reaching Greenland in 1368 (Netherton 2008). The possibility that Greenlanders would have seen new fashions from Europe is slim. Their gowns and other garments were based on antiquated European models, or else were hybrid Greenlandic interpretations. The medieval Norse Greenlanders appear to have incorporated patches and repairs into their dress that in no way deterred from their social messaging but instead reinforced group identity and the cultural values they held dear. Patching and recycling were simply part and parcel of tailoring, and people may have been unaware of any derogatory connotations of reuse and recycling in the rest of the world.

Wool Admixtures and Arctic Species in Greenlandic Textiles

McGovern's assertion that the Greenlanders never adopted Inuit garments still holds true, yet the incorporation of Arctic species into Greenlandic Norse clothing has slowly but steadily gained attention. The Norse Greenlanders, it is assumed, must have used furs and skins in their clothing due to the large number of Arctic species inhabiting those areas where the Norse settled (Østergård 2004:119). While this is probably correct (it would seem ridiculous for the Norse who were hunting local resources such as caribou and seal not to make use of these animals' skins), it is difficult to prove. Skins and skins with fur attached do not preserve in the same way as textiles, and few such items exist in the corpus.

Walton Rogers (1998:66–73) and Østergård (2004:82–83, 119–122) meticulously analyzed items that may have incorporated either furs or fibers of species other than sheep in the Greenlandic material. Their work demonstrated the wide range of species, domesticated and wild, whose fur, hair, wool, and hides were used in medieval Greenland. Walton identified goat, cattle, bison, caribou, musk ox, brown bear, polar bear, wolf, Arctic hare, and Arctic fox from Gården under Sandet alone (Walton Rogers 1998:70–73). Østergård (2004) published similar information, drawing from her collaborations with Walton Rogers in the identification of these species. Walton Rogers has since revisited some of the assumptions about fur use in the Canadian Eastern Arctic and Greenland in a coauthored publication with Greaves (2018).

The use of Arctic species, whether integrated into textiles or used alone, has been an appealing approach for demonstrating the adaptability of the Greenland Norse who, faced with severe hardships, managed to diversify and expand their subsistence strategies, going so far as to tap into extensive indigenous trade networks across the North to acquire these fibers. If they were able to procure fibers such as those of brown bear or bison that are not indigenous to Greenland, this would imply that they must have traded with indigenous peoples of North America at some point. This hypothesis has important ramifications for the debate regarding Norse/indigenous interactions in the Arctic.

Sutherland (2000), an archaeologist specializing in Dorset occupations of the Canadian Eastern Arctic, furthered this discussion of Arctic species use by describing a suite of finds that she argued demonstrated Norse contacts with indigenous Arctic cultures (both Dorset cultures, circa 500 BC–AD 1350) and the Thule phase ancestral Inuit (AD 1200–1500 of the contemporary Inuit). Before Sutherland's work, much of the debate about Norse/indigenous interactions had focused on interactions between the Norse and the Thule phase Inuit around AD 1000, and not on Dorset/Paleo-Eskimo groups. Norse finds in sites of the ancestral Inuit, Thule phase, included boat rivets, oak fragments, a carpenter's plane, chain mail, woolen cloth, and smelted metal objects from Ruin Island and Skraeling Island in far northern Greenland and Ellesmere Island, respectively (Schledermann 1980, in Sutherland 2000), but also scattered items of Norse manufacture from the western coast of Ellesmere Island (Sutherland 2000), the shores of Hudson Bay, scattered locations in the central Canadian Arctic archipelago (McGhee 1984), and northern Greenland (Appelt 1997). These finds, the majority of which date to the thirteenth or fourteenth century, hint at Norse-Inuit trade and interaction, which is not at all surprising, given the presence of Norse settlements in Greenland and documented hunting trips by the Norse into northern parts of Greenland, called the Nordsetur.

Sutherland (2000) also described other possible Norse finds that she had identified in previously excavated Dorset collections in the Canadian Museum of History and at Dorset sites that she excavated as part of her Helluland project. Based on their dates and the styles of Dorset objects found in them, these sites were generally thought to have been abandoned before the Norse established colonies in Greenland during the late tenth century. From the site of Nunguvik, on northern Baffin Island (excavated by Mary-Rousselière in 1976), Sutherland identified a 3-m-long piece of spun yarn, along with pieces of wood identified as white pine (not indigenous to the Arctic), two of which possessed iron-stained holes thought to have been made by square nails (Sutherland 2000). The spun yarn was analyzed by Walton Rogers, who concluded that the yarn combined Arctic hare fur and goat hair, a mixture comparable to the mixed-fiber yarns that she had identified from GUS in Norse Greenland. However, the yarns were radiocarbon dated to the seventh and eighth centuries, whereas the dates from the wood were medieval. Despite this discrepancy between the yarns' dates and the age of the Norse Greenlandic colony, Sutherland argued that the yarn had been a valued item, considered "a curiosity by Dorset people," and assumed these were items of trade from Norse settlers visiting Baffin Island because indigenous peoples did not possess the technological skill to spin yarn (Hayeur Smith et al. 2018; Sutherland 2000).

A small number of spun yarn pieces, plied but not woven, were also recovered across Davis Strait at Middle and Late Dorset culture sites including Nanook and Tanfield (Maxwell 1973:205, 1985:206), Willows Island 4 (Odess 1998:429), Nunguvik (Mary-Rousselière 2002:Plate 12b, 2009), Avayalik Island (Fitzhugh et al. 2006), and Cape Ray (Linnamae 1975:174–175; Figure 5.1). These initially elicited little attention. However, after the discovery of Norse material culture from the Thule-culture Skraeling Island site in the Canadian High Arctic (Schledermann 1980), the recovery of similar cloth from the early Thule Ruin

Island site in northwestern Greenland (Holtved 1944; Østergård 2004), and an apparent Thule carving of a Norseman from southern Baffin Island (Sabo and Jacobs 1980; Sabo and Sabo 1978), important questions were raised about the extent and timing of interactions between the indigenous Dorset, Thule Inuit pioneers, and voyagers from Greenland's medieval Norse colonies (Hayeur Smith et al. 2018; McGhee 1984). Sutherland's hypothesis about the spun yarns from these Dorset sites suggested that the sites yielding spun yarn were either Norse trading bases or the residential camps of Dorset Paleo-Eskimos who had learned to spin and perhaps weave fibers through sustained contact with Norse traders (Sutherland 2000, 2002, 2009).

Recent work, however, has forced reconsideration of these arguments. Walton Roger's assumptions that a wide range of Arctic species was used at GUS were proved incorrect by analyses conducted by Sinding and others (2015, 2017), who demonstrated through aDNA analysis that the bison identified at GUS was in fact horse and that the musk ox and bear were goat (Sinding et al. 2015). Sinding performed similar aDNA analyses on Greenlandic samples I had acquired through my research. He found, overall, that the material from Greenlandic sites that were excavated decades ago was inadequate for aDNA analysis due to the conditions under which the textiles were found and the conservation practices that may have damaged the aDNA (see Chapter 5). The only usable material came from sites such as GUS that had been preserved in permafrost and buried in sand. Out of 11 samples from 8 Greenlandic sites, Narsaq (Ø17a), Brattahlid (Ø29a), Abels Farm (Ø167), Qorlortup Itinnera (Ø34), GUS, Sandnes (V51), Niaquusat (V48), and Ujarassuit (Anavik) (V7), only two samples from GUS (KNK 1950 x776) preserved DNA suitable for analysis. These had previously been visually identified as mixtures of goat and Arctic hare by Østergård (2004) and Walton Rogers (1998), though aDNA analyses demonstrated they consisted of a fragment of sheep's wool with a strip of Arctic hare woven through the middle (Sinding et al. 2017:607).

In 2017 Sinding agreed to conduct similar aDNA analyses on the Baffin Island material reported by Sutherland (2000, 2002, 2009) using samples I had acquired with permission from the Canadian Museum of History. Once again, most of these samples were too damaged for their DNA to yield adequate results. Out of 12 samples from the Nanook (KdDq-9), Nunguvik (PgHb-1), and M-1 site (QeJu-1), only 3 provided usable results. The samples had all been selected on the basis of their materials, which for the most part appeared to be musk ox (which had been confirmed in similar material at Avayalik by Fitzhugh et al. 2006). However, from the Nunguvik site (PgHb-1), one sample had previously been analyzed by Walton Rogers, who identified it as a mixture of goat

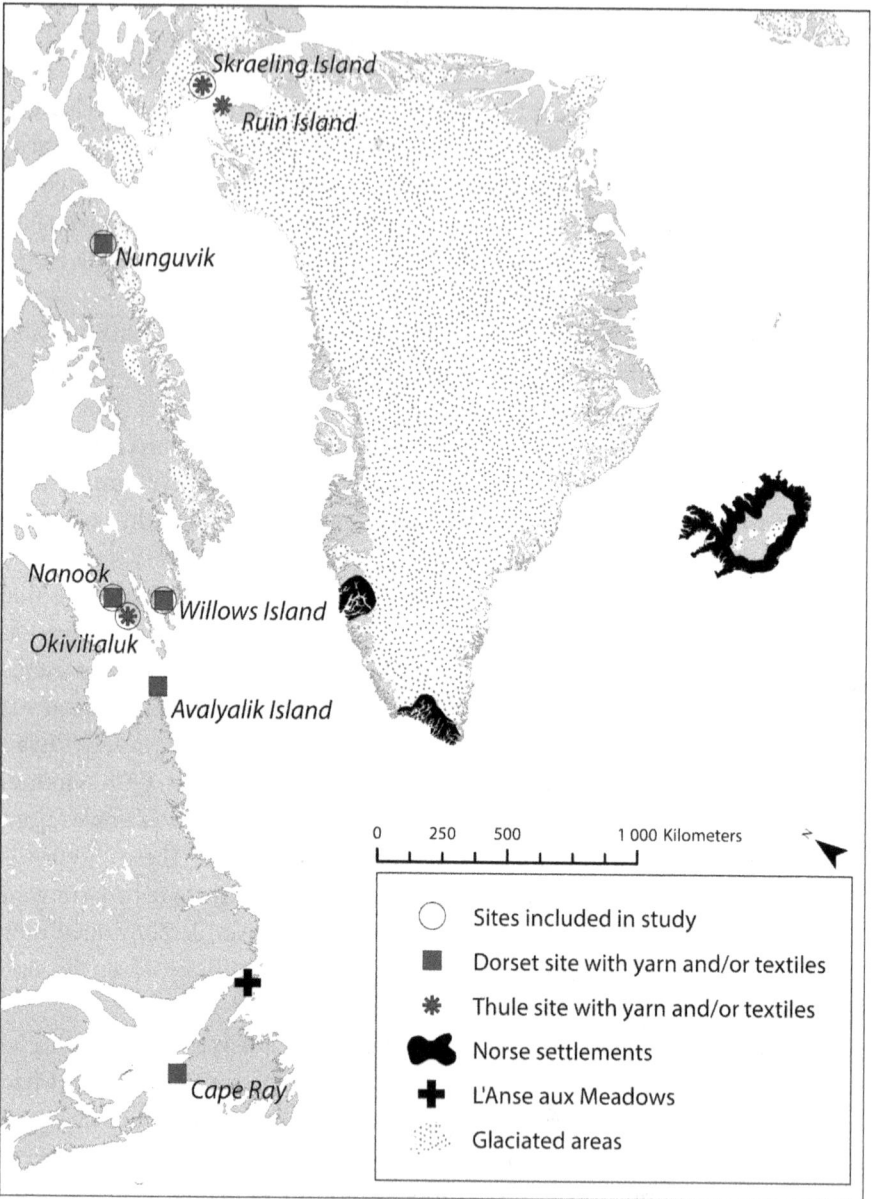

Figure 4.6. Map of Greenlandic and Eastern Canadian Arctic sites. (Map by Johan Eilert Arntzen, University of Tromsø. Reprinted from Hayeur Smith et al. 2018, with permission from Elsevier.)

hair and Arctic hare fur, similar to the sample from GUS (Sutherland 2000). The two remaining samples from the M-1 site (QeJu-1) and Nanook (KdDq-9) sites were made of plied sinew and their construction was similar to that of the woolen yarns. The analysis of these samples was of interest because if the Dorset were able to spin and ply sinew (usually used in garment construction), then the idea of applying this methodology to wool was perhaps not so farfetched. Sinding's results were unable to confirm the use of musk ox in any of the samples due to poor preservation of DNA. However, analyses of the sample from Nunguvik confirmed the presence of Arctic hare, but no goat. Walton Rogers and Greaves (2018) published a report after the publication of a coauthored article on the dating of the Dorset yarns that I wrote with Kevin P. Smith and Gørill Nilsen in the *Journal of Archaeological Science*. Walton Rogers argued that her first identification of the piece from Nunguvik was of goat and Arctic hare but felt that the publication of these results by Sutherland was premature. Further analyses confirmed no goat but following an analysis conducted using microscopy, Greaves at Microtex concluded there was caribou (Walton Rogers and Greaves 2018:24). It is worth pointing out, however, that molecular analysis may in this case be more reliable. Both sinew samples from the Nanook and M-1 sites analyzed by Sinding proved to be baleen from the bowhead whale, rather than sinew (Sinding, personal communication 2019).

Remarkably, all of the Dorset yarns were uniformly produced from initially spun and subsequently plied strands of varying lengths that had, for the most part, been spun Z with S as a final twist (Z2S). The fibers in these pieces of yarn appear to have been well combed or sorted, as the fibers are aligned and parallel with each other, a feature that was also noted at Avayalik (Fitzhugh et al. 2006:162; Hayeur Smith et al. 2018). In these assemblages, Z2S-plied yarn accounted for 98.1% of the 105 plied pieces from Nanook, Nunguvik, and Willows Island 4, whereas only 1.9% of all yarns in the corpus were spun S2Z. Thread diameters were also extremely homogenous across the Baffin Island Dorset material. Several pieces of plied yarn from Baffin Island also had ends that terminated in a small loop, suggesting they had been twisted (plied) on a stick or other implement. This feature is also present in specimens from Avayalik Island and Labrador (Fitzhugh et al. 2006) but has rarely been observed in the vast corpus (9,000± specimens) of Icelandic and Greenlandic Norse textiles (Hayeur Smith et al. 2018).

Even more revealing than the aDNA analyses on the Baffin Island samples were the AMS dates obtained on the spun yarns as part of this project (see Hayeur Smith et al. 2018 for full analysis). The results from this dating campaign, reported by Hayeur Smith and others (2018), demonstrated that all of the spun yarn samples from Dorset sites on Baffin Island were too old to be affiliated with the Norse, as had been previously suggested by Fitzhugh and others (2006) and Park (2004). Our investigations indicate that Paleo-Eskimo communities on Baffin Island spun threads from the hair and the sinews of native terrestrial grazing animals, most likely musk ox and Arctic hare, and from bowhead whale baleen, throughout the Middle Dorset period—in other words, for at least a millennium before any reasonable evidence of European activity in the islands of the North Atlantic or in the Arctic. There was no evidence for the transfer of fiber technologies from the Norse to the Dorset; instead, our findings suggest the existence of an unknown indigenous fiber technology that was present and widespread in the Canadian Eastern Arctic (Hayeur Smith et al. 2018). The only known and confirmed piece of Norse cloth to be found on indigenous sites came from Ellesmere Island, and it displayed the same features as the Greenlandic Norse textiles whose dates were contemporary with the Norse occupation in Greenland (Figure 4.7).

AMS dates on the Baffin Island yarn (presented in Figure 4.7) do not support Sutherland's theory but rather show that the Paleo-Eskimo cultures of the

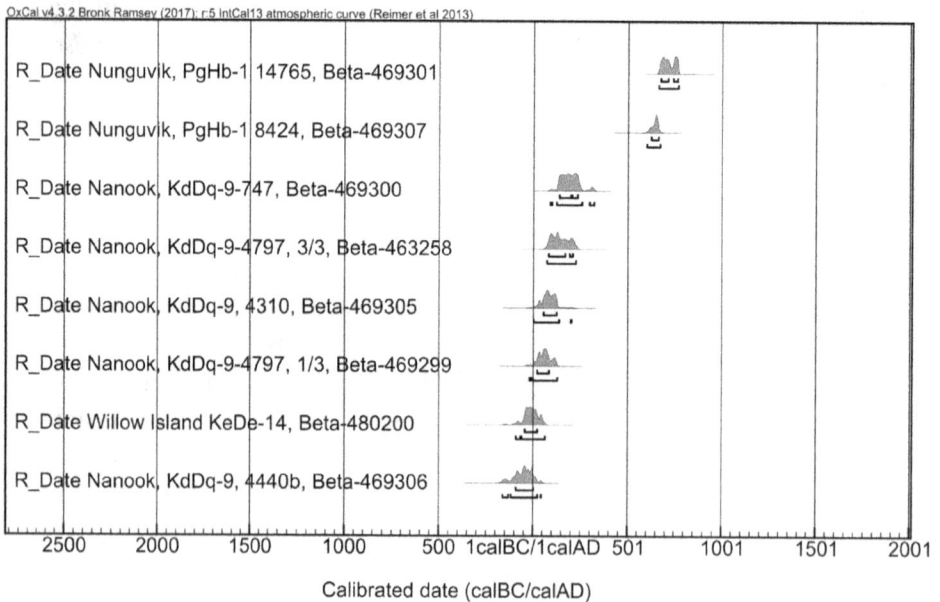

Figure 4.7. Calibrated AMS dates from Eastern Canadian Dorset sites. (Reprinted from Hayeur Smith et al. 2018, with permission from Elsevier.)

Eastern Canadian Arctic already possessed a knowledge of spinning (Hayeur Smith et al. 2018). I have always felt that spinning was a somewhat intuitive activity, and clearly these people possessed a fiber technology that is still largely unknown to Arctic archaeologists.

Currently, our knowledge and scientific abilities do not enable us to confirm the belief that there was a widespread mixture and use of Arctic species in Greenlandic Norse textiles, even though some pieces of woven cloth definitely show evidence of other fibers coming into contact with the cloth. From the site known as Abels Farm (in Vatnahverfi in the municipality of Qaqortoq), items Ø167 D24–1991 x56a and D24–1991 x54 both show evidence that some other species' fiber that had become stuck in the weave as if the cloth had been at-tached to a piece of fur. These fibers could be caribou hair, although without aDNA analyses, no conclusions can be drawn at present. Østergård (2004:120–121) identified a similar piece from GUS, KNK 1950 x497, as reindeer; another from GUS, 1950 x846, was described as an unspecified kind of fur, and KNK 1950 x606 was identified as fox. Additionally, D12560c from V7 Ujarassuit is fur of some sort, and several pieces from GUS (1950 x1084, 1950 x11, and 1950 x1545) appear to incorporate human hair. Østergård (2004:108) confirmed that 1950 x1545 was, in fact, a beautifully made circlet of looped and twisted human hair, said to have been found in the weaving room. The use of human hair in textiles or fiber work is also very common in Iceland, and in the recent past, women wove garters of their own hair to hold up their stockings under their skirts (Textile Museum of Blóndhuos, Iceland). There is something almost uniquely private and mystical about wearing a hidden accessory made of human hair. Østergård (2004:109) argued that the wearing of human hair carries with it spe-cial qualities and associations with magic, superstitions, and private emotions.

In conclusion, apart from a handful of items, Greenlandic women appear to have used and reused homespun woven garments as long as possible, patch-ing them to extend their existence. In some cases, the patches themselves may have held special meaning, as might be the case with the use of very old cloth to patch the crown of the Burgundian tall hat. The use of other fiber types in weaving and in other household implements seems to have been minimal, but the use of wool and hair from European domesticates was the foundation for Greenlandic textile technologies. The fact that the site of GUS produced more furs or textiles mixed with fur than any other site in Greenland may have to do with the excellent preservation at the site, which is not paralleled elsewhere in archaeological collections from Greenland. If so, this may sug-gest that wild species' fur and hair was more widely used in Greenland than can be documented in existing collections. However, the apparent rarity of well-documented fur and hair from Arctic species in sites such as Herjolfsnes, where textiles were well preserved, also suggests that the use of Arctic species' fur intermixed with European domesticates' wool and hair may indicate an otherwise undocumented norm at this site, or perhaps more widespread in Greenland's Western Settlement.

In Chapter 5 I further address wool and fiber types in Norse textiles, as well as issues of textile production in the face of climatic deterioration.

5

Cloth, Currency, Climate Change, and Subsistence in Greenland

In Chapter 4 I considered certain aspects of textile use in the Norse colonies of Greenland and touched only briefly upon the issue of cloth currency that was so integral to the economy of medieval Iceland. Greenland's textile data display patterns that are quite different from those of Iceland.

Greenlandic Cloth, Subsistence, Farming, and Goats

Zooarchaeological data acquired through excavations of Greenlandic farm sites over the past several decades provide additional information on subsistence strategies linked to the production of cloth in Norse Greenland that also contrast dramatically with Iceland. Overall, these data show that the Greenlanders became increasingly reliant on wildlife for subsistence as time passed (Koch Madsen 2014:22). Isotopic data on the skeletal remains of Norse Greenlanders support this conclusion and imply that fish and marine mammals became increasingly important in these colonies last centuries (Arneborg et al. 2012).

According to Smiarowski and others (2017), the Greenlanders brought European domesticates (cattle, sheep, goats, dogs, horses, and pigs) with them from Iceland at the time of settlement but rapidly developed into an export-oriented community in which the procurement of ivory and furs was a key goal and in which a dual strategy integrating both hunting and farming provided a mixed subsistence base. In contrast, Iceland was a dedicated pastoral farming community that supplemented its agricultural practices with fishing and a relatively minor hunting component (Smiarowski et al. 2017:151). This may be another reason why furs and other products of Arctic species are relatively rare in the textile corpus: for Norse Greenlanders, their money was not cloth but furs and ivory used for trade with Europe, a view shared by others such as Keller (2010). Furs were, therefore, probably too valuable for everyday use, and at least some were sent as tax payments to the Norwegian king (Dugmore et al. 2007:18; McGovern 1980:257–258).

Walrus maxillae from the region surrounding the tusk roots have been found on inland as well as coastal farms in Greenland, suggesting that all communities participated in the pursuit of walrus in the northern hunting grounds called the Norðursetur (Smiarowski et al. 2017:151; McGovern et al. 1996). Further, at the elite site of Garðar (Igaliku), a significant number of polar bear distal (third) phalanges were discovered to display cut marks indicative of the on-site tanning and finishing of bear skins (Smiarowski et al. 2017). Bear skins and walrus ivory were both in high demand at the courts of Norway and Northern Europe (Frei et al. 2015).

Zooarchaeological evidence for the ratios of goats to sheep on Greenlandic and Icelandic farms provides additional information about differences between contemporary Greenlandic and Icelandic Norse economic strategies. Goats appear to have been common members of mixed sheep and goat flocks in both Iceland and Greenland during the settlement period of the late ninth through tenth centuries. During these centuries, the ratios of ovicaprines (sheep and goats) to cattle were relatively low, implying that the pastoral economy was focused on the production of a mixed range of products, including meat, milk, and wool, without a clear focus on any one of these. However, by the mid-eleventh century, the ratios of ovicaprines to cattle on Icelandic farms changed, with increasing numbers of sheep and decreasing evidence of goats on most farms. By the thirteenth century, both goats and pigs are rarely documented in Icelandic archaeofaunal assemblages, sheep greatly exceed cattle, and large sheep, possibly wool-producing wethers, dominate the flocks (Koch Madsen 2014:24; McGovern et al. 2014).

In Greenland, however, the initial ratios of ovicaprines to cattle on sites that had characterized the island's early farming economic pattern remained relatively low throughout the Middle Ages, with a caprine-to-cattle ratio of 5–10:1 (McGovern et al. 2014), and goats were often more numerous than sheep on these farms from the beginning of the settlement onward (Smiarowski et al. 2017). Although ratios of goats to sheep did change over time in Greenland and from region to region, the numbers of goats kept on Greenlandic farms did not decline during the Middle Ages, as they had in Iceland (McGovern et al. 2014). In fact, goats are plentiful in Greenland's archaeofaunal records (Koch Madsen 2014:25; McGovern et al. 2014). Koch Madsen (2014) argues that this was due in part to the fact that goat flocks could benefit from the abundant shrubs in Greenland, as confirmed by the analysis of sheep and goat pellets from a farm in the Western Settlement (Ross and Zutter 2007:82, in Koch Madsen 2014:24). Koch Madsen and others have also attributed this increase in goats to climatic deterioration that made hay harvests unreliable but favored the growth of shrubs (Koch Madsen 2014:24; McGovern 1985, 1991; Vésteinsson et al. 2002). As climate deteriorated, the numbers of goats kept on farms increased and many farms also diversified their economies, intensifying efforts directed at the hunting of migratory seals after AD 1300 (Vésteinsson et al. 2002).

How did these interrelated patterns of climate change, stock raising, and trade specialization affect the products that Icelandic and Greenlandic women made and the amounts of time they spent spinning and weaving? It is one thing to note changes in the physical remains that we archaeologists see in our excavations and quite another to consider how that affected the day-to-day lives, work routines, and schedules of women and men in the past.

Clearly, data on assemblages of textiles from medieval Iceland parallel the zooarchaeological data gained from middens. As sheep bones come to dominate faunal assemblages, increasing amounts of standardized textiles begin to show up in middens and floor deposits at farm sites across the island (Hayeur Smith 2014b, 2018). However, within these assemblages, little variety can be noted in Icelandic cloth from this period. Standardized 2/2 twills dominate all of the assemblages examined to date, complemented by small amounts of tabby weaves. These 2/2 twills dominate because they are the currency known as *vaðmál* (Chapter 3).

In comparison, Greenlandic cloth is anything but homogenous and includes far more diversity in weave types and less concern with standardization than in Iceland. The Greenlandic corpus includes an abundance of 2/2 twills and 2/1 twills, as well as elaborate weaves such as panama weaves, diamond twills (both 2/1 and 2/2 variations), pile weaves, striped weaves, checked weaves, and smocking (or stitched pleats), and moreover includes more elaborate finishings such as tablet-woven piped edging, footweaving, and braiding (Østergård 2004:67–75, 104–107). Many of these features are so rare in Iceland during the same period that one might reasonably conclude that these features were not important in the Icelandic context, given the focus there of producing cloth as a standardized currency. In Greenland, however, more attention was paid to finishing details and the overall appearance of cloth because textiles were primarily for domestic use. In many ways, Icelandic cloth is interesting because of its sheer volume and ubiquity, whereas Greenlandic cloth is interesting for its diversity.

In recent archaeological reviews of the Greenlandic model, low caprine-to-cattle ratios and the large percentage of goats versus sheep in Greenlandic flocks have led to the conclusion that Greenlanders, both elite and common, switched from producing wool to producing food (McGovern et al. 2014). Koch Madsen (2014) suggested that the increase in goats involved the replacement of cattle as milk animals. Further, it has been suggested that goatskins may have been useful trade items, since they were in demand in medieval Norwegian markets

(Koch Madsen 2014:26). Mainland and Halstead (2005:117) also concurred that on the sites of Ø71s, V51, and V52a, goats were more important and that herding strategies there were focused primarily on the production of meat and milk, with some wool harvested from sheep that remained alive longer as meat and dairy animals.

While there may have been a shift toward the production of milk and meat in Norse Greenland, people still required wool to clothe themselves, and the plenitude of goats appears to have influenced textile production. Let us first explore the question of the quantity of wool that would have been needed in Greenlandic households, and the labor that would have been required for spinning and weaving it, since this is something rarely addressed when discussing household subsistence strategies.

Wool Needs on Norse Farms

A look at the quantities of wool needed for the production of garments in the Viking Age certainly suggests that significant amounts of wool were needed to clothe a household, assuming that each person had one new set of clothes a year, as was generally the case in preindustrial contexts.

Based on experimental trials done at the Historical and Archaeological Experimental Centre in Lejre, Denmark, Andersson Strand (2007:18) evaluated both the production time and the quantities of wool required to produce standard Viking Age garments and arrived at certain estimates. It is not clear what type of wool was used in the experimental trials or whether these were ancient Iron Age breeds akin to the Northern Short-Tail, but these experimental data provide a good starting point for considering labor and resource requirements. Andersson Strand estimated that one complete outfit required 3 kg of wool or flax, spun into 21,000 m of yarn. Her experiments suggest that this would have required 400 hours, the equivalent of 16.7 24-hour days of labor, or 50 days of labor for a woman spinning for 8 hours straight (Table 5.1).

Along with the experimental trials from Lejre, Andersson Strand based her calculations on Icelandic sources from the early nineteenth century (Aðalsteinsson 1990:286), which stipulated that one ewe produced 1.25 g of washed wool, whereas one wether produced 1.75–2.5 kg. For an extended household of 10 people, therefore, Andersson Strand's work suggests that clothing alone would have required 30 kg of wool and 167 full days, or 500 8-hour days, of spinning before weaving could begin.

The Icelandic historian Helgi Þorláksson (1991) calculated the annual needs of householders on a small farm in Iceland, based on various historic sources:

30–60 kg of wool for clothes

30 kg for bedclothes

10 kg for sails and sundries

12 kg for taxes and tithes

70 kg for land rent

Given that medieval Greenlandic taxes, tithes, and rents may have been paid in different commodities, and therefore that seventeenth- to nineteenth-century Icelandic values for these expenses might not be appropriate for estimating Greenlandic farms' needs, Þorláksson's estimates nonetheless suggest that a small household would have needed 70–100 kg of wool annually just for clothing, bedclothes, sails, and other items and up to twice as much wool for clothing than Andersson Strand used in her calculations.

McGovern and others (2014) also provided estimates of wool consumption in medieval Iceland, based on research by Vésteinsson and Þorláksson (1991) using documentary sources on medieval Icelandic sheep raising, especially as

Table 5.1. Production time and quantities of wool required to produce standard Viking Age garments

	Quantity of wool or flax	Meters of spun yarn	Hours of spinning	Days of spinning
1 complete man's outfit	3 kg of wool or flax	21,000	400	16.7
1 complete woman's outfit	3 kg of wool or flax	21,000	400	16.7
10 outfits	30 kg of wool	210,000	4,000 (12–20 sheep, if 1 ewe produces 1.25 kg, and 1 wether produces 1.75–2.5 kg.)	167

Source: Andersson Strand (2007:18, 2011:2).

Table 5.2. A tabulation of household wool consumption

Fleeces per person per year: ca. 4,5

Farm size	Household size	Fleeces
Small farm	4	18
Medium farm	10	45
Chieftain farm	20	90
Manor	40	180

Source: Based on McGovern et al. 2014:170.

discussed in medieval Icelandic legal sources. Their research pointed to quantities of wool greater than those calculated by Andersson Strand, with about 4–5 fleeces' worth of sheep wool needed each year to clothe an individual adequately; these numbers also subsumed additional fabric needs. McGovern' s team divided farms into four hypothetical size ranks based on household sizes: small farms with a household of 4, which would need the wool from approximately 18 fleeces annually; medium farms with 10 household members; larger chieftains' farms with households of 20; and manors, such as those of the bishops, with households of up to 40 individuals, requiring the wool from 180 sheep.

McGovern and colleagues (2014) were largely concerned with wool needs in relation to the size of the flocks of sheep or goats and herds of cattle kept on farms, whereas Andersson Strand was more concerned with the labor involved in cloth production. By combining these analyses and converting fleeces to spun yarn (since yarn and not fleece will be used to make the cloth), the hours of labor involved are as follows:

Table 5.3. Combined analyses demonstrating the hours of labor involved in spinning yarn

MODEL 1: McGovern et al. (2014:170) 4.5 fleeces/person/year, where 4.5 fleeces = 5.6 kg (1 ewe = 1.25 kg)		MODEL 2: Andersson Strand (2007:18) 3 kg wool per person	Spinning (McGovern et al. 2014: 170); Spinning (Andersson Strand 2007:18): 21,000 m of yarn spun per 3 kg	Spinning time: 21,000 m = 400 hours of spinning		
Farm size	Household	# Fleeces/ wool (kg)	Kilograms of wool	Meters (MG)	Meters (AS)	Hrs (MG)	Hrs (AS)
Small	4	18/**22.4** kg	12 kg	157,500 m	84,000 m	3,000 hrs	1,600 hrs
	10	45/**56** kg	30 kg	394,100 m	210,000 m	7,500 hrs	4,000 hrs
Chieftain	20	90/**112** kg	60 kg	787,500 m	420,000 m	15,000 hrs	8,000 hrs
Manor	40	180/**224** kg	120 kg	1,575,500 m	840,000 m	30,000 hrs	16,000 hrs

Notes: MG = McGovern et al. (2014). AS = Andersson Strand (2007).

Calculating the actual time required for producing the spun yarn with which to weave cloth suggests that Andersson Strand's figures may be more realistic in terms of the wool needed, even though she was largely focused on clothing production, as it appears that McGovern and Þorláksson's estimates would have created impossible labor constraints for any household. As demonstrated below, theirs may include additional wool needs that would have been addressed through cloth recycling.

The 12 kg of raw wool required to clothe a small farm of four, based on Andersson Strand's estimates, would have required the production of 84,000 m of yarn. Spinning this amount of yarn with drop spindles would have taken 1,600 hours, 66 days if the spinning was done for 24 hours a day without pause. Realistically, if spinners spun for 8 hours a day, it would have taken 198 days, more than half the year, just to spin the yarn needed to get started weaving clothing for the family of four.

The estimates provided by McGovern and others (2014) imply that supplying a farm of four would require 22.4 kg of wool to produce 157,500 m of spun yarn over the course of 3,000 hours of spinning. This is equivalent to 125 days of doing nothing but spinning, 24 hours a day, or 375 days, more than a year, of spinning for 8 hours a day. Þorláksson's estimates, requiring even more cloth than McGovern and others (2018) assumed, would have required women to spin for far more than a year to provide each year's cloth.

Bender Jørgensen (2012:117) cites experimental data indicating that it takes a good weaver, on average, 1 hour to weave 25 wefts on a warp-weighted loom, and that it would take 20 hours to weave 1 m² of cloth (either sailcloth or a 2/2 twill) which is also approximately the time it took me to weave 1 m of a plain weave. Although our discussion here centers on producing clothing rather than sails, the cloth used in sails was frequently a twill comparable to that used for clothing. Sailcloth was later treated with various animal fats and red ochre (*smørring*) to render it windproof (Cooke et al. 2002:208–209), but Bender Jørgensen's labor estimates for weaving cloth (20 hours per square meter) provide a useful estimate for producing the twills used for standard clothing in the North Atlantic.

According to Bender Jørgensen's calculations and my own conservative estimates at sewing garments, it would require about 4 m of cloth, 150 cm wide (as it is sold today), to make one complete outfit consisting of a long-sleeved gusseted garment and a pair of trousers. We know from the site of GUS that Greenlandic women wove textiles of about this width, as a complete long beam from the top of a loom was recovered there and measured 188 cm long (Østergård 2004:59). There are 34 holes for sewing the warp threads to the beam, and this portion of the beam, on which cloth was warped, measures 140 cm, roughly the same width as modern cloth. Thus, if 4 m of cloth are required, at 1.5 m width, the total amount of cloth used to make one complete outfit would be 6 m². Thinking back to Bender Jørgensen's estimates of 20 hours to weave 1 m² of cloth, it would take 120 hours to weave 6 m², enough cloth for one complete outfit, or 15 days of weaving at 8 hours a day, which might be considered a normal modern workday. The calculations of weaving time needed to outfit a household of 4 (McGovern's smallest household) are therefore as follows:

Table 5.4. Hours of weaving required to create enough cloth for individual garments

Item woven	Amount of wool needed for item	Hours to weave that amount of wool	Days to weave that amount of wool
Woman's outfit	6 m²	120 hours	15 days
Man's outfit	6 m²	120 hours	15 days
Third person's outfit	6 m²	120 hours	15 days
Fourth person's outfit	6 m²	120 hours	15 days
Total	**24 m²**	**480 hours**	**60 days**

Combining both spinning and weaving time together the workload would resemble something like the following:

Table 5.5. Combined time to weave and spin enough wool for garment construction

Household size	Spun yarn (meters of yarn*)	Spinning time (hrs)	Weaving quantities (6.5 m² cloth per person for clothing)	Weaving time (hrs)	Time to spin and weave garments (hrs)	Number of days, at 8 hrs per day	Number of adult women	Days of spinning and weaving per woman
Small (4 people)	84,000 m	1,600 hrs	24 m²	480 hrs	2,080 hrs	260 days	1 woman	260 days
Medium (10 people)	210,000 m	4,000 hrs	60 m²	1,200 hrs	5,200 hrs	650 days	2 women	325 days
Chieftain (20 people)	420,000 m	8,000 hrs	120 m²	2,400 hrs	10,400 hrs	1,300 days	4 women	325 days
Manor (40 people)	840,000 m	16,000 hrs	240 m²	4,800 hrs	20,800 hrs	2,600 days	8 women	325 days

Notes: * Assumes 3,500 meters of yarn per square meter of cloth, which is close to Andersson Strand's estimate (she says that 2 complete outfits require 42,000 meters of spun yarn). Therefore, 1 outfit requires 21,000 meters of yarn used to produce a garment with 6.5 m² of cloth, or 3,230 meters of yarn per square meter.

Would this be possible? In most preindustrial communities, adults make up 40% of the population, and children make up 60% (Weiss 1973). Half of the adults (20%) are women, and the other half (20%) are men. Adult women would make up roughly 20% of the population, and therefore a small household of 4, as defined by McGovern and others (2014) would have 1 woman, and a medium household of 10 people would include 2 adult women, a household of 20 would have 4 adult women, and so on. The numbers in Table 5.5 suggest that it would have taken one woman 260 days of labor to spin and weave the wool required to clothe her family of four, working 8 hours a day at nothing but spinning and weaving. McGovern's larger model household's labor time, could have represented 325 days of work per woman on the farm. This implies that work on textiles would have consumed the majority of most women's days throughout most of the year.

If spinning and weaving the cloth required just to clothe the household took this amount of time and labor, how would it have been possible to supply households with all of the textiles that they needed? The estimates produced by McGovern and others (2014) and Vésteinsson and Þorláksson (McGovern, personal communication 2014) assume that each family needed much more cloth each year than the amount needed just for their own clothes, and these estimates may well have exceeded the amount of cloth that one woman could have produced to supply her family. However, their estimates assume cloth replacement rates that may reflect modern sensibilities developed in an era of cheap textiles produced in industrial settings. Thus, factoring in the production of new bedding on an annual basis may be unnecessary, since it is unlikely that people replaced bedding and blankets yearly. In addition, since it appears that cloth recycling was so widespread in the North Atlantic, it is likely that textiles were reused and repaired over and over again. Archaeological evidence suggests that old cloth was reused for household furnishings such as bedding or pillows and new clothes may not have been produced yearly but repatched extensively, as was the case with the Burgundian hat and with many other Greenlandic and Icelandic examples. It is also unlikely that all farmers had ships or needed new sails every year.

This example provides an important demonstration that the production of cloth was an extremely important and time-consuming component of medieval Norse subsistence strategies, requiring as much time and labor as farming and hunting, and was as essential to survival in the cold and wet setting of the North Atlantic. If certain quantities of wool and certain numbers of sheep were needed, how did the Greenlanders manage their cloth needs if sheep were less numerous than goats? The work involved in making cloth is time and labor intensive, and even if wool was used only for domestic consumption in Greenland, Greenlandic Norse women undoubtedly managed not only by recycling cloth extensively (Chapter 4) but perhaps also by adding goat hair to their textiles.

Goat Hair and aDNA Research

Østergård (2004) suggested that Greenlandic textiles were frequently made with goat fibers, supporting archaeofaunal research. There were advantages to breeding goats rather than sheep in the Greenlandic environment, though their hair was not as soft as sheep's wool.

Goat hair garments have been recorded in collections from mainland Scandinavia, England, and Germany (Lübeck), as this material was also used to pack bales of cloth (Østergård 2004:75). In European Christian traditions, goat hair and goat hair garments, because they were coarse and irritating to the skin, were generally associated with mourning and penance (McKenna 2007; Østergård 2004:75). The term for this type of fabric made of either goat or cattle hair was "haircloth" or "cilice," a term derived from Cilicium, a covering made of goat hair from the Roman province of Cilicia (McKenna 2007). Despite the Greenlanders' Christian faith, these associations with penance and mourning must have carried little weight in medieval Greenland, since several garments and textiles were identified as goat fiber by Østergård (2004) and Walton Rogers (1998).

However, goat hair is notoriously difficult to discern from sheep's wool both microscopically and molecularly (Sinding, personal communication 2017). Østergård (2004) identified goat in roughly 29 items—or approximately 1 percent of the Greenlandic collection. Unsurprisingly, many of these were identified within the assemblage from GUS, which has preservation unparalleled in Greenland. Østergård (2004:75) also identified goat hair in several of the Herjolfsnes garments, and suggested that goats' hair was used in pile weaving, since the hairs are very waterproof. Given the high number of goats in the Greenlandic archaeofauna, the number of goat hair garments may be far greater than Østergård reported, but performing an extensive analysis of the entire collection to identify the frequency of goat's hair fiber would have been logistically impossible, and difficult using macroscopic or microscopic visual identifications alone. The difficulties of basing identifications on visible criteria, however, were demonstrated when some of Østergård's identifications were proven wrong, such as the striped textile from GUS (Chapter 4), which was believed to be made from goat hair with Arctic hare intermixed but which proved to be sheep's wool with two stripes of Arctic hare (Sinding et al. 2017:607).

My own efforts to use aDNA analysis to shed light on this issue also met with some difficulty and provided no conclusive results. With the help of Mikkel-

Holger Sinding from the University of Copenhagen's Center of GeoGenetics, a preliminary batch of 11 Norse Greenlandic cloth samples was tested for aDNA in an effort to determine whether we could identify the incorporation of goat's hair or other exotic fibers in the textiles.

The results were largely inconclusive, except for the sample from GUS containing Arctic hare; many samples contained abundant human aDNA contamination caused by excessive post-excavation manipulation, during conservation, or during the use and wearing of the cloth. Of 11 textiles suspected on the basis of visual characteristics to incorporate goat's hair, none were conclusively identified as goat using DNA. In each case where the use of goat hair was suspected, the results indicated that the fibers were either from sheep or that a sheep or goat match was equally possible. In 2017 Sinding conducted a second series of analyses on samples of Greenlandic cloth and others from Baffin Island. Again, most of the samples were difficult to analyze due to contamination, and Sinding was unable to identify species from the material, except for three items from Baffin Island that were produced by indigenous Dorset Paleo-Eskimo people from the hair of wild Arctic species, again without goat (see Chapter 4). The findings of this study, as reported by Sinding and others (2017), demonstrated that only the material from GUS provided adequate aDNA to carry out full species identification.

Weft-Dominant Cloth and Climate Change in Norse Greenland

Probably the Norse Greenlandic textiles whose characteristics have drawn the most attention are those that Østergård labeled "Greenlandic *vaðmál*." Norse textiles in Scandinavia, and wherever else the Norse settled, tended to be warp dominant, with 2–4 more threads per centimeter in the warps than in the wefts. However, at some point in time, Greenlandic women switched to weaving cloth with very high weft thread counts, outnumbering the traditional types of cloth they wove when they arrived from Iceland. Østergård (2004) attributed the stimulus for producing weft-dominant cloth, which appeared temporally later in her sequence, to attempts at making warmer clothing in the face of increasingly harsh winters (Østergård 2005:81, 2004:62–63, 1998:62, 65). Østergård (2005:81) felt that the use of more underwool that was then beaten more closely on the loom would have created a firmer and warmer product. However, in her analysis of Greenlandic cloth, she never pinpointed when this transition took place, only stating that it was a characteristic that could be used to identify Greenlandic *vaðmál* in other archaeological settings and that it seemed to appear in later medieval contexts.

Midden excavations from 2009 to 2010, undertaken by international crews working on the National Museum of Denmark's Vatnahverfi Project, at the site of Tatsipataa (Ø172) in the Eastern Settlement, provided an important collection of well-preserved textiles in a stratigraphic sequence. Analysis of these textiles yielded some tentative dating for this transition into the production of Norse Greenlandic *vaðmál*. The site, with its chronological sequence spanning several centuries, allowed for the tracking of this behavioral feature through time, despite its relatively small sample size.

For example, in Area B (Figure 5.1), no textiles with high weft thread counts were documented; all were like their Icelandic counterparts. However, Area B also contained far fewer textiles than Area C, so the absence of weft-dominant textiles in Area B may simply reflect sample size. By contrast, textiles from Area C show this shift in weaving patterns occurring in the second and third phases of the site's sequence.[1] Cloth from the deepest layers in Area C were warp dominant, as in Icelandic cloth from the late tenth and eleventh centuries. However, textiles from layer 114, at the end of Phase 1, incorporate some with equal thread counts. A similar mix of warp-dominant and equally balanced textiles came from layer 93, dated to the early part of Phase 2. However, through the course of Phase 2, evenly balanced and weft-dominant cloth become the principal types from the site as weft threads start to outnumber warp threads significantly, with thread counts of 10/15 or 8/13, and with the numbers of weft-dominant textiles increasing through time (Hayeur Smith 2014). Figure 5.2 displays thread counts for the various phases at Ø172: textiles from Phases 1 and 2 clearly mirror Icelandic *vaðmál*, yet by late Phase 2, change begins to occur, with an increasing amount of cloth produced using weft-dominant weaves. The only piece of cloth recovered from Phase 3 deposits has a weft-dominant weave, as was also the case with later Norse textiles from the site of Herjolfsnes, dated primarily to the fourteenth and fifteenth centuries, where this weft-dominance intensifies with extremely high weft thread counts.

The patterning seen at Ø172 suggests that weavers had been experimenting with this technological innovation before implementing it fully into their cloth tradition, as there is a clear, chronologically sensitive sequence from warp-dominant textiles in Phase 1 (AD 1000–1100) to equally balanced and weft-dominant textiles in Phases 2 and 3 (Phases 2 and 3 are dated to later periods, AD 1100–1300±).

To establish an approximate date for this shift in weaving, two fragments of cloth from Area C were sampled and submitted for AMS dating at Beta Analytic Laboratories (Figure 5.3). No. 1142b, from Context 93 (Beta-320126), produced a radiocarbon age of 600 ± 30 bp, calibrated at 1-sigma to calAD 1309–1398, and at two standard deviations to calAD 1297–1408. Internal probabilities suggest

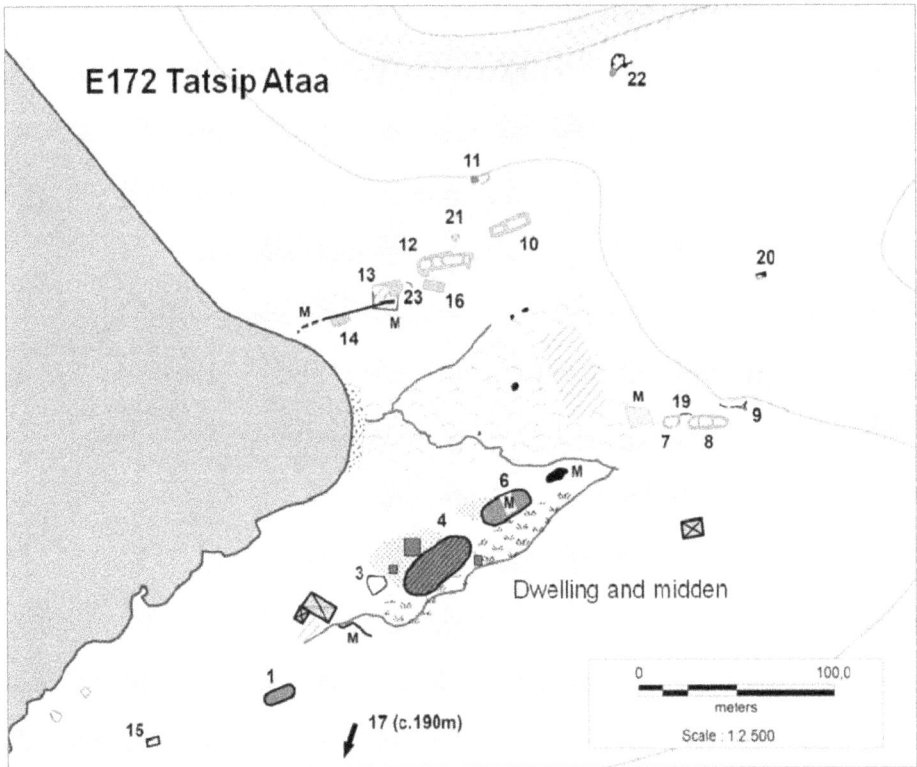

Figure 5.1. Ø172 site plan with excavation areas: Areas A–C comprise the largest square northwest of Structure 4. Area D is the smaller square northwest of Structure 4, and Area E is the small square southeast of Structure 4. (Plan by C. K. Madsen in Smiarowski 2012:6.)

the most likely estimate for its actual age is calAD 1309–1361 under the 1-sigma curve (p = 0.797), with a far lower (p = 0.202) probability of falling within the secondary curve, calAD 1386–1398. At two standard deviations, there is an internal probability of 0.74 that the date for this sample falls in the interval calAD 1297–1373. With fair certainty, the best estimate for the age of this sample is circa calAD 1300–1365 (Hayeur Smith 2014:71).

No. 1090, from Context 86 (Beta-320125), produced a radiocarbon date of 560 ± 30 bp, calibrated at 1-sigma to calAD 1323 1415, and at two standard deviations to calAD 1308–1428. Internal probabilities under the 1- and 2-sigma curves are almost split evenly between the intervals calAD 1323–1347 and calAD 1392–1415 (at one standard deviation) and calAD 1308–1361 or calAD 1386–1428 (at two standard deviations). Given the even internal probabilities under both curves, the best estimate for the age of Ø172-1090 is calAD 1323–1415 at 1-sigma and calAD 1308–1428 at two standard deviations (Hayeur Smith 2014:71).

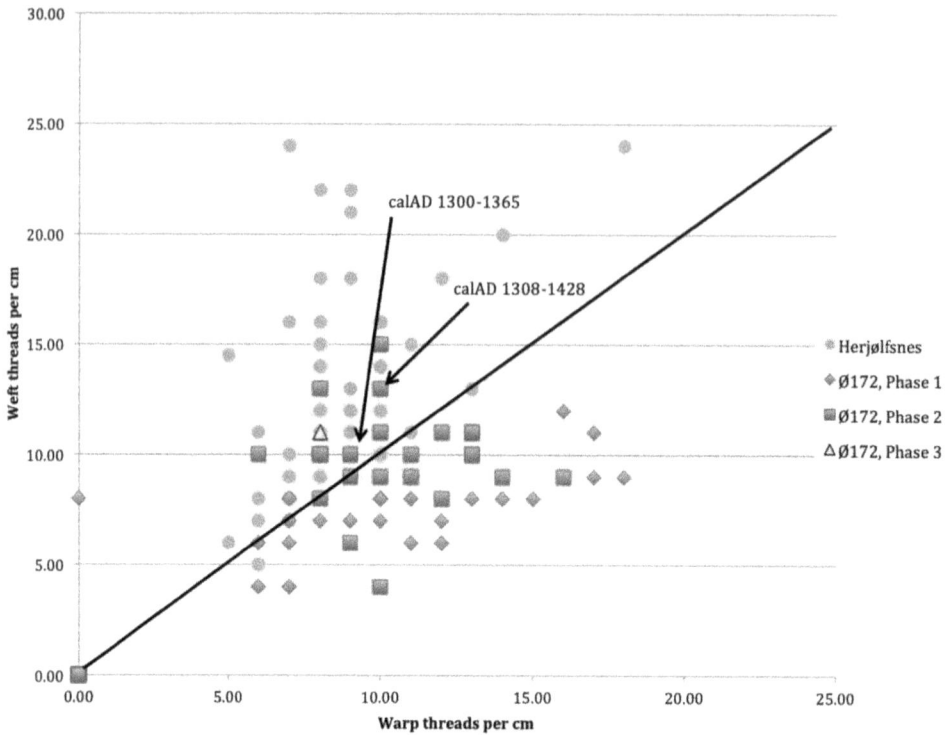

Figure 5.2. Thread counts recorded from Herjolfsnes (Østergård 2004) and Ø172 Phases 1–3 (Hayeur Smith 2014a. Courtesy Oxbow.)

These samples' ages are statistically identical at p >0.95 (T = 0.8888889). Given their stratigraphic comparability (based on the excavators' Harris Matrix placement), their similarity as the earliest Greenlandic weft-dominant cloth samples in the site, and the probability that the garments they represent were in use for more than a single (or even a few) years and may have been recycled and reused for quite a few years, an average of the two dates is reasonable, and may provide a closer approximation of the age of the later deposits from which both samples came (Hayeur Smith 2014:71).

The pooled average of these two samples, 580 ± 21 bp, calibrates to calAD 1320–1405 at 1-sigma, with a 68.3% internal probability under the 1-sigma curve that the actual date for these deposits falls within the interval calAD 1320–1349. At two standard deviations, the range for is calAD 1308–1413, with an internal probability of 67.5% under the 2-sigma curve that the most accurate age estimate for the initiation of the deposition of weft-dominant cloth at Ø172 commences

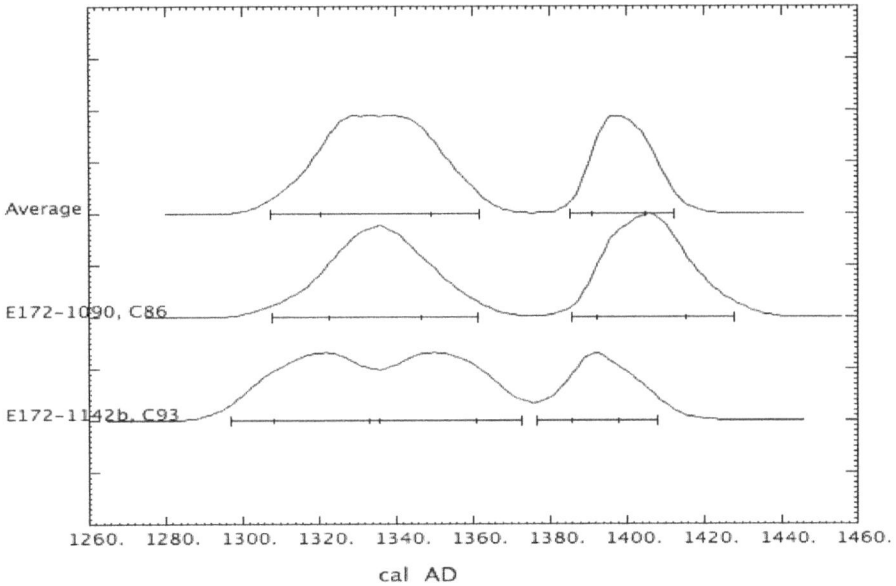

Figure 5.3. Probability distributions for calibrated radiocarbon dates on textiles from Ø172. (Hayeur Smith 2014a. Courtesy *Journal of the North Atlantic*.)

somewhere around calAD 1308–1362 (Figure 5.3; see Hayeur Smith 2014:71 for full discussion).

Archaeologists unfamiliar with using textiles for radiocarbon dating may not be aware of their value for monitoring certain cultural behaviors such as the transition to weft-dominant cloth, dating the sites and deposits in which they are found, or dating specific textile artifacts (Hajdas et al. 2014). However, textiles are produced from organic materials, hair, wool, or plant fibers, that are formed over single years and usually have relatively short use lives, so they should be perfect from the perspective of eliminating some of the "normal" problems with dated samples from the North, such as wood that grows slowly over very long times and may have been in use for decades or centuries. Unlike faunal remains, textiles do not require collagen extraction pretreatment stages before AMS dating, during which contamination can relatively easily enter the samples, due to the process itself. The smaller the amount of collagen available for dating, the more likely that a problem will arise from any such contamination (Wood et al. 2010). Hajdas and others (2014) provide an excellent review with relevant references to work performed using textiles for AMS dating since the 1990s.

However, woolen textiles can present the same problems for radiocarbon dating that may arise with "old" dates received from the bones of sheep that were foddered or grazed on seaweed. While bones can accumulate a Marine Reservoir Effect signal over the entire life of the sheep, wool is sheared off seasonally. If seaweed foddering is done as part of the winter feeding but the sheep are sheared in the late summer, the wool is more likely to have a summer fodder profile incorporating primarily carbon obtained from grazing on grass and sedges.

Ø172 (Tatsipataa) is a coastal site backed by extensive upland grazing. To check whether the wool used for making cloth at this site was obtained from sheep that had been foddered on seaweed, both carbon and nitrogen isotope ratios were calculated during the AMS dating process and compared to known isotopic ratios for Greenlandic terrestrial and marine resources. Both of the dates from Ø172 fell within the $^{13}C/^{12}C$ range for terrestrially fed herbivores, rather than the ranges linked to consumption of marine foods (K. P. Smith, personal communication 2014).

The dates from Ø172 fall within Phase 2 of the site, and bracket (AD 1309–1398 and AD 1323–1415) a double-sided comb (Smiarowksi 2012). Double-sided combs have been consistently dated across the Norse world between AD 1250–1350 (Andreasen 1980; Ashby 2010; Bigelow 1984:103–106; Hamilton 1956:189; Long 1975:21–25; MacGregor 1985:75; Wiberg 1977), suggesting that without a doubt the dates for this layer are AD 1250–1415 and could represent the last deposition at this midden. The presence of a suite of dates spanning the tenth to thirteenth centuries from Phase 3 (Smiarowski 2012:35), the surface layers of the site, could represent topsoil disturbance and site formation processes unrelated to the midden under analysis (K. P. Smith, personal communication 2019).

Although the data from Ø172 represented only one site, the pattern seen there appeared to support the trend that Østergård had suspected from her analyses of Greenlandic textiles, the transition to weft-dominant cloth was a feature that became widespread later rather than earlier in the settlement. Looking at the dating of weft-dominant cloth from other Greenlandic sites, including Narsaq 17a, GUS, Sandnes V51, Qaqortoq Ø83, Narsarsuaq Ø149, the Inglefield Land Site, Nipatsoq V54, Umiiviarsuk V52a, Brattahlid-Qassiarsuk Ø29a, Skraeling Island in the Canadian Arctic, and additional specimens from Herljofsnes Ø111, and integrating these with Ø172 (Figure 5.4), supports this conclusion, although additional observations can be made.

Combining data from Østergård (2004) with my own AMS dates suggests that weft-dominant cloth was present in the Greenlandic corpus but as a minor element in a diverse textile tradition at the beginning of the settlement, as early as AD 1001. Cloth with high weft thread counts was never widespread anywhere in the North Atlantic but was also present in very small frequencies in Iceland during the early medieval period, along with equally balanced cloth. Until the late 1200s and early 1300s, warp-dominant cloth was clearly the norm in Norse Greenland. The early fourteenth century marks a distinct shift to weft-dominant cloth, but both equal thread counts and warp-dominant cloth continue to have been produced sporadically. For example, cloth from Skraeling Island in the High Arctic was warp dominant (thread counts of 9/6), as was a piece of cloth from the Inglefield Land Site (thread count 8/6) and cloth from Umiiviarsuk V 52a (thread count 8/4); all of these textiles are from the thirteenth century and do not date to the early settlement. The patterns and trajectories of change are found across Greenland, with similar mixtures of weaving systems and dates from both the Eastern and the Western Settlement. Within this range, cloth produced with equal thread counts and weft-dominant textiles appear to have been present, but only as minor types, within the diverse repertoire of weaving styles brought to Greenland from Iceland. Rather than being later innovations, as suggested above, this suggests that Greenlandic women eventually experimented with these existing variations, promoting them over time to become dominant elements of Greenlandic material culture.

Therefore, some of the most interesting questions to arise from this attempt to date the transition to weft-dominant cloth in the later Norse settlements of Greenland pertain to the reasons why women switched their weaving methods from warp dominant to weft-dominant.

Globally, textile traditions, as already pointed out, do tend to change very little over extended periods of time (Adovasio 1986; Carr and Maslowski 1995; Drooker 1992; Johnson and Speedy 1991; Kuttruff 1988; Minar 2001; Petersen and Wolford 2000), unless some social or environmental cause motivates people to change their approaches. As argued by Østergård (2004), climate change linked to the start of the Little Ice Age was the most likely culprit behind the emergence of weft-dominant cloth as Greenland's most commonly produced textile.

The Little Ice Age affected Iceland and Greenland in different ways. According to McGovern (1980), Mann and others (2009), and Dugmore and others (2007), the North Atlantic experienced cooling effects from the Little Ice Age before AD 1500, with a first cold spell occurring sometime between AD 1320 and AD 1350 (McGovern 1980:246; Mann et al. 2009:1257; Dugmore et al. 2007). Greenland was particularly affected by this early, sustained drop in tempera-

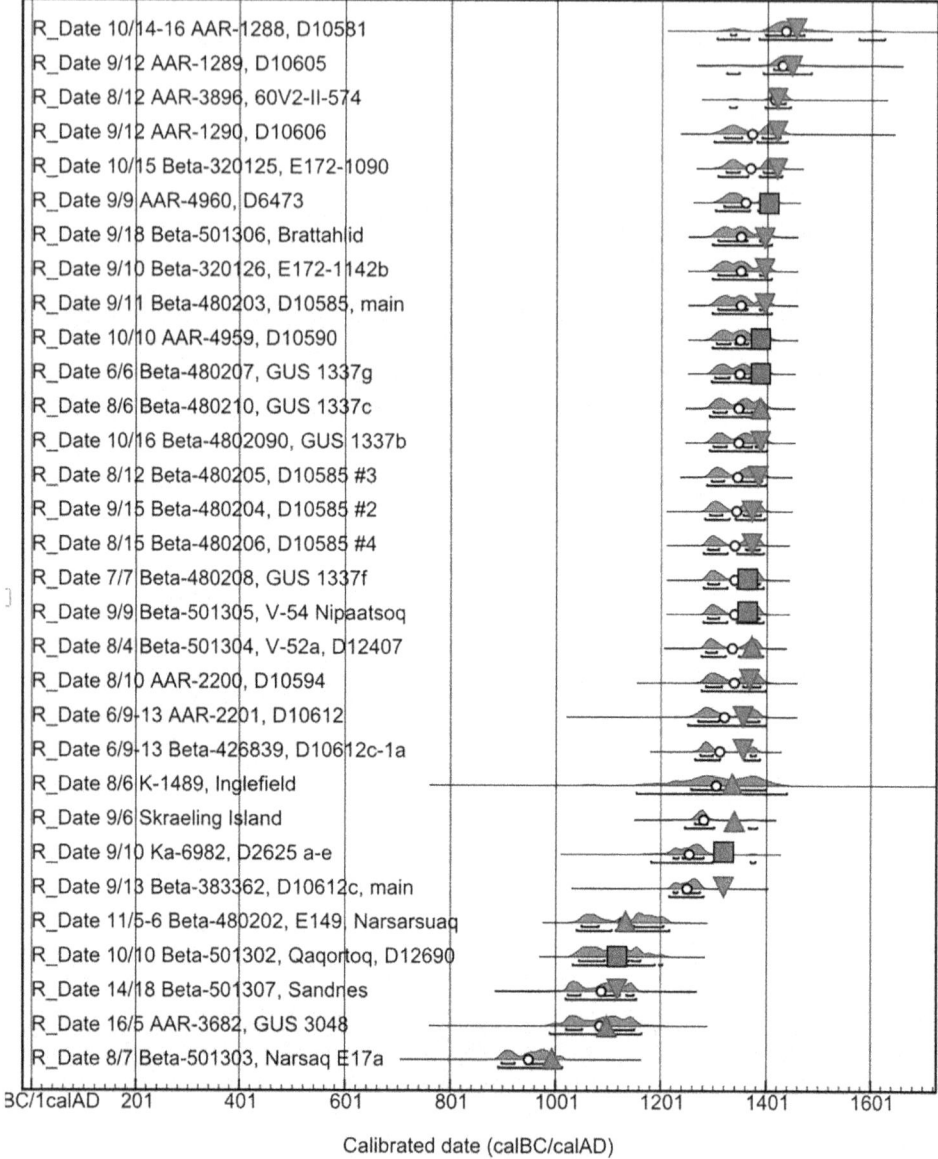

Figure 5.4. AMS dates showing the evolution of warp-dominant to weft-dominant cloth across Greenland in both the Eastern and Western Settlements. Triangles represent warp-dominant cloth; inversed triangle are weft-dominant cloth and squares, equal thread counts.

tures during the early 1300s, with the onset of a cold spell around 1340 that intensified to ruin crops and make subsistence generally difficult (see Figure 5.5), while Iceland only began experiencing sustained climatic deterioration between AD 1475 and AD 1520. While there were periods and years of warmth within the Little Ice Age, Greenland's Norse colonies disappeared by the mid-fifteenth century, while in Iceland, the sixteenth through late nineteenth centuries have been described, overall, as periods subject to extreme poverty and famine (Hayeur Smith 2012:14, 15).

Based on the data now available for dating trends in the production of textiles across Greenland, weft-dominant cloth appears to have become widespread between AD 1300 and AD 1362—well within the range noted for this first cold transition (Figure 5.5)—and its promotion from a minor type of cloth within the repertoire to the most common textile produced in Greenland appears almost certainly to have been a local response, undertaken by medieval Greenlandic

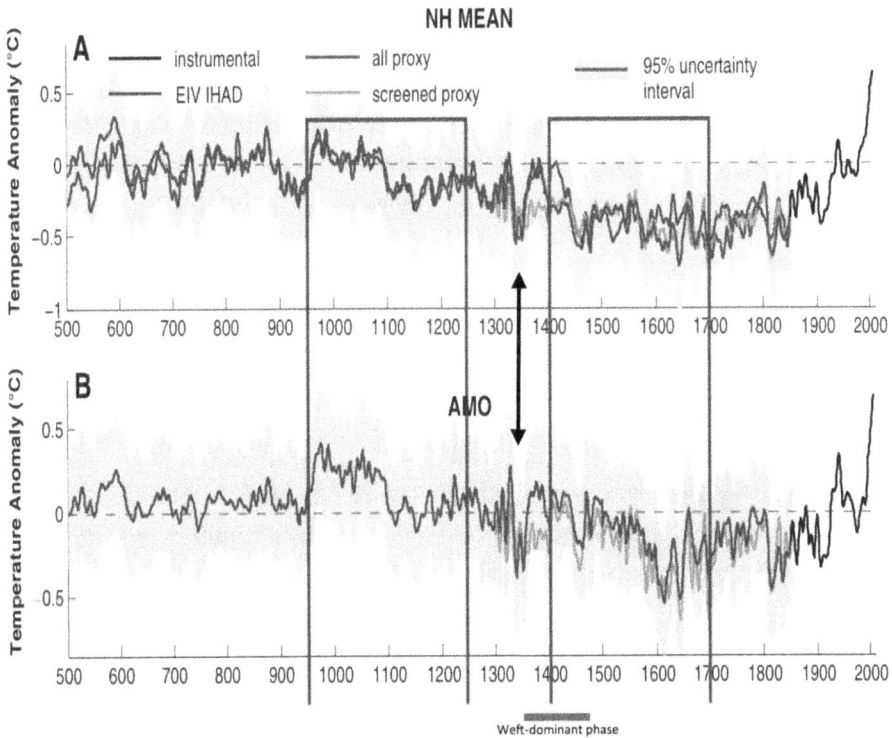

Figure 5.5. Climate deterioration in the Northern Hemisphere and North Atlantic from multiple proxy records. The arrow indicates the first drops in temperature that also coincide with the increase use of weft-dominant cloth. (Adapted from Mann et al. 2009.)

women to cope with cooling temperatures. This type of behavioral feature, so rarely visible in the archaeological record and so intimately linked to human perception of cold, reflects decisions and decision making that women had to undertake when changing how they produced cloth. When the weather began getting colder, how could they make warmer garments?

One solution was clearly to overpack the weft threads with the highly insulative inner wool, as Østergård (2004, 2005) suggested. Another adaptation would involve the inclusion of furs in clothing, and while such a trend was not widespread and is difficult to trace, it has also been documented in medieval Greenland. Creating greater numbers of *varafeldir*—pile-woven cloaks (Guðjónsson 1962:13)—was another option but would have been labor intensive and costly, requiring greater quantities of wool. Still, more examples of pile weaving exist in the Greenlandic corpus than the Icelandic one, suggesting that this, too, was adopted as a way of dealing with cold.

Other concerns might involve the overall conservatism of the late Greenlandic Norse population. Looking at the social dynamics of Norse Greenland during the periods leading up to the end of the colony, many features suggest that a powerful ecclesiastic elite could have contributed to the decline of the colony (McGovern 1980, 2000). Even as this elite certainly looked toward Europe for cultural contact with Greenland, it also consumed a disproportionate amount of the country's imported goods and was responsible for the construction of large manors and churches, such as that at Garðar, which had room for as many as 150 cattle (McGovern 1980:266, 2000:338). Smaller farmers, on the other hand, did not fare as well, and this elite may have monopolized most of the colony's resources while encouraging a cultural conservatism vis-à-vis indigenous people, who were moving into Norse settlement areas by the late thirteenth or early fourteenth centuries (McGovern 1980:266). This conservatism may have influenced the clothing and weaving traditions in Greenland and the refusal to adopt the efficient skin clothing of the Inuit in favor of European woolen garments that were not as well adapted to the worsening climatic conditions of the Little Ice Age (McGovern 1980:265). As a marginalized community at the edge of the Western world, Norse Greenlanders tried to adapt in a different manner, through their textile production, though without radically changing the overall appearance of their cloth.

This is clearly not the only cause of the decline of the colony in Greenland; as Arneborg (2003:177) suggested, several other factors that may have contributed, such as climate change affecting sustainability, failing exchanges with Europe, and changes in market conditions in Europe influencing the export of walrus ivory. With these ideas in mind, it is possible to draw up a list of priorities required for the transformation of cloth into something warmer by the women who produced it:

1. The new cloth should look nearly the same as the old cloth—dress styles in nonindustrial contexts are notoriously conservative. In this regard, weft-dominant cloth would have looked almost exactly like regular *vaðmál* from earlier periods and would have entailed no significant differences in the overall appearance of garments.

2. Making it should have required as little extra effort as possible and should have been something any farmer's wife might be able to do as part of her regular weaving chores. This would have been particularity important, given the long list of tasks these women had to perform around the farm, in addition to textile work and clothing their household. Adding more weft yarns does not change the weaving process dramatically, though it would have required more wool, and therefore more spinning, for every garment made. Norse women were very accustomed to working with the wool from the Northern Short-Tail sheep and knew well that the inner fibers are soft and fluffy and bind easily. As with Icelandic cloth, wool from the GUS textiles was combed or carded so that the two fiber types were separated, and the coarse outer hairs were used as warp yarns, with the fine underwool used as the wefts (Walton Roger 1998:66, 80). The shift to adding more weft yarns than warps (at Ø172, one finds 6/10, 8/13, and 10/13, for ratios of 3:1, 4:1, and even 5:1) only makes sense if, by using more of the underwool, the cloth was beaten closer on the loom to obtain a firmer and warmer product (Østergård 2005:81).

3. The final product could not be too different from the original *vaðmál* in terms of weight, thickness, and so on and not so thick as to adversely affect sewing and any other work involved in garment construction. It had to have the same properties as the cloth to which they were accustomed. Weft-dominant cloth appears to have been the Greenlandic answer to this conundrum.

This chapter wraps up the issue of cloth in Norse Greenland, from analyses of admixed goat and sheep fibers, the results of which remain unfortunately inconclusive, to the promotion of weft-dominant cloth as the textile that became characteristic of Greenlandic cloth during the latter phase of the settlement. How intensively the Greenlanders used furs remains unclear due to the uneven preservation of skins. However, it is useful to remember that fur was a trade commodity the Greenlandic Norse had to offer in exchange for other goods they needed. Therefore, the likelihood that most of it ended up as trade goods or as tax payment is high.

All of these issues characterize Greenlandic Norse textiles, textiles that were not produced for use as currency but that helped clothe the Greenlanders, and not a technology that they shared with indigenous people, but rather one they kept to themselves. It was not the most efficient form of clothing for the climate they lived in, but it was what they knew and it did reflect their own cultural traditions and heritage. A visual appearance that conveys messages of cultural belonging is not something people will give up lightly and, in the case of Norse Greenland, may have served to enhance their differences vis-à-vis indigenous populations whom they were encountering more and more often as time passed.

6

Textiles and Trade in the North Atlantic during the Late Middle Ages and Early Modern Period

The Greenland colony survived until ca. AD 1450, slowly unraveling as a society and suffering under harsh climatic conditions until its abandonment. Much research has been undertaken in the past 30 years to account for its demise, though a look at events on the other side of the ocean suggests that Greenland, along with the rest of the North Atlantic islands, was part of a larger political scenario playing out both internally within Norway and among the neighboring Scandinavian nations, diverting most if not all attention away from the northernmost Norse settlements.

From AD 930 to 1262, Iceland upheld its independence from the Norwegian king and became the Icelandic Free State. The Commonwealth period, as it is called, began with the establishment of the Althing (or parliament) and ended with the pledge of fealty to the Norwegian king in 1262 through the Old Covenant, one of the earliest agreements between a Norwegian king and his Icelandic subjects (Karlsson 2000). The final years of the Commonwealth are often known as the Sturlung Age, when conflict and warfare between local powerful chieftains brought an end to Icelandic independence. The Norwegian king himself may have played a role in the strife, aiming to annex the North Atlantic islands to Norway. After the Commonwealth period, Norway held sway over an impressive territory incorporating Greenland, Iceland, the Faroes, the Hebrides, Shetland, the Isle of Man, and Orkney (Karlsson 2000:100; Helle 2019:43).

Negotiations and alliances between Norway and Denmark eventually led to a shift in the North Atlantic islands from Norwegian to Danish colonial authority. This transition resulted in one of the longest colonial occupations in the world, lasting until 1814 but formally ending only in 1944 (Karlsson 2000:102). King Haakon VI (1355–1380) of Norway arranged a marriage with the Danish King Valdemar's 12-year-old daughter, Margrethe. Their 5-year-old son inherited the throne of Denmark upon the death of his grandfather and subsequently the throne of Norway and all of its territory from his father. In this way, Denmark became the colonial overlord of the North Atlantic islands, and for much of its history showed little or no interest in the affairs of its colonies. Greenland was forgotten, which may have contributed to its decline and certainly to its ever-shrinking population, unable to sustain itself in such isolation. Iceland was also ignored, which opened up opportunities for traders and merchants seeking access to the abundant supplies of stockfish in the North Atlantic. The Nordic countries were united under the Kalmar Union, so that by 1397, after Haakon VI's death, Norway had become a part of Denmark along with Sweden, until Sweden's withdrawal in 1520 (Karlsson 2000:102; Wylie 2014:17).

While Norse occupation in fifteenth century Greenland was dwindling into nonexistence, Hanseatic merchants were arriving in Iceland and the Faroe Islands to exert a strong presence there by 1430–1440 (Gjerset 1924; Karlsson 2000:123–127). They had previously shown a keen interest in the North Atlantic, and by 1300 Bergen was in the hands of the Hanseatic League, which negotiated between the Norwegian king and German ports of trade, but even then attempts were under way to curb their interest in the North Atlantic. In 1294 they were subjected to sanctions that were renewed in 1302–1348 and 1361 (Wiley 2014:18). Their interest was mostly in stockfish, but sulfur, falcons, and textiles also figured (Mehler 2015; Helle 2019).

For the Faroe Islands, once the North Atlantic was under Danish colonial oversight, so little interest was invested in these remote lands that the king of Denmark would "rent out" exclusive trading rights to eager traders for a fixed sum and duration (Wiley 2014:18). In 1529 this resulted in the establishment of a quasi-feudal overlord of the Faroe Islands, Thomas Koppen, a Hanseatic merchant from Hamburg.

Amid the Hanseatic traders in pursuit of stockfish in the fourteenth and fifteenth centuries were also English, Dutch, and Norwegian merchants. The English were particularly troublesome to the point that the fifteenth century in Iceland is called the "English century," and their presence was so significant that they are thought to have ruled Iceland for some time. Sources report that in the fifteenth century approximately 100 English boats a year would sail to Iceland in search of fish (Karlsson 2000:118). These boats were equipped with armed crews of approximately 90 men and room for 100–400 tons of goods. Attempts to stop English trade in Iceland were also undertaken, with pledges made to the English king, but these were ignored. Not surprisingly, clashes occurred between the English and Hanse off the shores of Iceland.

The situation during these centuries was somewhat chaotic and rendered even more so by European monarchs' disinterest in the region as a whole. The North Atlantic was far from Denmark and the affairs of a crown dealing with its own wars and domestic conflicts. This disinterest resulted in the forfeiture of Orkney and Shetland to Scotland in 1468, and the king eventually handed control of the region to the Hanse merchants, allowing them to rule in his name. But this method of governance did not last, and in 1602–1603 the Danes imposed an embargo on all trade in the region (Róbertsdóttir 2008). The Danish monarchy restricted commerce with Iceland and the Faroes to companies operating under direct and monopolistic royal authority. The Hanseatic expansion into the North Atlantic came at the tail end of their activity, which had begun with a boom in the trade of cities in the Hanseatic League around the Baltic a few centuries earlier. During this period, German merchants controlled much of that region's economy; analysis of the material evidence for this short-lived episode of German trade has been a topic of growing interest among archaeologists working in the North Atlantic.

The Textile Trade: Iceland

Documentary sources indicate that textiles were among the commodities imported to the North Atlantic by Hanseatic merchants and possibly by the English. Conversely, Icelandic households are known to have produced and traded woolen cloth that was exported to continental Europe and was much in demand in Norway, ending up in Bergen (Helle 2019). Various sources suggest that Icelandic cloth was also making its way to both Germany and England, quite abundantly, with references in the German sources about Iceland's "wadmal" that was cheap and used to clothe the poor (Gelsiger 1981), including a decree from Burchard, the bishop of Lübeck, dated June 12, 1294, addressed to a leper house ordering lepers to dress in Icelandic woolen cloth (Latin *watmalico*, or *vaðmál* in Icelandic) treated with sulfur: "Omnes autem simplici panno, scilicet griseo watmalico vel sulphurico vestiantur" (LUB III, no. 32, Grautoff 1871; Mehler 2015:194).

Tracing the movements of these textiles in both directions presents considerably greater challenges than monitoring the movements of other elements of Hanseatic material culture, such as ceramics or glass, due to the lack of comprehensive published information on Icelandic archaeological textiles.

The Hanse were notorious for their efforts to control the textile trade in Europe, moving cloth from one location to another in various stages of production. In this context, the question arises: what was the impact of this Hanseatic textile trade on Iceland? Further, why would Icelanders have felt the need to import more woolens, or other textiles, when they produced enough cloth to accommodate their own population and generate sufficient surpluses for foreign trade? At the same time, this local homespun had gained value as a unit of currency within Iceland throughout the Middle Ages (Chapter 3; Hayeur Smith 2012, 2014b, 2015, 2018; Hoffmann 1974; Þorláksson 1991).

Identifying Hanseatic cloth imports into Iceland or the movement of Icelandic textiles into Hanseatic ports is not easy without the use of isotopic analyses of the wool itself, which may provide opportunities to source the origins of the primary raw materials. Some isotopic work was commissioned as a pilot project for this work. The material presented below was published in 2019 and was part of the conference Hanseatic Trade in the North Atlantic held in Avaldsnes, Norway, in June 2013.

Identifying Foreign Cloth: The Cloth of the Hanse, Problems and Impediments

Mehler (2009:98) identified two types of Hanseatic material culture entering Iceland during the late fifteenth to seventeenth centuries. These were either artifacts produced in the Hanse core area by craftsmen from present-day Germany and delivered to Hanseatic merchants for further sale, from one of their Kontore (presuming their Hanseatic provenance can be identified) or else artifacts made from non-indigenous raw materials or by foreign craftsmen working outside areas of Hanseatic influence but transported by the Hanse. In addition to these, a third category of material culture found at Icelandic sites of this time consists of items that came to Iceland via trade with ships of other nationalities, such as English, Spanish, Basque, and Dutch whalers or fisherman and non-Hanseatic German tradesmen stocking up in Iceland and exchanging their wares for Icelandic foodstuffs, fresh water, or goods that could be resold in England or Europe as secondary products of their voyages (Gjerset 1924).

As mentioned, before the Hanseatic presence in Iceland, English merchants had conducted trade in this region for some time (Karlsson 2000:124). In 1490, however, the Danish-Norwegian state granted foreign merchants, including those from German and Baltic ports, licenses to trade with the Faroes and Iceland (Karlsson 2000:126; Mehler and Gardiner 2013:403). This presented a new set of challenges for the English, and between 1486 and 1532 they suffered increasingly violent clashes with German merchants (Gjerset 1924:274; Karlsson 2000:124; Mehler and Gardiner 2013:403). Archaeologically, the role of these foreign traders is apparent through the presence of imported material culture in sites and deposits from these centuries; less clear-cut is the question of who brought what. The types of cloth carried in the holds of Hanseatic ships for trade with North Atlantic communities were diverse and included wares made in England, Holland, and elsewhere in Northern Europe, as they had become textile suppliers and trans-shippers for much of the continent (Kijavainen 2009:93). Regarding trade goods in Finland, Kijavainen states that cloth was sent directly to Hanseatic towns such as Reval, Lübeck, and Danzig before reaching Turku. Munro (2003) and Maik (2009) both documented English cloth—specifically English woolen broadcloth and Kerseys—circulating abundantly in areas of Germany controlled by the Hanse, as well as in Central and Eastern Europe during the late fifteenth century.

English cloth itself was frequently the product of complex and nonlinear production processes. It could be woven in one location and sent elsewhere for finishing treatments, such as dyeing, fulling, teaseling, and so on (Egan 1987). Documentary evidence even suggests that Icelandic *vaðmál* imported to England was frequently sent out for such secondary treatments before it was resold to English or more distant consumers (Stuart Peachey, personal communication 2013). In the *Early English Custom System*, published by Norman Scott Brien Gras (1918), one encounters the term "wadmol" used frequently by customs officials, as in 1303: "De Snithewynd pro wadmol et cinere et vetere panno val" (roughly translates as "of Snithewynd wadmol ash and old rags"; £xxx [cust] vii.s vi. d.; Gras 1918:298; translation, Charles Steinman, 2019).

Despite these complexities, Walton Rogers (2012) argued that visibly identifiable English cloth was present in Icelandic textile collections from excavated late medieval and post-medieval deposits at the elite farmstead of Reykholt. Her insights suggested the potential for broader inferences about the role of foreign trade in textiles within Iceland, but these were limited by the scale of the collections. The absence of comparative data from across Iceland also limits the potential for assessing the significance of variability within the corpus from Reykholt.

Recognizing Indigenous Icelandic Textiles and Identifying Anomalies as Imports

From the early to late medieval periods (ca. 1060–1600), Icelandic homespun was used as a form of currency (Chapter 3). As late as the eighteenth century and even into the late nineteenth century (in a much sparser fashion), most of Iceland's homespun textiles were produced on all—or nearly all—farms across the country on warp-weighted looms (Andersson Strand 2014; Bek-Pedersen 2007, 2009; Bender Jørgensen 1992; Hayeur Smith 2014, 2018; Hoffmann 1974;

Róbertsdóttir 2008). No evidence survives in either documentary sources or the archaeological record for centralized workshops, and neither archaeological nor documentary sources support the idea that textile production was in the hands of elites or undertaken as a specialist industry. However, these textiles' qualities were legally regulated due to their use as a form of commodity currency (*sensu* Gullbekk 2011; Hayeur Smith 2014b:731). As a result, many attributes of Icelandic homespun textiles—spin direction, thread counts, panel widths, and units of measurement—were standardized to facilitate intra-Icelandic exchange and foreign trade. These patterns of standardization appear to be particularly rigid from the late eleventh to the late sixteenth centuries, when cloth was most commonly used as currency. All or most of these sites produce examples of weaving errors, starting bands, off-cuts, spun and unspun yarn, and other technological artifacts, such as spindle whorls and loom weights, that demonstrate cloth was made, not just consumed, at these farms, with no evidence for craft specialization in Iceland's textile economy (no fullers, dyers, or shearers).

During the analysis of these collections, samples were taken from select pieces of cloth for AMS dating. Strontium isotopic analysis was also commissioned from K. M. Frei at the National Museum of Denmark to answer certain research questions about cloth imports into Iceland.

Strontium isotopic work by Frei (2014b) on 17 samples (of which 5 were modern samples of Icelandic sheep, goat hair, plants, surface water, and soil) of Icelandic textiles and wool from the late medieval to the early modern period (resulting in 5 of 17 samples of nonlocal provenance producing values $>^{87}Sr/^{86}Sr$ = 0.7092). According to Price and others (2015) Iceland is composed of some of the newest land on earth, deriving from basalts that continue to form from the mid-Atlantic ridge (Price et al. 2015:121). Ratios measured from geological formations across Iceland provide values between 0.703–0.704; while ratios measured from the enamel of modern sheep range between 0.7059–0.7069 (Price and Gestsdóttir 2006). Other samples of barley, redshank birds, and archaeological samples of cattle and pig from across Iceland provide similar values. According to Frei (2014b), most of the 17 samples are of local Icelandic origin, while 5 have ranges above the Icelandic baselines and are of nonlocal origin. Possible places of origin where the sheep were grazed include Norway, Denmark, and the British Isles relying on baselines provided by Price and others (2015). The foreign cloth noted in the analysis are mostly from the early modern period, while three from Alþingisreitur could be applicable to the discussion of Hanseatic cloth, as they date from between 1500 and 1800 (Garðarsdóttir 2010). Further AMS dating would help clarify this, as Garðarsdóttir's date ranges are broad and lack precision.

Table 6.1. Strontium isotope values of nonlocal cloth

Name of site	87 SR/86SR	Date of site	Nature of site	Appearance of the cloth
Aðalstræti	0.71078	1740	Weaving workshop established after the Danish trade monopoly	Fine brown tabby
Alþingisreitur	0.71273	1500–1800	Harbor	Red fine tabby
Alþingisreitur	0.71105	1500–1800	Harbor	Red fine tabby with surface finish
Alþingisreitur	0.70997	1500–1800	Harbor	Fine tabby, dark brown
Skálholt	0.70993	1700–1800	Icelandic bishopric	Tabby weave

Source: Frei 2015.
Note: The fine tabbies noted in the collection have always been unlike local Icelandic cloth and are confirmed to be imported items into Iceland, with possible places of origin being Norway, Denmark, and the British Isles, according to the baseline analysis by Price et al. (2015).

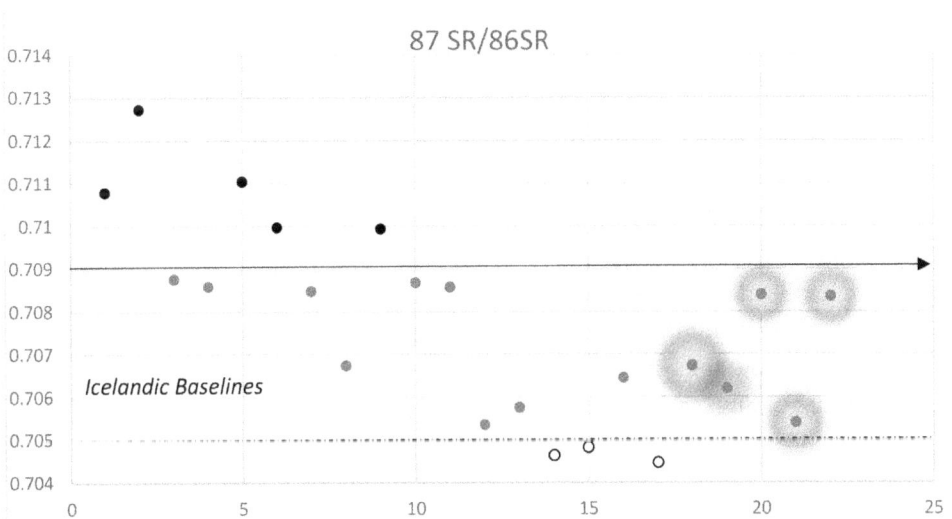

Figure 6.1. Diagram inspired by Frei (2015) depicting the strontium isotope values of the wool samples from the textile fragments. Values above the black line represent nonlocal cloth, those with gray halos are modern samples. (Hayeur Smith 2019b.)

Without strontium isotope analyses, how does one recognize non-Icelandic cloth types archaeologically or cloth types that are referred to in written sources? Maik (2009) felt that the weaving techniques used in Western and Central Europe were so similar that it was difficult to identify textile imports visually in collections. Swatches attached to pattern cards, letters, and contracts are useful aids when available, but in cultures such as medieval Iceland's, with non-industrialized textile traditions, these aids are nonexistent. Icelandic legal documents, medieval exchange lists, and other literary sources provide clues to the types of cloth—indigenous and imported—that circulated or were recognized as economically significant from approximately the late twelfth century onward. These documents provide clues to the kinds of textiles that might be found archaeologically, but not on their ubiquity or even frequency in use, let alone their representation in the archaeological record. Nor can it be assumed that these sources refer to all of the textile types imported to or manufactured in Iceland, as the number of such references is relatively small, and the agendas behind their creation are quite varied and frequently obscure.

Against these limitations of the documentary record, my work on Icelandic textiles has generated a sizable corpus of analyzed textiles, textile fragments, and weaving debris from farm sites across the country. This corpus provides strong evidence for the range of textiles produced in Iceland, their diagnostic attributes, the characteristics of wool produced by Icelandic sheep, and changes through time in all of these variables (see also Hayeur Smith 2012, 2014b, 2015a, 2016a, 2018).

As we have seen, preindustrial societies tend to produce little variety in textiles or weaving techniques over time (Minar 2001:382). My analyses of assemblages from across Iceland suggest little regional differentiation in weaving styles and considerable uniformity in the composition of textile assemblages nationwide. Major changes in assemblage composition or in the introduction of new textile manufacturing strategies, such as the appearance of knitting or the use of plied yarn in weaving homespun, appear to happen nearly concurrently across the country. Given these similarities and their predictable patterning, the presence of unusual elements, differences in materials or surface treatments, or unusual weaves in a site's assemblage suggest foreign intrusion into the mix. However, identifying foreign cloth visually in any site's assemblage requires a good knowledge of indigenous collections and textile traditions.

As discussed in Chapter 2, cloth was predominantly made of wool, with 2/2 twills dominating all assemblages. Despite the presence of other weave types, it was also largely spun Z/S. Silks, velvets, or fine textile types such as worsted twills and cloth woven with finer fleeces suggest imported cloth from the mainland and contrast clearly with these indigenous textiles in Icelandic collections. Far more abundant, however, are the tabbies, often with visible finishing, that occur frequently in collections and are also of probable foreign origin (see Table 6.2). These are finely woven, made of softer fleeces, have very high thread counts, and are frequently dyed red. Occasionally, they are spun differently from Icelandic cloth and are S-spun in both warp and weft systems or Z-spun in both systems. In fact, the late medieval and early modern samples with these characteristics from the sites of Alþingisreitur, Skálholt, and Aðalstraeti have all been confirmed by isotopic analysis as nonlocal, suggesting that the earlier examples in the Icelandic corpus are also probably nonlocal. Table 6.2 lists these elements and compares them with Icelandic homespun from the eleventh to the nineteenth centuries. Several of these types of cloth were identified in the collections from Reykholt, Stóraborg, and Gilsbakki and are discussed along with other possible cloth imports identified at these sites. Stóraborg was a wealthy coastal farm in southern Iceland, and Reykholt and Gilsbakki are both elite residential sites and parish centers located in the interior of western Iceland. These three sites were chosen because they offered significant numbers of textiles with recent and reliable AMS dates and data on textiles from the Hanseatic period in Iceland.

Table 6.2. Local Icelandic homespun compared to possible imports

Icelandic homespun from eleventh to nineteenth century	Possible imports
2/2 twills predominate; fewer tabbies	Tabbies, felts, 2/1 twills
Weaves not balanced–greater number of warp yarns than weft	Even and balanced weaves (equal numbers of warp and weft yarns (11 × 11 common)
Z/S-spun (Z-warp, S-weft) in early modern period this becomes Z2S/S (plied)	Predominance of S/S with some Z/S
Seeming lack of dyes	Frequent evidence of dyes: red (madder) and some blue (indigotin/woad)
Some surface treatment but not consistent	Heavy surface treatment: fulling, teaseling, and shearing on one or both sides
Wool: coarse warp yarns and fine fluffy wefts (Icelandic dual-coated sheep)	Fine wool, or unusual fibers and/or combination fibers, linen, silk

Source: Hayeur Smith 2019b.

Foreign Cloth from Stóraborg, Gilsbakki, and Reykholt: A Case Study and Discussion

Stóraborg

Stóraborg was a middle-ranked farm site located on the southern coast of Iceland that was abandoned in 1834 due to coastal erosion (Snæsdóttir 1991). Rescue excavations were carried out in 1978–1981 by Mjöll Snæsdóttir, as the site was being destroyed through the encroachment of a meandering river channel. The large, exceptionally complex, *tell*-like farm mound incorporated the remains of at least four major, superimposed farm complexes and 17 building phases representing rebuilding episodes within a continuous occupation that spanned at least 800 years, from the early medieval period (perhaps as early as the tenth century) through the early historic period. The final report for this important site is currently under completion (see Hayeur Smith 2019b).

The textile collection from Stóraborg is substantial, with roughly 518 find numbers recorded and nearly 1,000–1,100 actual fragments of cloth. The phasing of this site and the dating of its phases have been slightly problematic due to the scale of the site itself and the context of its excavation. Given the rapid pace of erosion, the priorities of each year's excavation had to be based on the shifting locations of the erosion fronts, rather than a more structured expansion of previous excavation units. Despite losses to erosion and discontinuities, the general structure of the phasing is clear, though links between deposits and their dating are still being assessed. The AMS dating of textile fragments (Table 6.3 and Figure 6.2) has helped clarify some of these questions, confirming that Phases 2/3, Phase 3, and the very earliest parts of Phase 2 represent the centuries during which Hanseatic commercial activity was most prevalent in Iceland. Phase 2/3 is an arbitrary phase that I developed as part of this analysis and is a layer with material found between the floors of Houses 14 and 18, dating to 1500/1550–1600, though this material may have belonged to Phase 3 (see Hayeur Smith 2019b). The sample used here consists of approximately 300 items of cloth from this targeted period and was used to give a glimpse into the social reality of textile production and import at the site.

At a site such as Stóraborg, located on the southern coast where fishing was widely pursued and a trade in locally produced dried fish supported most farms, it might be expected that the Hanse presence would have been felt through direct or indirect trade. As expected, several of the finely woven and probably imported tabbies described above were identified within the sampled collection and found in layers associated with the Hanseatic presence in Iceland.

Table 6.3. AMS dates run on textile fragments from Stóraborg, from Phases 2, 2/3, 3, and 4

Sample ID	Lab Number	Material Dated	Δ13C °/oo	Radiocarbon Age (BP)	1 sigma calibrated mean [median]	2 sigma calibrated mean [median]
ST-1979-443	Beta-344499	Textile House 14 Phase 2	-23.8	120 ± 30	1910–1927 (8.7%) 1809–1889 (40.6%) 1718–1731 (6.9%) 1685–1709 (12.0%) **1814 [1832]**	1800–1940 (62.8%) 1679–1765 (32.6%) **1814 [1832]**
ST-1981-182-639b	Beta-344502	Textile House 19 Phase 3	-22.9	350 ± 30	1481–1523 (29.4%) 1572–1630 (38.8%) **1550 [1555]**	1458–1531 (41.3%) 1539–1635 (54.1%) **1550 [1555]**
ST-1981-182-421	Beta-344501	Textile House 18 Phase 2/3	-24.2	410 ± 30	1441–1486 (68.2%) **1488 [1468]**	1591–1620 (12.1%) 1578–1583 (0.5%) 1430–1522 (82.8%) **1488 [1468]**
ST-1981-182-225a	Beta-344500	Textile House 14 Phase 2/3	-23.1	430 ± 30	1435–1469 (68.2%) **1464 [1453]**	1601–1616 (4.1%) 1507–1511 (0.6%) 1421–1499 (90.7%) **1464 [1453]**
ST-1985-322	Beta-339969	Textile House 33 Phase 4	-22.2	500 ± 30	1414–1437 (68.2%) **1421 [1425]**	1398–1449 (94.7%) 1333–1337 (0.7%) **1421 [1425]**
ST-1985-299	Beta-339968	Textile House 28 Phase 4	-23.3	960 ± 40	1135–1151 (11.9%) 1083–1127 (34.8%) 1024–1050 (21.5%) **1088 [1093]**	997–1164 (95.4%) **1088 [1093]**
ST-1985-231	Beta-344503	Textile House 28 Phase 4	-22.8	990 ± 30	1142–1147 (3.3%) 1095–1120 (19.6%) 1013–1045 (43.8%) 999–1002 (1.5%) **1060 [1038]**	1080–1153 (38.0%) 989–1053 (57.4%) **1060 [1038]**

Source: Hayeur Smith 2019b.

The majority of imported textiles from the late fifteenth- to early seventeenth-century deposits are from Phases 2 and 3. Phase 2 (Figure 6.3) is dominated by the remains of nine attached houses or rooms forming a large turf-house complex of typical southern Icelandic type, initially thought to date between ca. 1600–1700 (Snaesdóttir, personal communication 2013). The AMS dating

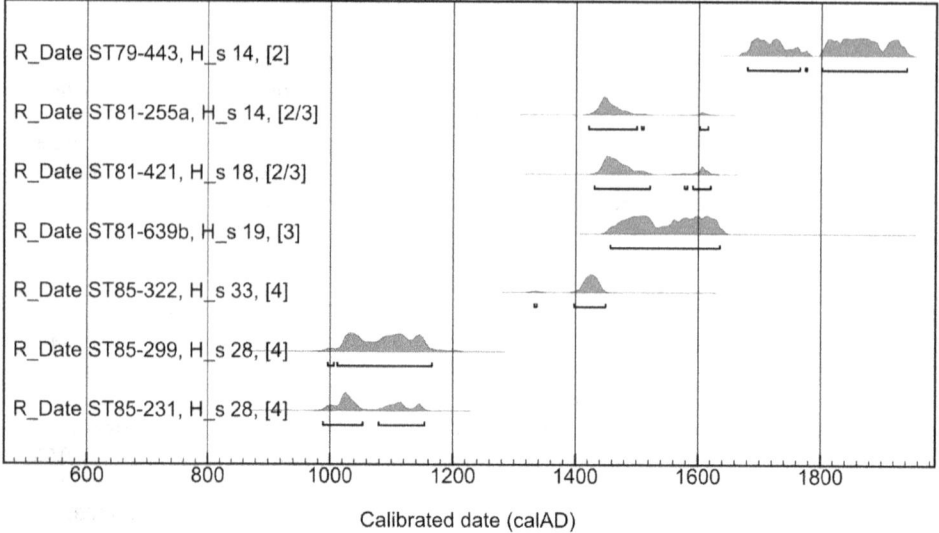

OxCal v4.2.2 Bronk Ramsey (2013); r:5 Atmospheric data from Reimer et al (2009);

R_Date ST79-443, H_s 14, [2]

R_Date ST81-255a, H_s 14, [2/3]

R_Date ST81-421, H_s 18, [2/3]

R_Date ST81-639b, H_s 19, [3]

R_Date ST85-322, H_s 33, [4]

R_Date ST85-299, H_s 28, [4]

R_Date ST85-231, H_s 28, [4]

600   800   1000   1200   1400   1600   1800

Calibrated date (calAD)

Figure 6.2. AMS dates run on textile fragments from Stóraborg from Phases 2, 2/3, 3 and 4. (Hayeur Smith 2019b.)

of textiles from its deposits confirmed this, with dates spanning 1600–1750. From this phase, textiles were found in rooms 9 and 14. Phase 3, underlying the Phase 2 farm, comprises deposits and architectural units beneath Phase 2 that represent an earlier range of turf-walled buildings laid out in similar orientation to the overlying Phase 3 farmhouse. Continuously accreting deposits between rooms in the Phase 2 and 3 farms and a similarity in the placement of the farms' walls and rooms strongly suggest that Phase 3 represents a major rebuilding of the Phase 2 farm, while the intervening Phase 2/3 deposits represent repairs and floor accretions between the initial construction of the Phase 2 houses and the Phase 3 rebuild. Artifact types, tephra, and stratigraphic considerations suggest that Phases 2/3 and 3 involved the period 1500–1600, whereas AMS dates on textiles suggest that these layers span a slightly longer and earlier range, 1450–1600. Textiles from Phase 3 were found in House 18 (Figure 6.3).

Textiles from the Hanse period, both locally made and imported, are clearly concentrated in the same parts of these superimposed houses, suggesting a continuity of nearly two hundred years in the activities occurring within these rooms, indicating that this may have been a *stófa*, or workroom, where women produced or otherwise modified textiles, along with other manufacturing activities, though the excavator also mentioned the possibility of a separate weaving area (Hayeur Smith 2019b).

Figure 6.3. (a) Phase 2; (b) Phase 3 constructions and 2/3 for those textiles found between the floors. Numbers refer to the rooms of the house and were given during excavation. (Illustration by Mjöll Snæsdóttir, modification by Hayeur Smith).

At Stóraborg, 33 of 300 samples of analyzed fragments appear to be imports displaying the characteristics described above, clearly separating them from more typical Icelandic homespun textiles. Many of these were tabbies spun and woven differently from their Icelandic counterparts or made with much finer wools or other exotic materials (Figure 6.4), including silk. Many appear to have been dyed red and in some cases teaseled and sheared indicating the work of specialized craftsmen in Europe (Walton Rogers, in Sveinbjarnardóttir 2012). The tabbies described here compare well with foreign woolen imports and with material evidence for Hanseatic trade items identified in Eastern Europe by Maik (2009) and others.

Figure 6.4. Possible imported textile found at Stóraborg, National Museum of Iceland. (Photo by Hayeur Smith.)

Reykholt

Reykholt, best known as the farm of Snorri Sturluson during the thirteenth century, is located in the western interior of Iceland, approximately 40 km from the coast (Figure 6.5). Reykholt was an elite ecclesiastic center throughout the medieval and post-medieval periods (Sveinbjarnardóttir 2006), which eclipsed its early medieval rival Gilsbakki in regional affairs during the early modern period. Excavations of the farm and its church were undertaken by Guðrún Sveinbjarnardóttir over a span of 20 years (1987–2007). Textiles from the farm were analyzed by Walton Rogers, whereas textiles recovered during the excavation of the church were analyzed by me and published as a specialist report in 2016b (Sveinbjarnardóttir 2016).

The total assemblage from Reykholt is considerable, including 340 fragments from the excavation of the farm mound and 408 from the church excavation (Hayeur Smith 2016b; Sveinbjarnardóttir 2016). Imported textiles were identified in the farm mound's Phase 4 (sixteenth- to seventeenth-century) and early Phase 5 (seventeenth- to nineteenth-century) deposits.

Despite near contemporaneity with the textile assemblage from Stóraborg, the foreign cloth in these phases, according to the classification by Walton Rogers

(2012), suggests an assemblage somewhat different, including worsted twills (both 2/2 and 2/1) with a satin-like finish that are said to have originated in northern Germany and that spread across Europe in the fourteenth century, remaining popular for centuries (Tidow and Jordan-Fahrbach 2007). In addition to these, the farm mound produced silks from the Eria and Atlas silk moths, felts said to be from either Flanders or England, and lastly, finely woven tabbies (Walton Rogers 2012).

The church excavations demonstrate a slightly different phasing, with imported textiles most common in Phases 3 (fourteenth to sixteenth century) and 4 (sixteenth century to 1886). Foreign imports were far less numerous in the excavated deposits from the church, presumably because most of the site's textile work, including sewing and the making of textile items from both local and foreign cloth, took place within the farm rather than the church. Worsted twills and silks were identified in the assemblage from the church, although from much later phases, while fine tabbies dominated the foreign cloth assemblage from the period of Hanseatic trade. Overall, the assemblage of imported cloth from Reykholt displayed greater variety and more luxury items, whereas imports at Stóraborg were of a more utilitarian nature (Hayeur Smith 2019b).

Gilsbakki

Gilsbakki is located 15 km east of Reykholt and was a powerful chieftains' center from the Viking Age until the early thirteenth century, when it was absorbed into the expanding polity of Snorri Sturluson, who consolidated power over the Borgarfjörður district and, around 1205, removed Gilsbakki's dynasty (the Gilsbekkingar) from power. The farm continued to be an important and wealthy regional estate and ecclesiastic center until 1907, when its church—most likely founded in the eleventh century—was decommissioned. Gilsbakki is still occupied, but unlike many former elite sites in Iceland, Gilsbakki's demotion from its early role as a regional political center transformed it into a regular farm, which it remains today. As a result, the farm was not subjected to extensive construction in the twentieth century and contains deeply stratified cultural deposits that are well preserved throughout the central core of the farm mound. Two trial trenches were excavated at the site in 2008 and 2009. Trench 1 was set in a deeply stratified midden where the majority of textiles were found, while Trench 2 appears to have been located on top of, and adjacent to, the foundations of turf ruins from one or more of the site's medieval farmhouses (Smith 2009).

Textiles were found in damp deposits, as is frequently the case in Iceland, encased between layers of turf blocks from the demolition of turf houses, where acidic environments were favorable for textile preservation. In total, 126 fragments of textiles were found at the site; these were analyzed by me and Margaret Ordoñez from the University of Rhode Island.

Compared with Stóraborg and Reykholt, imported cloth items were very infrequently recovered at Gilsbakki (Table 6.4). These included two items of felt, as well as one 2/1 twill and one very fine tabby, but all were in deposits quite late for the Hanseatic period. Yet despite the absence of textiles, Gilsbakki clearly had access to the material culture of German and Hanseatic trade. Pottery of German, Dutch, and southern Scandinavian origin first appears at Gilsbakki around 1490 and 1520 but becomes more common after 1550, along with other items of dress and consumption from this region.[1] Kevin Smith (personal communication 2017) suggests that the appearance of this "Germanic" assemblage at Gilsbakki may reflect, rather than a passive acquisition of Hanseatic material culture, conscious efforts by the site's priests to adopt visual symbols and personal accoutrements (e.g., redware and stoneware ceramics, leather-heeled shoes, an enameled bronze knife handle, lead pistol shot, early clay tobacco pipes) that expressed their alliance with the Protestant movement and emulated the possessions of Lutheran bishops and administrators sent to Iceland after the tumultuous decades of the Reformation (of 1550) and during the subsequent century and a half in which the crown consolidated power, confiscated ecclesiastic properties, and executed heretics. While these objects were relatively few in number, they almost completely replaced earlier forms of material culture at the site and seem to have been highly valued, as many were quite old when they entered the archaeological record, having been repaired and kept in use for more than 150 years (Smith 2009). It is important to note in the context of this examination that the range of imports at Gilsbakki clearly shows the site's strong links to international trade through the Hanseatic period, yet the site's textile assemblage, unlike those from Reykholt and Stóraborg, consists almost entirely of locally woven homespun.

There may be more than one reason for the discrepancy between Gilsbakki's textile assemblage and those of the other two sites, as well as between its "German" material culture and its indigenous cloth profile. Gilsbakki was an ecclesiastic center, and its occupants may have felt that forms of material culture other than textiles were better suited for signaling their status within the emerging German or Lutheran social environment (Hayeur Smith 2019b). However, since Gilsbakki was an ecclesiastic center, its households may have been inclined to adhere more closely to the conservative sumptuary laws in effect across Europe at the time. Sweden observed many such laws, particularly during the sixteenth and seventeenth centuries, singling out foreign textile goods as a dangerous influence, and foreign merchants as purveyors of dangerous new fashions that undermined

Table 6.4 Percentage of foreign imports per site

Stóraborg:	Reykholt: church and farm	Gilsbakki: from 2 trenches
300 items of cloth analyzed (total cloth fragments estimated at 1,000)	*526 fragments of cloth analyzed*	*126 fragments analyzed*
33 items of foreign cloth	37 items of foreign cloth	4–0 items of foreign cloth
11%	7.03%	3.2–0%

Source: Hayeur Smith 2019b.

existing traditional dress styles. Women were particularly targeted in these laws (Andersson Strand 2014). Similar conservative concerns regarding dress may have operated at Gilsbakki, as the limited discussion of sumptuary laws in Iceland's post-medieval law code, Jónsbók, cautioned Icelanders about the "objectionable practices which men have taken into custom" regarding "fancy" dress (Schulman 2010:153). Jónsbók warned of the dangers of adopting new, frivolous styles of dress that could result in large debts or in people freezing to death. Therefore, strict guidelines were imposed on people according to their wealth:

> Anyone who has twenty hundreds and not less, whether he is married or not, may wear a jacket with a hood made of costly material; and whoever has forty hundred may wear in addition a tunic made of costly material; whoever has eighty hundreds may wear in addition a coat or a cloak with a hood double lined, yet not with grey fur; whoever has one hundred hundreds, he may wear freely all of this clothing, except learned men may wear whatever clothing they wish as may the king's retainers who have all the weapons which they are required to have. And those men who have travelled abroad are allowed to wear the clothing which they themselves bring back while they last, even if they have less property that what was said before, but they shall not buy more clothing than was stipulated before. But if someone wears finery who has less property or otherwise than here is indicated then he is fined two ounce units for each piece of clothing he wears beyond what the law indicated, unless the clothing is given to him. (Schulman 2010:153)

These laws clearly limited the use of "costly materials" and imported clothes to the uppermost echelons of medieval and post-medieval Icelandic society, as 20 hundreds was the value of 20 cattle, 120 sheep, or a moderate-sized "independent" (non-tenant) farm. While Gilsbakki's Hanseatic-era residents may have simply wanted to respect these conservative sumptuary laws, the farm's wealth would most likely have exempted its core household members from the sorts of restrictions that Jónsbók prescribed, and this behavior seems to contradict the conspicuous display of other forms of imported material culture that make this period stand out in the site's archaeological record.

Other explanations for the lack of foreign cloth at Gilsbakki may involve the geographic location of this site and its distance from the sea. Geographically, both Gilsbakki and Reykholt are located quite far inland, whereas Stóraborg sits directly onshore. Gilsbakki and Reykholt, which were both elite farms, had such an abundance of grazing land for their sheep that they may have had no need for foreign cloth, except to denote status in some circumstances—as seems the case at Reykholt, where worsteds, satin-finished twills, and silk were present, albeit not plentiful. Textile debris, distaff fragments, spinners' discarded work, and so on are also abundant at both of these sites, suggesting they may have produced more than enough cloth for their own needs and were producers of textiles for export, rather than import, and focused their efforts on acquiring imports and more visible items of material culture for their households and personal use to denote and emulate specific German, Hanseatic, and Northern European associations (Hayeur Smith 2019b).

Finally, the differential representation of imported cloth at Gilsbakki and Reykholt may reflect differences in the trajectories of these parish farms within the social and economic lives of their district. While Reykholt's parish expanded throughout the post-Reformation period and retained its role as a regional and national cultural center, Gilsbakki slowly slipped into a lower rank within the ecclesiastic and political structure of rural western Iceland. Until 1605, for example, farmers on the southern side of the river Hvítá, in the commune of Hálsasveit, were required to bring their dead to Gilsbakki for burial, as they had done since at least the thirteenth century. However, after 1605 the community buried its dead at a smaller church on Stóri-Ás, one of its farms, and this became a part of the parish of Reykholt. Thus, as Reykholt's role expanded, Gilsbakki's status declined, and although its household acquired and consumed smaller amounts of material goods acquired through trade with the Hanse, any foreign cloth its household members acquired may have been too valuable to discard, rework, or consign to the archaeological record to the same extent that a wealthier farm like Reykholt could afford. At the same time, Gilsbakki owned far more grazing land than Reykholt. The ready availability of woolen cloth from its own flocks and those of its tenant farms may have made using local textiles a reasonable compromise that perhaps also signaled some assertions of tradition and Icelandic values. At the same time, the use of imported

Hanseatic status symbols such as tableware, beverages, and personal items may have signaled this land-rich but lower-ranked parish farm's allegiance to the new Lutheran ecclesiastic structure and its privilege relative to its parishioners (K. P. Smith, personal communication 2017).

Stóraborg, however, had little grazing land. Based on the site's archaeofaunal assemblage of more than 100,000 identifiable fragments, the farm appears always to have been engaged in large-scale fishing (McGovern 1990). The large number of tabby weaves of foreign origin at this site is, therefore, striking and suggests the possibility that Stóraborg's inhabitants may have been engaged in trading their dried fish (*skreið*) at the harbors of Eyrarbakki and the Westman Islands for cloth and other goods, as Mjöll Snaesdóttir (personal communication 2013) has suggested (Figure 6.5).

A remarkable number of cloth seals has, in fact, been recovered from the southern coast of Iceland in the vicinity of Stóraborg, and these may offer additional insights regarding the disproportionate amount of cloth imports from the fifteenth- to seventeenth-century layers at this site. These seals' iconography and inscriptions are not always easily identifiable, and they are infrequently found in Iceland, but they have been recovered from Bessastaðir (the colonial

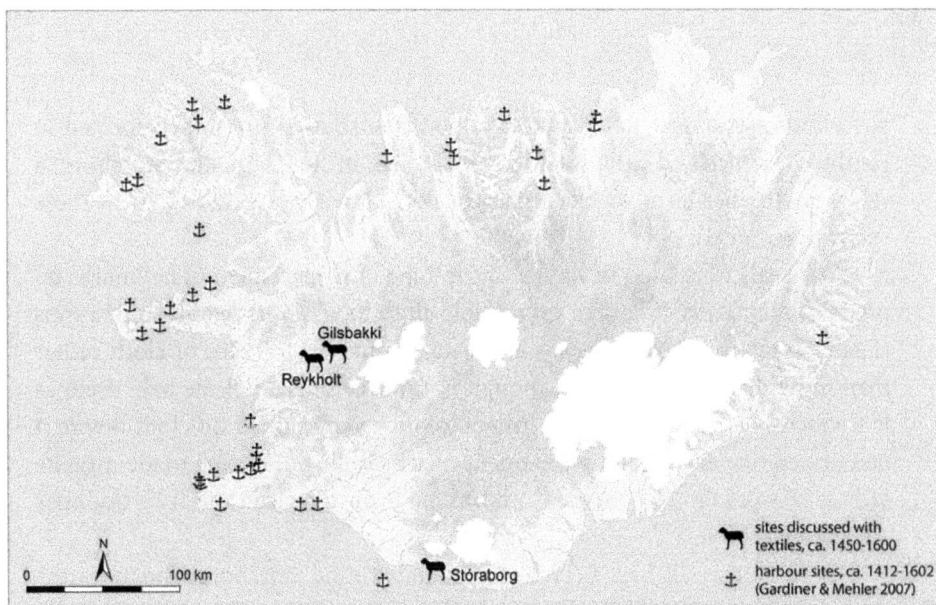

Figure 6.5. Map of Iceland with the location of sites discussed. (Map by Joris Coolen, in Hayeur Smith 2019b.)

Figure 6.6. Cloth Seal from Reykholt (2004-25-356) made of a thin sheet of metal folded over. The inscription "Carsay 66" (for the year 1666) is located on one section of the seal. Dimensions 31.5 mm × 15 mm maximum, weight 8.21 g. National Museum of Iceland. (Photo by Jónas Hallgrímsson.)

governors' estate near Reykjavik), Skálholt (the southern bishopric located in southwestern Iceland), the wealthy parish farm of Reykholt, and Stóraborg, a relatively smaller farm where, paradoxically, relatively large numbers of these seals are recorded.

Cloth seals were used in ways comparable to the placement of hallmarks on precious metals and were put on saleable cloth to verify its quality and origins (Egan 1987). These cloth seals were usually attached to bales of cloth rather than individual bolts of fabric, though not on the outside of the bale itself, as is frequently assumed. In some instances, they were placed on cloth before it had undergone any finishing treatment such as fulling or dyeing to identify the factory or workshop where the cloth was made or to register the taxes or duties already paid on it.

Several cloth seals have been found in and around Stóraborg. The most legible of them was found in the excavation of the same rooms that produced the probable imports dating to the Hanse period. This seal has a heraldic lion carrying a staff on one side and the initials VL on the other. The inclusion of Roman numerals could indicate the weight of the parcel in pounds or the alnage officer's privy mark (Egan 1987). A cloth seal from Skálholt has a similar VL on one side, suggesting that both of these may have accompanied cloth shipped from the same area in Europe.

The Stóraborg seal was dated to the seventeenth century by Þórláksson (2010:144), who concluded it was German. No parallels are known in comparative data from Britain or Bremen (Egan 1987; Hittinger 2008). Fourteen seals have been found at Stóraborg and from the sands along the coast near Stóraborg, where Þórður Tómasson, curator of the Skógar Folk Museum, collected them after storms battered the farm mound at Stóraborg and several smaller nearby sites. Most of these no longer have any inscriptions or are highly corroded fragments with the exception of one from Sanhólmagjá on display at the Skógar museum, which appears to have the obscure inscription *fordh norlic*. Although it is thought to date to the sixteenth century, no European comparisons or comparable inscriptions have yet been identified. An additional four seals were found at Skálholt, also located in this southern coastal area. These were thought to belong to the sixteenth and seventeenth centuries for the most part (Bankhead 2016).

Despite our current inability to identify their specific countries of origin, the diversity and number of cloth seals recovered from this small region suggest that its households, especially at Stóraborg, were involved in a complex pattern of trade networks. While I am not arguing that Stóraborg was a trade center for Iceland, the available data clearly suggest that this coastal area had more access to foreign textile products in bulk quantities than did more inland sites such as Reykholt and Gilsbakki. If bales and cloth were fitted with seals, the bales presumably had to be broken up into smaller units of cloth before they could be used or resold through local trade. The numerous cloth seals found in and around Stóraborg suggest that during the Hanseatic period, Stóraborg, a wealthy farm but not a parish center, may have played a pivotal role in the regional redistribution of cloth and other goods obtained in exchange for fish. Perhaps the farmer at Stóraborg acted as a middleman, during and after the Hanseatic period collecting fish from neighboring farms and in return distributing items of trade such as cloth. This may explain the abundance and diversity of textile activity evident in Rooms 9 and 14 of the site's second phase, in Room 18 of Phase 3, and in the deposits between them. It was also in deposits of Phase 2/3 that the cloth seal was found.

A model similar to that of the coastal marketplace as posited for Stóraborg was discussed by Callow (2010:213–29) regarding the earlier medieval site of

Dögurðarnes in Western Iceland. Callow's research involved an in-depth analysis of written sources about the region; he concluded that smaller sites such as Dögurðarnes may have acted as a sort of small market and distribution center outside the control of chieftains, with more imported objects reaching a greater audience than previously expected.

It is worth asking whether the "foreign cloth" from these sites represents Hanseatic trade, and especially whether the presence of English or German cloth in sixteenth-century deposits at these sites represents products carried in Hanseatic merchants' vessels. It seems most likely that such cloth was, or could have been, given the Hanseatic merchants' dominant role in Iceland's trade and also their active efforts to transship English cloth, a preferred item of cargo. But could the turbulent upheavals of the Reformation, taking place during that same hundred-year period, combined with the eventual triumph of Lutheranism in Iceland, described as "brought on by force" and "not welcomed by the Icelandic people" (Hjálmarsson 1993), have driven the Icelanders, particularly on elite ecclesiastic farms under constant threat of land seizure, to embrace whole heartedly material culture stemming from the Lutheran countries (K. P. Smith, personal communication 2017)?

Material culture in this case becomes a symbolic visual manifestation of the victors in a religious and political struggle that established the Danish monarchy's authority to rule by divine right rather than papal authority and eventually made the crown Iceland's biggest landholder. By "consuming" their material culture, centers such as Gilsbakki may have been conveying public messages of acceptance of the new faith and the new order, thus avoiding confrontation. The pottery at Gilsbakki hints at this, but textiles from this site tell us nothing. In fact, neither do those from Stóraborg or Reykholt reveal anything in this regard, though at one site the occupants consumed ordinary European woolens, and at the other, finer imported cloth. If the adoption of Hanseatic material culture represents a deliberate act of messaging and identity-formation by consumers rather than the passive acquisition of what merchants made available to them, this is surprising, as dress and visual appearance are among the more effective ways of displaying cultural identity and a sense of belonging or conforming. Furthermore, dress styles changed drastically at the time of the Reformation in Iceland, and one would think that people would seek out foreign cloth far more in line with European Lutheran dress practices of the time in order to do so. Or perhaps some Icelanders, as suggested by Hayeur Smith and others (2018) and summarized in Chapter 7, chose to ignore Lutheran dress guidelines and consuming foreign cloth by actively declining these goods, demonstrating humility, making visual statements about local identity and national identity, facing economic realities, or signaling adherence to both the sumptuary laws of the period and the more austere values of the new religious ideal.

The sixteenth century was a period of intense political and social upheaval in Iceland, as elsewhere in Northern Europe. By continuing to produce Icelandic homespun—a commodity that had been vitally important for centuries—on farms that could afford to do so, people may have been expressing a form of resistance to change, to direct colonial rule, or to the new faith, by not changing their dress immediately except in their cut and tailoring, instead using homespun to reflect their identity as Icelanders.

The Faroe Islands

The textiles collection from the Faroe Islands is the smallest from the North Atlantic, with a mere 142 items from the Viking Age to the early modern period. Most of the collection is from the early modern period (74 items); there is a striking lack of textiles from earlier periods.

A surprisingly large quantity of textiles (n = 40) were spinners' waste, clumps of raw wool; the rest were mostly textiles from the early modern period. Certainly cloth was not used as currency on these small islands as it was in Iceland, and when asked where the archaeological textiles were, the curators of the National Museum of the Faroe Islands replied that it had all been traded abroad according to medieval documentary sources (Símun Arge, personal communication 2015). Wylie (2014:26) argued that the Faroes had two economies, the most important being the export trade in wool, which was increasingly sold to foreign merchants. Such woolens were also collected from Shetland and sold in Bergen (Helle 2019).

Not a lot can be concluded about such a small assemblage, except that the early modern material from the seventeenth century, as is the case in Iceland, is well endowed with imports (n = 30), based on the knowledge of foreign imports and visual recognition described above. The medieval material, on the other hand, is not, and therefore a comparison between sites in the Faroes, as

Table 6.5. Faroese cloth over a 900-year period

Total	Early Modern	Medieval	Viking Age
142	74	44	0

opposed to Iceland, is not possible, though the islands were heavily controlled by foreign merchants from the 1300s to the early seventeenth century, when the Danish monarchy imposed its trade monopoly. From that point on across the North Atlantic islands, Danish colonial authorities took a sudden and great interest in the wool industry, and realized the profits that could be attained from all this wool if only it were produced like European broadcloth with production methods that had been in place in Europe since the fourteenth century. This led to an interesting cultural revolution in both Iceland and the Faroes, which ultimately altered and transformed the roles of women in these societies. This transformation is discussed further in Chapter 7.

7

The Danish Trade Monopoly in the North Atlantic and the Transformation of Women's Roles in Textile Production

In 1603 the Danish crown had had enough of foreign merchants controlling and profiting from the resources of the North Atlantic and enacted a trade embargo forbidding them from doing business in the region altogether. Several previous attempts to evict German merchants had mostly failed, until King Frederik II leased out specific harbors to individual merchants for specific periods of time (Karlsson 2000:138). While the Germans were said to profit from this arrangement, so did others, such as Danes, and from Iceland's perspective this created an active trade environment with all harbors in use (Karlsson 2000:139). King Frederik II's successor was Christian IV (1588–1648), who preferred a policy of mercantilism and sought to improve foreign trade in Denmark and its territories. He imposed a monopoly on foreign trade that included both Iceland and the Faroes and that endured for 186 years. To sum up its main principles, 1) trade was restricted to Danish citizens and mostly Copenhageners, and 2) competition between merchants was excluded as far as possible.

This policy exerted a tremendous impact on the North Atlantic textile trade and marked a massive influx of imported cloth into both Iceland and the Faroe Islands. Luxury items appear more abundantly in the seventeenth century than ever before, with, among textile types, silks, velvets, linens, fustians, and worsted twills making their way into people's households. But among the imports, homespun survived despite the Danish crown's active attempts at eradicating this cottage industry in favor of modern tools and industrial-style textile workshops.

Social Change and the Industrialization of Iceland

Textiles dating from the trade monopoly of 1603 differ considerably from those of the late medieval period, and to any observer poring over these vast collections, they mark the beginning of a new era in Iceland and the North Atlantic. Medieval textiles were produced in the home by women, but by the seventeenth and eighteenth centuries, a shift occurred with the introduction of new tools and technologies, along with an attempt to establish a regulated system with a standardized product combined with centralized textile workshops and trained craftsmen. The shift in production, therefore, not only affected the tools used in creating textiles but also organized the making of textiles into a more centralized and regulated activity, as had happened in Europe. The new tools included the treadle loom and spinning wheel, which were introduced in Iceland by the early 1700s in the bishoprics of Skálholt and Hólar and became widespread by 1750 (Róbertsdóttir 2008:30).

Additional changes in social organization were directed toward augmenting textile production so as to increase exports of Icelandic woolens and worsteds and decrease imports (Róbertsdóttir 2008:69), though the archaeological record reveals that the opposite occurred. This resulted in the creation of the Privileged Icelandic Company (PIC), which was interested in modernizing Iceland's wool industry and which created the Innréttingar or the Nýju Innréttingar (New Enterprise) in 1751, with local officials reporting back to the king of Denmark (Róbertsdóttir 2008:29). The PIC established a central policy that regulated wool in general and items made of Icelandic wool that were to be sold within the Danish empire, to which Iceland and other North Atlantic islands belonged. This affected knitted goods (in the Faroes particularly), spinning, and weaving. The PIC also set up textile workshops in Reykjavik in 1750, and in its early years there were two main workshops with facilities for shearers, a fulling and stamping mill, and dye works (Róbertsdóttir 2008). Worsteds were woven, as were fustians and linens, and a "putting out system" was established so that people across the countryside (mostly women) could partake in the modernization process and carry out the spinning for these workshops. A sheep farm was also established in 1756 and was run for a decade with the king's support to develop a better breed of sheep with higher-quality wool to benefit the whole country, according to Róbertsdóttir (2008:136). The textiles produced underwent quality inspection and were frequently sent back to Copenhagen for quality control and then returned to Iceland (or elsewhere) for resale (Róbertsdóttir 2008:134). In 1764, however, a large fire swept through Reykjavik, reducing the number of workshops to one; by the end of the century, production had ceased entirely.

From a social perspective, this meant that the PIC influenced the production of textiles, and also the training of specialized weavers in Denmark, almost all of whom were men. These efforts were most active between 1720 and 1790. But what did the removal of textile production from women and its allocation to men mean to Icelandic women? Were women losing ground to men? Women in Iceland had been weaving and spinning for 800 years, and the country had relied on them for its economic well-being. In Chapter 1 we discussed the implications of old Norse religious practice on weaving and how weaving may have been tied to beliefs surrounding life, death, and fate. In the early medieval period, when the gendered *dyngja* had been abolished with the introduction of Christianity and with the thriving cloth currency economy, women brought their weaving indoors but continued to work in the *stófa* with little to no male involvement. People forget ancient beliefs, yet sometimes these beliefs continue to permeate society and influence cultural attitudes toward certain activities. For example, in the early modern period of Northern Europe, spinning was considered a form of subjugation and punishment for women, according to Schneider (1989:177), and fear of spinning was expressed in numerous fairy tales, such as Rumpelstiltskin. Are these fairy tales and other stories about supernatural beings and the intervention of fairies in the textile world simply a reflection of deeper and older beliefs connected to female, pre-Christian textile work that was opportunistically demonized by Christianity? In Norse society, as discussed, weaving and spinning were related to the goddess Freyja, to the *völvur* or seeresses, and to the Norns who controlled fate, but in these Christian and male-dominated societies of Northern Europe in the early modern period, such religious beliefs were branded as the work of the devil, and I would propose that the tale of Rumpelstiltskin and many others emerged in part as an attempt to reinforce a male and Christian agenda and ideology by ostracizing more ancient belief systems that still lurked in people's attitudes and cultural beliefs. Schneider (1989), on the other hand, perceived these stories differently, as a reflection of the situation in which women found themselves vis-à-vis spinning during the Industrial Revolution.

To better understand how women might have reacted to the sweeping changes underway in Iceland (were they pleased by a reduced workload and greater access to luxury goods and wealth, or did they perceive this as a usurpation of their traditional status?), it is useful to look at the situation of women who experienced a similar transition in mainland Europe during the Industrial Revolution and earlier. But even there the situation is not clear-cut.

Berman (2007:10) argued that spinning was the great bottleneck in industrial textile production and that the spindle and distaff would not always provide enough yarn to weave a piece of cloth. The time allocated to spinning in Greenland's nonindustrial context was disproportionate to the time required for weaving, so these were plainly very real concerns (Chapter 5). Berman (2007:18) also argued that it would take the work of eight village women spinning to support the work of a single male weaver operating a treadle loom. In the early Icelandic model, where each household produced its own yarn and textiles, and where households owned their own products, all able-bodied women and probably children spun. In the new economy of the eighteenth century, following European models, women were paid to spin for men who were engaged in more specialized work with wool, either in the workshops of Reykjavik established by Skúli Magnússon and the Danish colonial authorities or in small rural workshops. Faced with a similar situation in Europe concerning the spinning of flax, merchants and other investors in the cloth trade singled out children and young women as the most promising laborers and promoted "feminized" autonomous spinning institutions (Schneider 1989:190–191). They went so far as to argue that younger women left at home alone were unruly, but in harnessing their skills "'away from home, they might be more productive,' for 'when so many are employed in sight of each other' and with proper encouragement, 'small and great' will strive to excel" (Haines 1677:14, in Schneider 1989:191). Spinning was encouraged in various contexts: it was taught in orphanages and workhouses, and because spinning wheels were portable, women congregated in "spinning bees," working together in the evening to economize on light, space, and fuel, and enjoy the conviviality of each other's company (Schneider 1989:193). These spinning bees were reportedly also conducive to courtship, with men dropping in to flirt or accompany women home (Schneider 1989:194). Eventually both the Protestant and Catholic hierarchies attacked these workplaces as "dens of vice" and seduction and called for parental oversight (Schneider 1989:195). However you look at it, spinning then or during the Viking Age was perceived as a dangerous activity linked to female reproductive power!

While some accounts of women's involvement in spinning were positive, an equal number, particularly from New England, describe atrocious conditions for spinners in mills, especially for children. Galbi (1996) addressed the working conditions of women and children in England during the mid-nineteenth century. In his analysis, he argued that the transition from cottage industry to large-scale enterprise was more difficult in the cotton industry and that working conditions were horrific. Employees (including children) were forced to labor roughly 15 hours a day during the week with a 35-minute break for breakfast and a 55-minute break for dinner, with another 9 hours of work on Saturday (Galbi 1996:144–146).

Mills on that scale never operated in Iceland, and it is difficult to know exactly how people felt about their new, more industrialized way of life. Moreover, Icelandic workshops required the assistance of the countryside for spinning and also involved the oversight of entrepreneurs commissioned by the Danish colonial authorities (Róbertsdóttir 2008:138). In this manner, manufacturing could have been a means to discipline and educate the locals on how to be efficient and useful subjects. By 1775 the Danish authorities had come to exert their influence over households directly and encouraged wealthy farmers to set up domestic-scale weaving workshops on their farms, using professional weavers, and modern tools and production techniques to supplement the output of mills and workshops in Reykjavik (Róbertsdóttir 2008:139). It was thought this would help modernize Icelandic wool-working traditions and probably force a transition from the warp-weighted to the flat treadle loom. To this end, tools and training were offered free of charge. The authorities wanted to support quality spinning instead of knitting, which had been a widespread activity until then. This phase of government-controlled production eventually died out with the abolition of the trade monopoly in 1787 (Róbertsdóttir 2008:142). Beyond this thumbnail overview of the situation, however, the everyday reality was more complex and nuanced: nothing has been reported on how the people affected felt about these transitions, let alone the women who were suddenly thrust into a new way of life. The archaeology may hold some answers.

Although the Danish presence also asserted itself in the Faroe Islands, introducing the same new technology for spinning and weaving as in Iceland, the Faroes never experienced the same level of reorganization of the wool industry as did Iceland (Róbertsdóttir, personal communication 2017). In contrast to Iceland, the primary focus in the Faroes remained the production of knitted goods for export, particularly in the form of knitted stockings in the seventeenth and eighteenth centuries (Wylie 2014:26).

Homespun Cloth and the Case of Textile Imports at the Site of Skálholt, the Icelandic Bishopric: A Working Example

Analyses of archaeological textile data from 1600–1800 reveal that homespun on the warp-weighted loom was far from obsolete, and people continued to work as they had for the past 900 years, despite efforts by the authorities to impose changes. Some of the data presented here regarding Skálholt were published in a paper coauthored with Gavin Lucas and Quita Mould in the *Journal of Social Archaeology* during 2018.

Skálholt was one of two episcopal seats in Iceland and possessed a school where sons of the elite were educated; many of the students became priests or government officials (Hayeur Smith et al. 2018). In the excavations carried out between 2002 and 2007 (yielding material from the seventeenth to nineteenth centuries), textiles were a significant category of artifact, with up to 3,462 fragments of cloth.

The majority of textiles are scraps of cloth or spinners' waste, such as raw wool and spun yarns, suggesting that some textile work was taking place on the site. Whether or not that was the case, these textiles were used in a household context, perhaps initially as garments, and then progressively devolving into household rags. Some were garments belonged to students or the staff of the school, and possibly even the bishop, and many of these clothing remains did not originate at Skálholt but in elite households across the island from which the boys had come (Hayeur Smith et al. 2018).

Overall, woolen textiles dominate the assemblage, with 3,236 fragments (93.4%). This is an inaccurate estimate of textile consumption on the site, however, because linens and cellulose-based fibers, another important category of textiles do not survive and tend to degrade much more quickly than woolens unless they have been burned or mineralized to metal artifacts. Figure 7.1 shows the distribution of woven textiles; ribbons and bands are often made of wool, but this category includes silks as well. "Textile waste" refers to raw wool and fragments of spun yarn, often suggesting that textile production occurred on the site. Twills are for the most part 2/2, followed by plain weaves. The felts include both pounded examples for which no weave is visible and those derived from woven cloth. Many are imports. The twills are the largest category in the assemblage, and at Skálholt, in keeping with other early modern sites, it is often difficult to determine whether these twills are locally produced homespun, industrially woven imports from the mainland, or professional worsted twills from the workshops of Reykjavik in the 1750s (Hayeur Smith et al. 2018).

Textiles from the early modern period are among the more complex in Iceland's textile corpus and reflect the complexities of an industry dominated by the Danish trade monopoly and the reorganization of textile production. It is interesting to ponder what percentage of textiles at a site like Skálholt was imported. What percentage was produced locally in the Reykjavik workshops? And how much homespun was in circulation in Iceland at the time? One might think that the students, priests, and bishops residing at Skálholt, as members of the elite, were dressed in European styles with imported and often lavish or elaborate textiles (Icelandic *vaðmál* was perceived in Europe as a cheap and coarse type of cloth), yet the textile data point to something else altogether. A

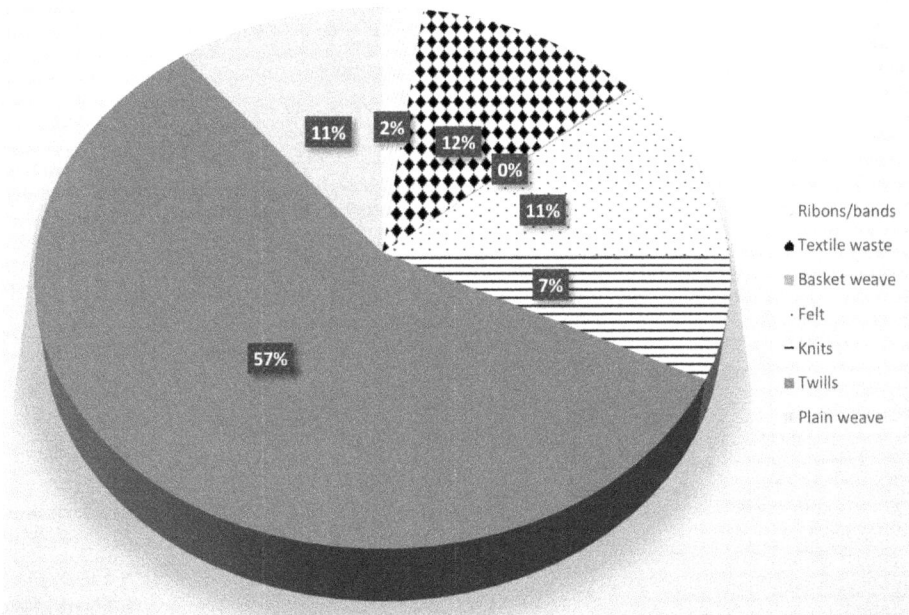

Figure 7.1. Distribution and percentages of weave types at the site of Skálholt, the seat of the Icelandic bishopric. Ribbons/bands (often made of silk): n=70; textile waste: n=384; basket weave (panama weave): n=5; felt: n=374; knits: n=238; twills: n=1,876; plain weave: n=347.

good way to understand consumption patterns of textiles is by looking at thread counts in the archaeological data (see Chapters 2–5).

At Skálholt, the examination of thread counts over several centuries is quite revealing. The data from these centuries are divided into archaeological phases comprising AD 1650–1700, AD 1700–1750, and post–AD 1750. From AD 1650 to 1700, thread counts of twills suggest a pattern consistent with medieval Icelandic homespun and textiles produced on a warp-weighted loom, that is, warp dominant fabrics, with warp thread counts similar to those of earlier medieval examples: 4–14 warp threads per centimeter, reflective of high standardization and the use of textiles as a currency (Chapter 3; Hayeur Smith 2014b, 2018). Homespun items generally lacked the surface finish of the European-style worsteds (Chapter 6). As in the medieval period, textiles from AD 1650–1700 cluster around 4–14 warp threads per centimeter, but at Skálholt, additional pieces with higher thread counts are also present, suggesting possible imports (Figure 7.2). Based on the data from Skálholt, coarse homespun cloth—not unlike medieval *vaðmál*—seems to be the dominant textile at Skálholt between 1650 and 1700 (Figure 7.2), and not the luxurious textiles depicted in paintings.

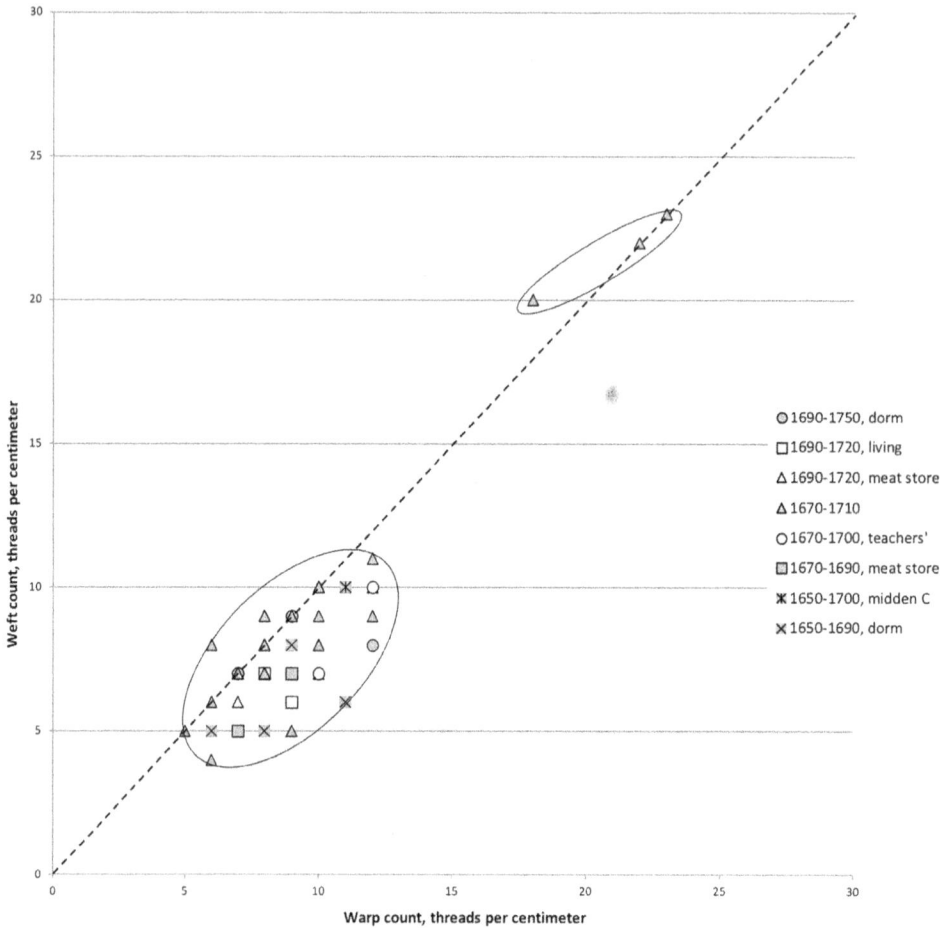

Figure 7.2. Thread counts of textiles from AD 1650–1700 at Skálholt. (Hayeur Smith et al. 2018. Courtesy *Journal of Social Archaeology*.)

Between AD 1700 and 1750 (see Figure 7.3), a change in thread counts is noted, with the inclusion of a greater range of higher thread counts as well as more balanced weaves (with equal thread counts), suggesting the use of the new treadle loom, which is more efficient and produces more regular and balanced cloth. The cluster identified in Figure 7.2—between 4–14 wrap threads—is still relevant, but with far more diversity in thread counts, which may reflect the increased availability of textile types other than homespun in Iceland, possibly as imports, as the weaving workshops of Reykjavik were only established in the 1750s. The period of 1700–1750 seems to reflect the greatest prevalence of imported cloth at Skálholt, whereas post-1750, the situation changes yet again.

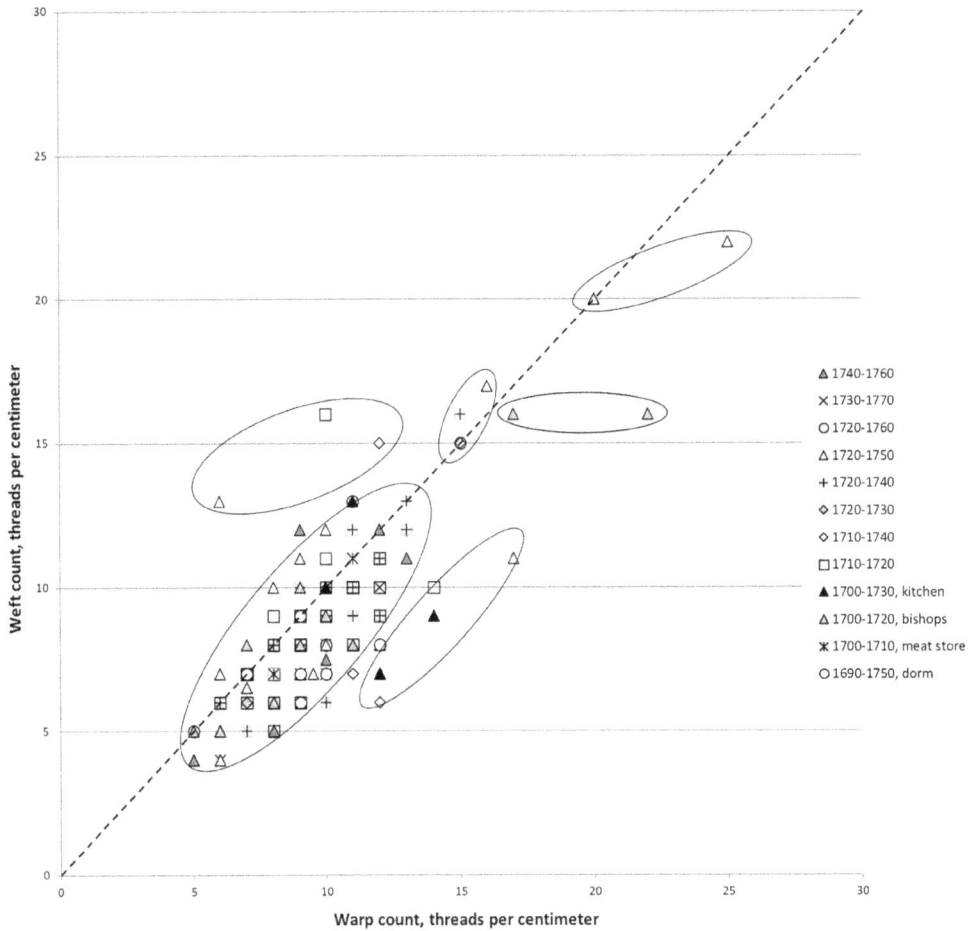

Figure 7.3. Thread counts from textiles at Skálholt, AD 1700–1750. (Hayeur Smith et al. 2018. Courtesy *Journal of Social Archaeology*.)

By 1750 (Figure 7.4) twills restabilize around the core cluster, but in a slightly different way. Textiles are more numerous in this group, and display more balanced weaves. Visually the textiles from this period resemble European imports, as the manufacturing technology is the same in both locations. Do the data from after AD 1750 perhaps indicate that these textiles were produced in the workshops of Reykjavik?

Thread counts help track the movements of cloth imports and the consumption patterns at Skálholt, and Figures 7.2–7.4 indicate that homespun cloth continued in use throughout the centuries, regardless of sanctions and new reforms to curtail it. This suggests that attempts at modernization and at abolishing the

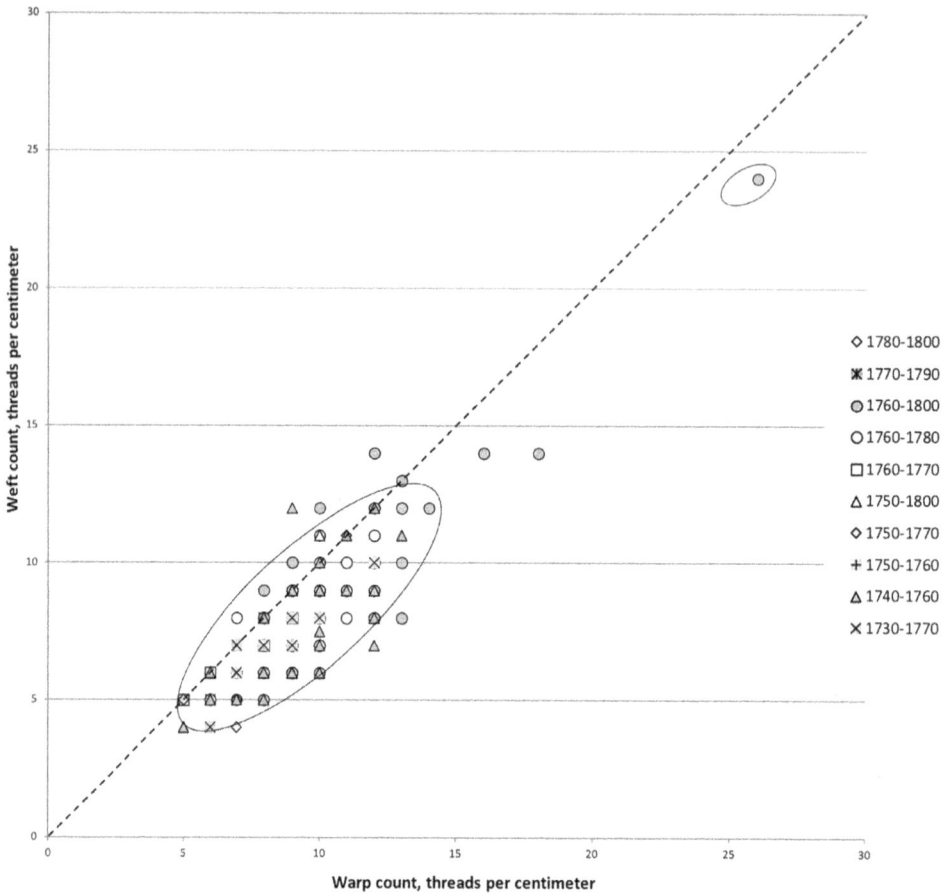

Figure 7.4. Thread counts of textiles from AD 1750–1800 at Skálholt. (Hayeur Smith et al. 2018. Courtesy *Journal of Social Archaeology.*)

old looms were not resoundingly successful; furthermore, the workshops were short-lived, operating for only 50 years.

Examining the data on spin direction at Skálholt may shed more light on the issue of homespun consumption. Textiles from this period are not spun like their medieval counterparts, which were always spun Z/S, whereas these are spun Z2S (plied) in the warp and S in the weft. This manner of spinning first emerged in Iceland during the late fifteenth century; long before the introduction of the new loom, women were weaving homespun cloth with plied warps in one system or the other (Z2S). This technique is found across Iceland and may be attributable to increasing climatic deterioration in the fifteenth century at the onset of the Little Ice Age, since adding plied yarns makes cloth heavier and warmer (Hayeur Smith 2012).

Out of 3,236 woolen textile fragments, approximately 1,343 had plied warp yarns Z2S, while 563 were Z-spun in the warp. In a previous analysis of Skálholt textiles, the issue of spin direction and plying was addressed in a smaller sample of 383 fragments dating from the seventeenth to nineteenth centuries (Hayeur Smith 2012). Plied textiles progressively dominate the assemblage during the eighteenth century but become far less common in the nineteenth century (Figure 7.5). The use of plied yarns in either warp or weft is a feature that was also noted in homespun at most sites of the same period across Iceland, and its presence in the Icelandic corpus represents an innovation in terms of earlier medieval textile production.

Only at the site of Stóraborg (Chapter 6) did this pattern of plying differ, though there too a long-term use of homespun cloth was noted. The largest quantity of textiles from that site (45%) is from the latest level, Phase 2, dated between 1600 and 1750. Stóraborg, unlike other parts of Iceland during the early modern period, continued to produce cloth in the medieval style, using single yarns Z/S (78% of the total amount), whereas cloth with plied yarns in one or both systems (warp or weft) amounts to only 7% of the total corpus. It is unclear why this is the only site to resist plying, as all other sites with substantial textile remains (homespun), such as Bergþórshvoll, Reykholt, Gilsbakki, and Skálholt, show a propensity toward plying as time progresses. Stóraborg also contains more tabby weaves spun S/S or Z/Z with elaborate finishes than at any other site, implying European rather than Icelandic production. This could reflect Stóraborg's special role in the Icelandic economic landscape, as it was in close proximity to two substantial trading posts, Eyrarbakki and the Westman Islands, and may have served as a redistribution center of imported goods (see previous chapter).

The innovation of adding plied yarns to homespun, though more labor intensive, developed before the introduction of the modern loom and represents a new approach to yarn manufacture in most of Iceland, aimed at producing cloth and clothing with new qualities and features (Hayeur Smith 2012).

The data from Skálholt and other sites show that homespun cloth continued to be produced despite efforts by the Danes to abolish it. The data further suggest that elites in Iceland dressed with the same cloth that had been in use for centuries and that luxury goods enjoyed limited circulation and may have been restricted to certain people for specific occasions. Knitting is also surprisingly rare, with only 238 knits in the entire corpus. It is often argued that knitting became widespread during the eighteenth century (Róbertsdóttir 2008) and was used to make garments. However, most knits probably made their way to

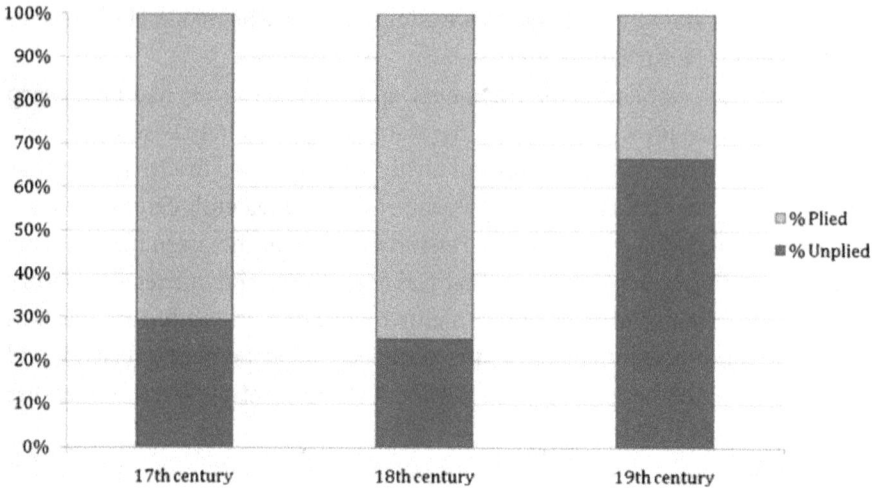

Figure 7.5 Percentages of plied versus unplied yarn at Skálholt. (Reprinted from Hayeur Smith 2012, by permission from Springer Nature.)

Copenhagen as export products, and Icelanders during this period, were probably more focused on spinning and textile work. Complete knitted garments became common only after the eighteenth century when the textile mills in Reykjavik shut down, and fewer and fewer people knew how to weave using the old looms, while flat looms required specialized training.

Homespun Use and Dress Styles in Iceland in the Early Modern Period, Based on Visual Evidence

A look at tailoring in early modern Iceland also reveals more about the use of homespun and its integration into everyday dress. Women's reactions to the new imposed changes are perhaps more visible through dress overall than through specific textiles and textile production itself, whereby women were directly impacted either positively or negatively. As the colonized, they were in no position to react to these changes except in discreet and subtle ways. Women were responsible for clothing manufacture from the Viking Age onward, a role they maintained during the trade monopoly. If dissatisfaction, resistance or even nationalism vis-à-vis their colonizers was to be expressed in some tangible form, clothing was as good as any. An examination of Icelandic men's clothing for this period demonstrates how both clothing and cloth formed a potent symbol of national identity.

Icelandic textile collections hint that fifteenth century dress in Iceland may have had elements in common with European dress of the same period. From the site of Bergþórshvoll, for example, several pieces were identified with "dagged" edges that are cut in square shapes, a decorative feature often added to sleeves, hoods, and *houplandes*, a long garment worn with long sleeves. But more evidence is available for the sixteenth century, when more radical changes in dress are evident in Northern Europe. This is largely due to the Reformation, which brought clearer guidelines about dress practices, or rather dress restrictions, when introduced to Iceland in AD 1550. Sumptuary laws were a part of the Reformation in Northern Europe, and religious authorities were eager to control dress, feeling that people impoverished themselves with lavish apparel (for sumptuary laws in Iceland, see Chapter 6; Cox 2006). Earlier extravagances and ostentatious clothing associated with Catholicism motivated the authorities on moral and religious grounds to establish what should be worn, particularly among the clergy, and to advocate for moderation and decency, "a decorum in appearance which pleased God" (Murdock 2000:182–188). The authorities promoted models of simple dress, leaving the body well covered, and they discouraged the use of bright colors, instead promoting long, dark gowns.

The main analysis of male dress and costume in Iceland for this period was published by Æsa Sigurjónsdóttir (1985), and in 1999 Fríður Ólafsdóttir published *Íslensk karlmannaföt, 1740–1850* on male clothing in Iceland. Sigurjónsdóttir drew on contemporary depictions and descriptive text from various sources, which can, however, be biased in favor of elites.

The non-clerical dress of men in the sixteenth century, according to Sigurjónsdóttir, was influenced by Spanish style, though the Spaniards enjoyed bolder colors such as crimsons, tawny, and mulberry (Ribeiro 2003:665). Ribeiro argued that northern taste, differing from the Spanish, opted for more exaggeration in style, such as doublets padded with decorative "slashings." These were worn with a high and frilled collar—also of Spanish and French origin and favored by European elites—that grew considerably larger as the century progressed (Ribeiro 2003:665–666). The doublet in Iceland was called a *treyja*, and in common with Northern European trends was worn with a ruff collar (*kragi* in Icelandic) made of starch and lace (Ribeiro 2003; Sigurjónsdóttir 1985; Thursfield 2001). In Europe longer garments were frequently worn over tighter ones as "informal fashion" (Cox 2006). According to Ribeiro (2003:667), the trousers in Europe that complemented this outfit assumed various forms: "rounded like an onion, flared out like a short stiff skirt, or longer, more oval in shape." A well-shaped leg was an important asset to men, often enhanced by stockings, many of which came from Iceland and the Faroes, whose workers began knitting stockings for trade around that time.

Portraits of Iceland's sixteenth century officials and ministers did not depict such tight-fitting garments; looser, longer robes continued to be the norm. This style of dress was customary for clerics and ministers in Northern Europe, according to Murdock (2000). In 1574 Scottish ministers were banned from wearing decorative elements on their clothes, light-colored hose, or velvet breeches. They were restricted to black or somber colors, eschewing anything brighter comported more appropriately with their roles as models of self-control, discipline, and moral authority (Murdock 2000:184, 186). The ruff or collar, worn by such officials, may have been used in Iceland as an emblem of social ranking and to show connections with the outside world and European elites, as many of these officials were educated in Denmark.

The sheriff Magnús Jónsson (died AD 1591) from Bæ á Rauðasandi was depicted with his family in a commemorative painting (ca. AD 1580–1600) now at the National Museum of Iceland (Þjms 2060). While entirely in black, he clearly wears imported cloth in the form of a silk damask black floral-patterned cloak and the infamous ruff collar—clearly violating European Lutheran ideals in choice of textiles, but perhaps this is how Iceland set itself apart (Hayeur Smith et al. 2018).

By the early seventeenth century, the English and Dutch development of this style became more fashionable in northwestern Europe. It included longer breeches, a looser-fitting jacket flaring out at the waist, and a flattening of the ruff into a broad linen collar gummed with shellac, known as a *velona*, which rested on the shoulders (Cox 2006; Ribeiro 2003:673). Sigurjónsdóttir (1985) described the new jacket (*kjöll*) that dropped to the knees and featured more pockets and buttons, exhibiting Asian influences. It was less padded and more muted than the earlier version (Ribeiro 2003:673). With the final addition of a waistcoat (*vest*), this new ensemble constituted the emergence of the three-piece suit, which remains fundamental to the male wardrobe to the present day, albeit undergoing multiple changes in style and cut (Hayeur Smith et al. 2018; Kutcha 2002). Breeches now fastened below the knees, and high-heeled boots and long hair came into vogue (Ribeiro 2003:673; Sigurjónsdóttir 1985). It is said that the overall look entailed a more casual elegance and less structure (Ribeiro 2003:673).

Icelandic paintings from this period suggest that the ruff collar did not disappear in the early seventeenth century; nor does it disappear in Holland or Denmark, which is where the Icelandic elite are said to have derived their sense of style. Bishop Steinn Jónsson, the bishop of Hólar, is depicted circa 1711–1739 wearing the same ruff collar as in earlier periods. His garments are not form-fitting, and he too is in black, with a buttoned overcoat or possibly a loose-fitted

Figure 7.6. Painting of Gísli Þorláksson, bishop of Hólar, and his three wives: Gróa Þoleifrsdóttir (d. 1660), Ingibjörg Benediktsdóttir (d. 1673), and Ragnheiður Jónsdóttir, who survived her husband. Copenhagen, 1685. (National Museum of Iceland, þjms 3111/1888–118.)

jacket in the European fashion. In a painting from 1685, Gísli Þorláksson is accompanied by his three wives (þjms 3111/1888–118). This painting was produced in Copenhagen, according to the museum description, and is very similar in topic to another at the National Museum of Denmark, depicting Ole Worm, a Danish physician, professor, and antiquarian. In both cases, the men are wearing the ruff collar, as are the three wives in the Icelandic portrayal (Figure 7.6).

The resistance to changes in dress may have had some bearing on the persistence of the ruff collar. The bishop of Skálholt, Brýnjolfur Sveinsson (1639–1674), expressed severe displeasure at modern fashions and established strict guidelines for his priests, including the appropriate length of hair (Hayeur Smith et al. 2018; Sigurjónsdóttir 1985:37). Halldórsson (1903:10) stated that the bishop's own clothing was simple, and he promoted the idea that God had given the Icelanders wool from their sheep, and so clothing should be made of homespun (Hayeur Smith et al. 2018). Brýnjolfur Sveinsson may or may not have influenced dress practices at Skálholt, but the next bishop, Þorður Þorlaksson (1674–1697), seems to have furthered Brýnjolfur's ideas, judging by a contemporary portrait (Mms-4677; Sigurjónsdóttir 1985:44), though he was also a bishop with considerable experience in the outside world, having been educated in Denmark and Germany. At Skálholt, he hired a foreign chef to cook for him and was responsible for bringing musical instruments back to Iceland (Halldórsson 1903:10). While he may have dressed according to religious requirements, his attitude toward his students and household may not have been as doctrinaire, given his openness to foreign culture (Hayeur Smith et al. 2018).

Late seventeenth-century resistance to these changes in dress was not ubiquitous among secular officials. A portrait of Jón Þorlaksson, a county sheriff and the district commissioner of Berunes in 1688, depicts a man who thoroughly adopted the French style, with a buttoned coat possibly made from silk, long hair, and a lace neckcloth (Sigurjónsdóttir 1985:43). The ruff collar had been abandoned. The one restraint to be retained seemed to involve color: elites in England and particularly France opted for lighter hues, whereas black and darker colors were normal in Northern Europe (Ribeiro 2003:676), as in Iceland.

By the turn of the eighteenth century, French fashions dominated Europe and seemed to have spread among Iceland's elite. According to Ribeiro (2003:682), this century, before the French Revolution, reflected a taste for the artificial, exemplified by the popularity of powdered wigs. For European men, the style in the earlier eighteenth century continued to incorporate long, structured, heavy waistcoats, with large cuffs and flapped pockets (Ribeiro 2003:684). Very soon, apparel began to tighten up; the coat lost its waist and its heavily pleated look and by the late eighteenth century had become narrower in cut and shorter and the breeches tighter fitting. By 1780 the coat's hemline was a few inches below the waist. Large wigs gave way to smaller ones with curls at the sides, and tied at the back of the head with a silk ribbon.

The eighteenth-century bishop of Skálholt, Jón Viðalin (1698–1720), wore one of the earlier-style wigs, and although the subsequent bishop Jón Árason (1722–1743) was rather more austere in his tastes, his complaints about students wearing wigs indicate this was a fashion among many of the young, elite men in Iceland (Sigurjónsdóttir 1985:52). Even if formal ecclesiastical dress remained somewhat conservative, secular attire clearly followed mainland trends over the eighteenth century for elite males; although dark gray and black remained the dominant colors, red and blue became more common, particularly in women's clothing.

The dress of commoners and poorer farmers, however, was rather different and, on the whole, much more conservative. They continued wearing buttoned, short, waist-length jackets (*treyja* or *peysa*). Breeches and stockings continued to be worn by all. By the end of the eighteenth century, better evidence emerges for the three-piece suit, reserved for special occasions by lower- to middle-status men (*spariföt*) and later forming the basis for the male national costume (Hayeur Smith et al. 2018). It consisted of a short, collarless jacket (*mussa* or *treyja*) with a double row of buttons, a similarly cut double-buttoned waistcoat (*vest*), neckcloth (*kluta*), and buttoned breeches and stockings (Sigurjónsdóttir 1985:59).

In terms of material, Sigurjónsdóttir (1985) argued that wool was the dominant fabric for jackets, breeches, and stockings, though wealthier males would certainly have used silk or velvet. Archaeologically, the use of knits does not seem to be widespread for clothing before the nineteenth century, and homespun outnumbers all other textile types. For shirts, wool, linen, and later cotton, and for neckcloths, linen, silk or lace would have been the main materials.

Examples of Contemporary Dress in Iceland and Scotland and the Use of Homespun in the North Atlantic

Occasionally textile collections can be more than bits of cloth and can bring complete garments to life or provide enough information to reveal dress practices in the past. After a trip to the National Museum of Copenhagen in March 2017, where I was working with Greenlandic material, the curators brought to my attention a poorly known and complete knitted garment from eighteenth-century Iceland that was donated to the museum by a trader in 1823 (Museum catalogue number V181; Jette Arneborg, personal communication 2017). It was alleged to be from the Mývatn area and may have belonged to a wealthy farmer. It was originally augmented by leather shoes and a helmet of some sort, which have since been lost. Today what remains of the outfit are a pair of knitted stockings, knitted breeches, a knitted jacket, and a waistcoat made of *vaðmál*. This outfit is clearly a *spariföt*, as described by Sigurjónsdóttir (1985). The appearance of the jacket is very much like those examples in the artwork of Iceland and among comparable jackets in Scottish collections.

Both the jacket and the vest are double-breasted, with rows of matching pewter buttons. Neither garment has a collar. The sleeveless vest, presumably worn on the inside, is straight in cut and relatively short and gently follows the curvature of the body, whereas the outer jacket is flared like those from Scotland. These garments are reminiscent of today's three-piece suits. The breeches are knee length, with three buttons to fasten them tightly around the calf. They also feature a front flap held in place by two rows of the same buttons. The knit stitch of the outer garments is stockinet and very finely done, but there is some patching on the inside of the outer knitted jacket made of woven cloth, possibly homespun tabby weave. The finish on the inside of the outer jacket and breeches has not been knitted but is of an industrial-looking blue and white denim-type material, possibly linen. The overall garment resembles those described above, again suggesting that tailoring in Iceland during the centuries under discussion followed European designs and styles.

Similar garments are depicted on a colored-ink drawing said to be from the eighteenth century (but may be earlier based on the hats worn, which are

Figure 7.7. Colored-ink drawing from the eighteenth century depicting outfits similar to the one found in Copenhagen. (National Museum of Iceland, permanent exhibit.)

not dissimilar to the hats from Skógar [page 176]), on display at the National Museum of Iceland. Farmers haying their fields wear the same outfit shown in Figure 7.7, supporting the idea that the styles of ordinary people in Iceland were much like those of Europe, but made of local woolen products, either *vaðmál* or knitted Icelandic wool.

Garments such as V181 from the Mývatn area have also been found in peat bogs in northern Scotland, and date from the seventeenth and eighteenth centuries. From Caithness county, at Quintfall Hill, Barrock Estate, one of the more spectacular finds of male dress, dated to the late seventeenth century (based on coins found with the body), was unearthed in 1920 (Wilcox 2016). The remains of a man's body and all of his clothing came to light during peat cutting. The man in question was dressed in much the way described above, with a jacket that flared at the waist and knee-length breeches. He had two woolen jackets worn one on top of the other, along with two pairs of woolen breeches also worn one over the other. He had short woolen stockings, the remains of a pair of leather shoes, and a woolen bonnet. Wilcox (2016) suggested there may have been additional garments of linen that did not survive the conditions of the bog.

The Barrock find was not the only instance of well-preserved garments dated to the early 1700s from a bog in Scotland. Additional finds include those from Arnish Moor and Gunnister. Without going into a full description of the garments from these bog finds, all the bodies recovered appear to have worn jackets and garments similar to those described here, although the Gunnister find also involved a long coat worn to the knees with cuffed sleeves. Wilcox (2016) argued that the coat was tailored along the lines of fashionable elite coats but was, like all other bog finds, made of the same coarse textiles.

As in Iceland, the dress styles and tailoring in Scotland and probably most of the North Atlantic from these centuries appear to be universally European, but the uniqueness of Icelandic dress, as demonstrated by the archaeological data, was defined by the material selected in producing the garments. According to Hayeur Smith and others (2018), and as noted in Chapter 6, not only did homespun in Iceland and specifically at Skálholt serve to emphasize a certain ambivalence, even a resistance, toward the modernizing attempts of the Danes, but it was also the cloth of choice in Skálholt's elite community. This incipient nationalism may have been fueled in part by women resisting the changes being imposed by the Danish colonial authorities, so while little evidence survives of their displeasure at their new roles as spinners, they did continue to weave on the old looms, despite the attempts of administrators to persuade Icelanders to adopt typical European imported textiles and dress and despite attempts to abolish the old looms (Hayeur Smith et al. 2018). Whether or not the clerics of

Skálholt were also behind this nationalistic trend, I believe that encouraging the use of homespun versus imported cloth could be perceived as a form of resistance to the Danish colonial authorities.

The old looms gradually went out of commission during the nineteenth century, and the Danish efforts of introducing new tools eventually succeeded in taking over and abolishing the old ones, until no one remembered how to warp or weave on a warp-weighted loom. The Icelandic outfit V181 from the National Museum of Denmark belongs to the end of the eighteenth or early nineteenth century, that is, to the period when the old looms were on the decline and the workshops had disappeared. I believe Icelanders turned toward extremely finely knitted garments to compensate for the decline in traditional homespun and the loss of local mill production. They could and probably did rely on cloth imports in urban settings, but for a society that had been involved in self-sufficient wool production for 1,000 years, I see the finely knitted garments introduced into Iceland in 1500s as a way of keeping some of these traditions alive.

Conclusion

This book about the roles of women and textiles in the economies and political systems of the North Atlantic Norse colonies has spanned a millennium from the ninth to the eighteenth centuries. Over this period the North Atlantic region's climate shifted from the temperate conditions of the Medieval Warm Period (ca. AD 800–1200), when Scandinavian colonies extended from Shetland and Orkney to Greenland and the coasts of North America, to the big chill of the Little Ice Age (ca. AD 1300–1800), which devastated the communities of the North Atlantic and sped the demise of Greenland's Norse colony. A considerable amount of recent archaeological research in this vast region has focused on subsistence strategies and adaptation to climatic deterioration by analyzing human choices and decision-making relating to farming, animal husbandry, and hunting or has been set within the context of power relationships and the struggles of the elite trying to impose their authority and privileges within and over these remote colonies.

Instead, I have examined the other side of this coin: material culture and the products resulting from these subsistence strategies. I have looked specifically at the wool that the people of the North Atlantic used to clothe themselves and trade for other essential goods. Investigating wool and the cloth produced from it has also brought the women of the North Atlantic to the forefront, reversing and correcting tendencies seen in many studies to ignore their roles in these North Atlantic societies. History in the North Atlantic was written down by men and was concerned largely with men's lives and struggles, so that archaeologists working in the North Atlantic are blessed to have an extensive body of medieval literary sources to supplement their data and to help guide their research. But the perspectives presented in these sources are largely male, and archaeology, too, has become more often than not about what men did—women are frequently forgotten.

This book has attempted to bridge that gap. I felt that by looking at a product that was made by women I could access women's lives, particularly in a society where textile work was so gendered and fraught with superstition and taboos. I have followed the data where they have taken me and have tried to draw out the roles that women played in phenomena as diverse as the symbolic meanings of cloth for the Norse of the North Atlantic; mythological associations between women, men, cloth, and fate; Viking Age Iceland's mixed cultural community that was literally woven together via the cultural phenomenon that was *vaðmál*; the economy of these islands; subsistence strategies in Greenland; the interactions of climate change, trade, and resistance to Danish colonialism; and ultimately homegrown nationalism.

In the secondary literature of historians and archaeologists, the term *vaðmál* has often been used loosely to describe any cloth made in Iceland or as a term for all archaeological textiles, or to denote an economically important but somehow "invisible" product described in the medieval documentary records and law books. Generally speaking, *vaðmál* was something abstract that had been studied by male scholars, working with documents written by men, who focused exclusively on the economic and legal implications of *vaðmál* as currency, while forgetting that behind the cloth were the women who made it. This study has enabled me to work directly with the actual products of women's work in an effort to gain insights into women's motivations, decisions, and roles in the North Atlantic and to pinpoint the true definition of *vaðmál* by ascertaining its physical characteristics (a 2/2 twill, Z/S-spun woven with 4–15 warp threads per centimeter) through painstaking analyses of textiles in the storage facilities of Iceland's National Museum. The huge collection that existed there—a rarity unto itself given how infrequently organic materials are preserved in the archaeological record—awaited nothing more than careful analysis of most of this vast corpus to bring women to the forefront in the Norse settlement of Iceland and in that nation's development. Because *vaðmál* was a currency produced by women, it was not just a product traded by men but was the result of a symbiotic relationship between the sexes, in which both women and men were heavily invested in the making and distribution of this resource, which provided a mechanism through which Icelanders could survive. In its role as a form of commodity currency, ultimately based on Norwegian models, *vaðmál* became part of a larger economic system built upon commodity exchange that linked Icelandic households to ports, markets, and consumers in Norway, the British Isles and Europe from the end of the Viking Age in the eleventh century until the rise of early modern globalized networks for textile trade in the seventeenth century and the emergence of industrialized production of cloth in the eighteenth century.

Greenland's cloth story was different from that of Iceland. The colony was smaller, conditions were harsher, and the Greenlanders had to contend with an earlier and more severe onset of the Little Ice Age, which greatly impacted their farming and subsistence strategies. Greenlandic cloth was initially much the same as its Icelandic counterpart, reflecting their shared Scandinavian roots and the origins of most of Greenland's settlers in Iceland's nascent society. Both islands' cloth was made on the warp-weighted loom, but in Greenland it was never used as currency or standardized to the same degree as Icelandic cloth. The Greenlanders' cloth traditions became more focused on extending the life of textiles through various mechanisms: cloth recycling, patching, and hanging on to older pieces of cloth because of their emotional value as heirlooms or because there was no choice. Clothing was extensively patched, maybe because materials were scarce, and integrating goat hair in woven cloth became a common practice because goats had gained importance in the Greenland colony as animals better suited to the terrain. For the Greenlanders, making and using cloth was about keeping warm and avoiding waste, not about stockpiling *vaðmál* to pay taxes and tithes. The focus on warmth eventually led women to opt for the creation of weft-dominant cloth, taking Norse textile traditions to a whole other level and direction. This was particularly noticeable in the late thirteenth and early fourteenth centuries as cold weather became more frequent and more severe with the initial onset of the Little Ice Age. Through the incorporation of more weft yarns in the traditional twills and tabbies of the Norse textile tradition, Greenland's women created a denser product that helped their wearers stay warm. The invention of Greenland's weft-dominant cloth was the result of women taking direct action to devise survival strategies in the face of depleting resources and climate fluctuations. At some level, weft-dominant cloth represents a vital female statement in a world where female expression was suppressed.

Iceland suffered during the Little Ice Age as well, but its impact seems to have been felt later, with the coldest phases mostly during the late fifteenth through nineteenth centuries. At the start of this period, Icelandic women slowly integrated plied yarns into homespun cloth to make their textiles heavier and warmer. Thus, Greenland's women and Iceland's weavers responded to similar climatic stresses through different approaches, though they drew on shared traditions of weaving and clothing manufacture. How frequently do archaeologists have the privilege to observe such human responses and decisions firsthand in the archaeological record?

Contrary to the popular image, the Greenlanders did not incorporate a lot of fur from Arctic species in their cloth, even though they hunted and were surrounded by wild animals. Furs were wealth, and recent archaeological evidence suggests that furs and walrus ivory were more likely to be kept in reserve for trade with Norwegian merchants or to be sent to the king of Norway for the payment of taxes. Sporadically, archaeological examples of Greenlandic Norse cloth incorporate elements of caribou fur or Arctic hare but there are only a handful of examples of this. Differences in the degrees to which fibers and furs preserve in the archaeological record clearly play a role in how well we perceive their use of fur, but the middens of Greenland preserve large quantities of leather, as well as tufts of animal hair and woolen cloth. While there is still little that can be said about the use of furs in Greenland, there is currently little evidence to support the idea that the Greenlanders turned away from using the wool and hair of their domestic animals to produce their clothing or that they wove fibers from the wild animals of the Arctic abundantly into their clothing as conditions worsened.

The Greenland colony disappeared around 1450, and while approximately 1,000 or more fragments of cloth have provided insights into the lives of its women and their choices in the face of environmental decline, these fragments reveal nothing about the end of the colony except at Herjolfsnes, a late Norse burial site of the thirteenth to fifteenth centuries, where the deceased were wrapped in the garments of their predecessors, an instance where clothing was transformed into shrouds or cloth-coffins because little wood was available. Historical sources suggest that fewer and fewer boats came to Greenland from Europe or Iceland as the Little Ice Age deepened—the last written record of life in Greenland comes from the report of an Icelandic ship's captain who came to Greenland to trade and witnessed a wedding there in September 1408. Through the fourteenth century and into the fifteenth, plague and dynastic turmoil embroiled and weakened the Kingdom of Norway and transferred Iceland and Greenland to a new colonial power, Denmark. As the last generations of dead were being buried at Herjolfsnes, mainland Scandinavia's elites were forgetting about Greenland, and in this process the Greenlanders began leaving without anyone recording whether some migrated back to Iceland or whether they stayed on their farms until there was no one left to tend them. By the middle of the fifteenth century, the Greenlandic Norse were gone. Fortunately, the textiles from Herjolfsnes were preserved, and the Greenland Norse, amid their demise, left us the most extensive collection of medieval garments known today.

The Faroes featured only briefly in this book, in large part because the collections are so small, yet the most noticeable thing about those collections is a singular absence of actual cloth despite the presence of unspun wool. Most Faroese cloth is said to have been sent to Norway, and new research is exploring this hypothesis, but the Faroese people must have worn some of the cloth they wove. Still, little of it has been preserved.

The Faroe Islands and Iceland both provide information about the chaotic nature of trade in the mid- to late medieval period, which was marked by political unrest in Europe, changing colonial powers sending merchants and administrators into the North Atlantic, warfare between European nations based on commercial, political and religious disputes, and widespread conflict over the products of the North Atlantic islands, notably stockfish, which was in high demand across Northern Europe. Fish was clearly the most important commodity, and in this period the role of cloth as an export product has often been ignored in light of an academic consensus that cloth was no longer used as a form of currency in Iceland after the thirteenth century, when fish exportation took over. Yet the archaeological record documents that cloth never lost its importance during these periods, especially in Iceland, where its use as currency actually continued until the late seventeenth century. *Vaðmál* continued to be produced in Iceland as a highly standardized export product until the early modern period and, along with other types of cloth, had an ongoing role in Iceland's commerce, since quantities of woven cloth, raw wool, and eventually knitted goods were shipped in bulk to European ports. Icelandic or north Atlantic *vaðmál* is consistently mentioned in medieval and late medieval documentary sources in Europe as a desired import product.

Significant players in the later medieval movement of goods throughout the North Atlantic were the Hanseatic merchants and the English, who fought each other for control of trade networks, ports, products, and profits. These often-bloody clashes and the dynamic relations with various trading partners they created offered a profitable environment for the Icelanders (Karlsson 2000) and also laid the groundwork for the slow integration of the North Atlantic islands into the industrialized world. It was clear from research into the textiles produced, used, and traded at different Icelandic sites from this period that certain farms enjoyed privileged positions in trade and played critical roles in the redistribution of trade goods, notably cloth, across Iceland.

In 1603 the Danes, then the colonial overlords of the North Atlantic islands, took a sudden interest in the resources of this area (possibly realizing they were missing out on vast profits to be had from stockfish and wool or reasoning that they could benefit by reducing the conflicts roiling their colonies) and imposed a royal monopoly over trading that lasted almost 200 years. In contrast to the preceding chaotic centuries, the glory days of commerce came to a grinding halt with the Danes controlling every item imported or exported to and from the islands. As explored in Chapter 7, during this time of direct colonial rule, the production of wool was transformed dramatically from a cottage industry into an industrial operation. While the Danish efforts were short-lived—just about 50 years—the changes they wrought exerted lasting impacts on gender relationships in Iceland. Women were removed from the process of weaving textiles and were forced into spinning thread and knitting, though evidently not without resistance. While they continued to create and sew garments for their families and households using imported textiles or cloth woven in Reykjavik's new weaving factories, they also continued to use and weave the old traditional cloth, incorporating it into garments that used modern tailoring to make statements about Icelandic national identity in the face of colonial domination. Iceland's elite also partook of this movement, as demonstrated by the material recovered from Skálholt, Iceland's wealthiest ecclesiastic estate, where homespun cloth dominated the assemblages from all parts of the site.

The continued use of traditional cloth in early modern contexts, alongside increasingly cheap factory-made imported textiles, surely expressed women's resistance to the changes imposed on them, specifically to the loss of power they had derived from textile work, and pride in local identities. From their earliest roots in North Atlantic Norse society textiles constituted a female mode of expression, without which women lost an important part of their cultural identity. In the context of the Danish colonial monopoly and efforts to "modernize" the Icelandic economy through the creation of weaving factories where men wove the cloth from threads women spun, women continued to resist and express themselves and pushed for the ongoing use of traditional cloth as a symbol of nationalism and cultural identity. Eventually, however, efforts to abolish the old loom on which this cloth was woven were successful, and by the late nineteenth century few people knew how to operate it.

Why Cloth?

Throughout this work, women and cloth have been the focus, but why cloth? Textiles and their use once held paramount importance in the North Atlantic and in many ancient societies, where they were tied intricately to all aspects of cultural life. This stands in contrast with perceptions today, since the Industrial Revolution cloth has been produced on mechanized looms hundreds of times faster than it could be made by hand, and concerns with textiles and dress are considered frivolous or peripheral to our daily lives or of interest and important mainly to women as their primary consumers. It was in part the Industrial Revolution that sealed the fates of women as second-class citizens and ensured that Western society would become so vehemently patriarchal.

In today's world, cloth has been transformed into a billion-dollar industry, to the point that its manufacture and waste products are threatening the environmental well-being of our planet. But throughout its history, cloth—whether valued or not, whether linked to power or not—has remained important, triggering some of the world's most profound cultural and historic movements, from the beginnings of globalization in Europe and the North Atlantic to the continental spread of the North American fur trade, in which animals' skins were sought both to replace and to enhance textiles used in dress, for status, and for the adornment of the human body.

Draping, dressing, decorating, covering, or modifying the human body have been universal concerns in all human societies (Turner 1993:15). As recounted earlier in this book, Terence Turner saw the modification of the human body and its surface as reflecting a symbolic boundary between the individual as a biological and a social entity. The surface of the body is therefore perceived as the frontier of society, and by modifying its surface, the social self can emerge as the body offers a platform on which socialization is enacted. The term Turner used for this process was production of the "social skin," whereby all forms of modification, draping, and ornamentation aid in the socialization process. Cloth is an integral part of this system and is probably the one item most befitting the label "social skin," since cloth mimics skin as a second "cultural" envelope, helping to integrate the individual into his or her society.

From its fundamental role as a "second skin," cloth came to symbolize the binding of social relationships associated with the "making" of social beings, parallel to the making of biological beings. Birth, life, death, and fate became intertwined, and the metaphors for weaving and social order became numerous. Homer recounted how human destinies were determined by the gods or fates at birth, just as the Nornir of Norse mythology spun the fates of men before birth, such that lives were predestined. According to Weiner (1989:33), the Tongans of western Polynesia have a saying that "Humankind is like a mat being woven." The poem "Darraðarljóð" quoted in Chapter 1 offers the similar metaphor of a piece of cloth woven of entrails, so that the living bodies and fates of those who were to fall in battle became woven together as cloth, and there is also the cloth drenched in blood holding the life essence of Höskuld in *Laxdaela Saga*.

In the Norse tradition, cloth relates to fate and was central to women's lives from its creation to its distribution and, as it is in many cultures, cloth was undoubtedly linked to those symbolic systems that evoke female power (Schneider and Weiner 1989:21). The propensity of women cross-culturally to become weavers may have arisen from the demands of childcare, facilitating their adoption of this task (Wayland Barber 1994; Gale and Kaur 2002). However, I feel a more likely explanation relates to cloth as an extension of the human body, a body part unto itself, evoking ideas of birth, reproduction, and death. These are commonly ascribed female themes, particularly the giving of life, though in many societies men too have been weavers. In the Norse context, to weave, to spin, and to distribute cloth were all actions associated with female power. According to some scholars, the production of cloth was also a means by which women could express themselves because they otherwise could not and had no opportunity to tell their stories in a patriarchal society that valued poetry and the spoken word of men (Norrman 2008). Men spoke while women wove. Some see the result of weaving cloth or the tapestry as the written word of women and point to etymological connections that exist between "text" and the Latin verb *texô*, "to weave." This point is visually represented in one of the most common and romanticized images to emerge from nineteenth century Iceland's reversal of women's roles—the image of the *kvöldvaka*, where women spin, knit, or fix clothing in the *baðstofa* (the main room of the house) while the master of the house oversees their work and reads aloud the sagas or the Bible by candle light.

This is a book about women in the past, not about the general circumstances of Viking women. It does concern the specifics of women's actions, because in each of these North Atlantic islands women assumed different social roles connected to textiles at different times. Norrman (2008) was correct in stating that women in Norse society expressed themselves through weaving, and this mode of expression did give them power from the Viking Age until work on the warp-weighted loom ceased. The ability to keep themselves and others warm and alive represents significant power over nature, so the struggle was both physical and spiritual: to create a social canvas in the form of clothing as part of the socialization process that ensures the cohesion of the group is a vital skill in itself.

The power these women held is of relevance to women today. In our modern world, women have departed from their traditional roles as makers of cloth and clothing. As women grapple to gain power and respect through the #MeToo movement, some are returning to the fiber arts of their grandmothers, finding solace and strength in the quiet, repetitive work of sewing, knitting, weaving or spinning, and sharing their resistance with other women in knitting or embroidery groups, like the spinning bees of the Industrial Revolution. Popular culture continually addresses the issue of the loss of fiber arts in women's lives. At the end of December 2018, as this book was starting to take shape, E. Tammy Kim wrote an op-ed piece in the *New York Times* (29 December 2018) titled "The Feminist Power of Embroidery" that seems fitting as this book comes to its end: "When I picked up needle and thread, I joined a long line of women who have turned the domestic arts into political expression." In a world where women feel the pressure of male aggression and attempt to fight for respect and equal rights, turning back the clock to the era of our grandmothers and great-grandmothers revives a uniquely female mode of expression, bringing us back to a time when women held power and were respected for their abilities to create a vital resource and master these lifesaving skills.

Glossary

balanced weave: A textile with equal numbers of warp and weft yarns.

bóndi (pl. bændur): Free-farmer or freeman, equivalent to the English "yeoman farmer." In Iceland the *bóndi* was allowed to carry weapons and attend the Althing (Alþing), or general assembly or parliament held annually in the summer at Þingevellir in southern Iceland. *Bændur* had to own a specified amount of wealth, cattle, or fishing gear to ensure the sustainability of their households.

Commonwealth period: The period of Icelandic history from AD 930–1262, when Iceland was independent of external political governance and operated under its own set of laws. The starting date for the Commonwealth period is the traditional date for the establishment of the Alþing, Iceland's unique parliamentary system; the end of the period is set by the date at which Iceland became tributary to the Norwegian king.

diamond twill: The most complex of the twill fabrics; the finished appearance is a series of small diamond motifs (see **twill**).

Dorset: A prehistoric indigenous archaeological culture in the North American Arctic. The Dorset culture is the endpoint of a sequence of cultures sometimes grouped together under the term "Paleo-Eskimo." Sites of the Dorset culture are found from the islands of the Canadian Arctic down the coast of Labrador to Newfoundland and around the coasts of Greenland. The Dorset culture developed from earlier Paleo-Eskimo cultures around 800 BCE, flourished for more than 2,000 years, and disappeared between 1200–1300 CE, as the ancestors of contemporary Inuit communities migrated across Arctic Canada. Stories among historic Inuit about the Tuniit, semi-mythical people their ancestors encountered as they settled into Canada and Greenland, probably refer to the last of the Dorset. Their names for themselves are unknown.

dyngja: Weaving hut, a structure reserved for women exclusively used for textile production that fell out of use in Iceland shortly after the introduction of Christianity in AD 1000.

early modern period: The period from the end of the Middle Ages, which occurs roughly after the Reformation (c. 1540) in the North Atlantic colonies until the end of the Danish trade monopoly.

ell (Icelandic öln/ölnir): A unit of measure for cloth used in England and in Iceland. The ell changed dimensions several times throughout the Middle Ages, from 46.0 cm to 56.0 cm and eventually back down to 49.2 cm.

ergi: A concept that does not exactly equate with homosexuality but refers to "unmanliness" and femininity. Certain activities culturally associated with women, such as textile work, are full of *ergi* for men. Some queer theorists gloss *ergi* as "queer," as pushing against the boundaries of established gender categories.

gjaldavöð: *vaðmál* suitable for legal payments.

klæðavoð: *vaðmál* suitable for clothing.

landnám period: *Landnám* means "the taking of land," and the *landnám* period is therefore used as a term for the periods of Iceland's, Greenland's, and the Faroe Islands' initial colonization and settlement. In Iceland the *landnám* period begins around 870 CE; in Greenland it conventionally begins in 985 AD, while the dating of the Faroe Islands' initial settlement remains unclear but may have been as early as 750 AD. The settlement or *landnám* period in Iceland lasted until the establishment of the Althing in AD 930.

nið, niðingr: A type of formal insult or curse that put into question a man's sexual orientation and masculinity through implications of behavior in actions linked with *ergi*. According to Price (2002:211), *nið* could be communicated in more than one way, either verbally or with a *tréníð*, a wooden *nið*, which could involve runes carved onto a wooden sculpture depicting men engaged in sexual acts or as a pole topped with a decapitated horse's head facing in the direction of the person being cursed or insulted.

Norse: A general term that refers variously (1) to the Scandinavian peoples during the Late Iron Age and Viking Age before the establishment of the modern kingdoms of Norway, Denmark, and Sweden; (2) to Old Norse, the language spoken by these communities before they divided into the ancestral forms of the modern Icelandic, Faroese, Norwegian, Danish, and Swedish languages; (3) to the settlements established by these people across the North Atlantic region; and (4) to the medieval Scandinavian occupations of the North Atlantic after the Viking Age.

Norse Greenland: Post-Viking Greenland settled by Scandinavian settlers. "Norse of the North Atlantic" is a more general term for inhabitants of this period from the end of the tenth century to the fifteenth century when the colony in Greenland disappeared.

North Atlantic: Here defined as the chain of islands settled by people from Scandinavia (Sweden, Denmark, and Norway) in the late Iron Age (or Viking Age) and the oceans connecting them. This region includes Iceland, Greenland, the Faroe Islands, parts of the United Kingdom such as Scotland, including Shetland, the Hebrides, Orkney, Caithness and the Isle of Man, parts of Ireland, and briefly Newfoundland and the coasts of Labrador and Arctic Canada. Scandinavian settlement of the North Atlantic region began in the last decades of the eighth century AD and continued into the tenth or early eleventh century. The discovery and exploration of Vínland (thought to be parts of the region surrounding the Gulf of St. Lawrence, including Newfoundland) around the year 1000 AD marked the date that the Viking Age migrations reached their farthest extent, at the westernmost end of the known world (Koch Madsen 2014). The first regions to be settled were Scotland and Shetland, followed by the Faroe Islands, Iceland, and Greenland. No permanent settlements are known from the areas of North America that were explored by the Norse during the Viking Age.

North Atlantic colonies: Settlement areas in the North Sea occupied by Scandinavian settlers coming from mainland Scandinavia and Scandinavian settlement areas in the British Isles. The North Atlantic Norse colonies of Iceland, the Faroe Islands, and most of Greenland had no known indigenous populations when the Norse colonized them.

Scandinavians: The inhabitants of Sweden, Norway, and Denmark. For the eighth to sixteenth centuries I am referring to similar geographical borders and people as today, not including Finland or the North Atlantic regions.

seiðr: A type of divination, witchcraft, and magic practiced by women during the Viking Age and apparently also connected with textile work and tools.

smávoð: A finer quality of cloth, with higher thread counts and finer yarn that could be used in the Middle Ages for paying tithes to the church.

Thule: The name given by archaeologists to the ancestral culture of the Inuit communities that migrated into the Eastern Arctic (Canada and Greenland) from Alaska and easternmost Siberia starting around AD 1200.

tóg and þell: Icelandic terms used to identify the different fibers in the fleece of the Icelandic sheep breed—the Northern Short-Tail. *Tóg* refers to the coarse outer, or guard, hairs, while *þell* is the term used for the soft, fluffy, inner coat.

twill: A type of cloth used extensively in Northern Europe and the second most basic weave that can be made using a simple or warp-weighted loom. To produce twill, each warp yarn crosses two or more weft yarns with a step or offset between rows, creating a diagonal pattern. If two weft yarns cross two warp yarns this is referred to as a 2/2 twill; if two weft yarns cross one warp yarn, it is designated 2/1. In the twill family, one can produce 2/1 twills, 2/2 twills, diamond twills, and herringbone twills.

vaðmál: Literally, *vað* means "cloth," and *mál* means "made to measure." *Vaðmál* was a type of cloth that was used as currency from the eleventh-seventeenth centuries in Iceland and was both legally regulated and highly standardized. *Vaðmál* was a 2/2 twill with a thread count range of 4–14 warp threads per centimeter.

vararfeld (pl. vararfeldir): Literally, "cloaks made as wares for sale"—a shaggy pile-woven cloth made in Iceland and traded extensively with Norway during the Viking Age.

Viking Age: A period from the eighth century to the eleventh century when people currently inhabiting the countries of Norway, Sweden, and Denmark expanded beyond their homelands and engaged in various activities ranging from piracy to trade to colonization. The period is traditionally established in AD 793, when the first documented raid took place on the Northumbrian island of Lindesfarne (Graham-Campbell and Batey 1998), though there is evidence of earlier raids. The end of the Viking Age is sometimes set locally, based on the date at which Christianity was adopted as the main religion within the Scandinavian countries and their colonies across the North Atlantic, but at other times the end of the Viking Age is set approximately at 1050 or 1066, marking the end of Viking involvement in England (Graham-Campbell and Batey 1998).

vöruvoð: Marketable cloth, a term for common *vaðmál* made to legal standards and suitable for use in commercial trade or in payment of debts.

warp-dominant cloth: Cloth woven with more warp yarns than wefts.

warp-weighted loom: A type of vertical loom that stands upright or could be propped against a wall, consisting of three beams and several heddle rods. Warp threads are hung from the top beam of the loom and are held taut by weights of stone, clay, or bags of sand tied to the ends of the warp threads.

weft-dominant cloth: Cloth woven with more weft yarns than warps.

Notes

Chapter 1. "Cold Are the Counsels of Women": Bloodied Warps and Gilded Wefts; The Engendered Economy of Cloth in the North Atlantic

1. Bek-Pedersen (2007, 2011) has argued, to the contrary, that the association of the Nornir with textile production is simply absent in the historic texts, and while they may not have been spinning under the World Tree, the Nornir and related beings are associated with textile work, as illustrated in the "Darraðarljóð".

2. Iceland converted to Christianity in AD 1000, roughly the same time as the Faroe Islands, while Greenland was settled by Christians; thus no pre-Christian burials have been found in Greenland.

Chapter 2. Weaving in the Viking Age: Iceland and the North Atlantic Expansion

1. The exact number of textiles is not established as I have not analyzed all collections (approximately 90%) to date. Further, new textiles emerge with each new excavation.

2. Mineralization has been described by Chen and others (1998) as the replacement of the physical shapes of fibers with minerals. When partially replaced, they are referred to as "mineralized," and when completely replaced and the fiber structures have disappeared, they are termed "pseudomorphs."

3. Spinning clockwise results in Z-spun yarn, and counterclockwise, S-spun. Spinning is technologically neutral: either direction will produce usable yarn.

4. Thread count is one of many methods used in textile analysis, and to quote Andersson Strand and others (2010:150), "a textile is not simply a binary system of spun, twisted, or spliced fibers, but first and foremost a result of complex interactions between resources, technology and society." Thus following preliminary basic visual analysis, a combination of analytical techniques is used to supplement information on the use, wear, and function of textiles. These can include SEM analysis, fiber and dye analysis, and molecular analyses such as aDNA and strontium.

5. In the early twentieth century, Jan Pedersen devised an extensive typology for

Viking artifacts that is still used today to identify particular styles of object categories. Oval brooches were worn by Norse women from the eighth to tenth centuries, always in identical pairs that were usually cast from the same mold. They were highly stylized and appear throughout the Viking world. They were probably the result of early "mass production" in trade centers such as Ribe, Birka, Hedeby, and Kaupang, where numerous molds were found. Worn usually at breast level, they secured the pinafore or apron. These brooches were most likely not simply functional and may have indicated the married status of women, as they do not occur in the graves of very young women. The iconography on these brooches pertains to the goddess Freyja and may have symbolized notions of reproduction and fertility (Hayeur Smith 2001, 2004, 2015, 2019). With nine metal bosses, they resembled the nipples of a lactating mammal.

6. Osteological and isotopic analyses of the skeletal remains were undertaken by Joe W. Walser III with a team from Durham University led by J. Montgomery and T. Jacob. This research is ongoing: Karin Frei from the National Museum of Denmark performed an isotopic analysis of the textiles; I carried out the analysis of the textiles, jewelry and dress; Kevin P. Smith of the Haffenreffer Museum of Anthropology at Brown University performed AMS dating and calibration; and Sandra Sif Einarsdóttir reanalyzed the records of the site's excavation.

7. Tablet weaving is a technique where tablets or square cards are used to create a shed.

Chapter 4. Textiles in Greenland during the Medieval Period

1. Exact numbers are difficult to assess, given that the purpose of this study was not to perform a full reanalysis of Greenlandic textiles but rather to shed new light on previously published research material. As a starting point, I used the catalog compiled by Østergård (2004), which is lacking in some items because Østergård often chose not to analyze examples comprising multiple fragments, simply referring to fragments as "and several more." Additionally, new textile material has come to light since the publication of this book, notably from sites Ø172 and Ø171, as well as others. Østergård's book is nonetheless the most comprehensive and thorough analysis of the Greenlandic corpus, covering all aspects of Norse textile technology.

2. Two additional Icelandic hats were discovered in the context of research about this Greenlandic hat at the Skógar Folk Museum in southern Iceland. Both of these hats (F1 and F2) were recovered from the same site, Fornusandur, on the southern Icelandic coast, and both were sampled and dated. F2 is the closer match to the Greenlandic tall hat, while the latter, with a more peaked appearance, has equivalents in Icelandic medieval and post-medieval illustrations. However, both are dated later than the Herjolfsnes hat and also postdate Memling's and Nørlund's Burgundian models. Two identical AMS dates on these Icelandic hats, calAD 1530–1795 (with the highest prob-

abilities at 1619–1670 [53.1%]), are consistent with historical documentation for this farm's occupation and, together with Falk's (1918) and Arneborg's (1996) interpretation of the sagas' references to tall hats, suggest such items of dress remained "in style" for centuries in the North Atlantic.

3. The dates of Østergård (2004) were based on those of Arneborg (1996). No additional dating was performed in 2004.

Chapter 5. Cloth, Currency, Climate Change, and Subsistence in Greenland

1. Note that the phasing at Ø172 is still under analysis, and Phase 2 may prove to be part of an earlier Phase 3 and Phase 3 to extend later into the fourteenth century. I am grateful to Konrad Smiarowski and Thomas McGovern for sharing these unpublished data.

Chapter 6. Textiles and Trade in the North Atlantic during the Late Middle Ages and Early Modern Period

1. Ceramic identifications from Gilsbakki were reported by Colic (2010).

References Cited

Aðalsteinsson, S.

1991   Importance of Sheep in Early Icelandic Agriculture. *Acta Archaeologica* 61:285–291.

Adderley, W. P., I. A. Simpson, and O. Vésteinsson

2008   Local-Scale Adaptations: A Model Assessment of Soil, Landscape, Microclimatic and Management Factors in Norse Home-Field Productivities. *Geoarchaeology: An International Journal* 23(4):500–527.

Adovasio, J.

1986   Artifacts and Ethnicity: Basketry as Indicator of Territoriality and Population Movements in the Prehistoric Great Basin. In *Anthropology of the Desert West: Essays in Honor of Jesse D. Jennings*, edited by C. J. Condie and D. D. Fowler, pp. 43–88. University of Utah Press, Salt Lake City.

Almqvist, B.

2000   I margfinalen till Sejd. In *Sejd och andra studier I nordisk själsuppfattning*, edited by G. Gidlund, pp. 237–71. Hedemora: Kungl. G.A. Akademien/Gidlungs Förlag, Uppsala.

Anderson, S. M., and K. Swenson

2002   *Cold Counsel: Women in Old Norse Literature and Mythology: A Collection of Essays*. Routledge, New York.

Andersson Strand, E.

2003   *Excavations in the Black Earth, 1990–1995: Tools for Textile Production from Birka and Hedeby*. Riksantikvarieämbetet, Stockholm.

2007   Textile Tools and Production during the Viking Age. In *Ancient Textiles: Production, Crafts, and Society, Proceedings of the First International Conference on Ancient Textiles held at Lund, Sweden, and Copenhagen, Denmark, March 19–23, 2003*, edited by Carole Gillis, pp. 17–25. Oxbow, Oxford.

2011   Tools and Textile-Production and Organization in Birka and Hedeby. In *Viking Settlements and Viking Society: Papers from the Proceedings of the Sixteenth Viking Congress, Reykjavik and Reykholt, 16–23 August 2009*, edited by A. Holt, G. Sigurðsson, G. Ólafsson, and O. Vésteinsson, pp. 1–17. Hið Íslenzka Fornleifafélag, University of Iceland Press, Reykjavik.

2014   Foreign Sanctions: Sumptuary Laws, Consumption and National Identity, in Early Modern Sweden. In *Fashionable Encounters: Perspectives and Trends in Textile and Dress in the Early Modern Nordic World*, edited by T. E. Mathiassen, M. L. Nosch, M. Ringgaard, K. Toftegaard, and M. Venborg Pedersen, pp. 17–27. Oxbow Books, Oxford.

Andersson, T. M., and W. I. Miller (editors)

1989   *Law and Literature in Medieval Iceland: Ljósvetninga Saga and Valla-Ljóts Saga*. Stanford University Press, Stanford, California.

Andreasen, C.

1980   Nordbosager fra Vesterbygden på Grønland. *Hikuin* 6:135–146.

Appelt, M.

1997   Construction of an Archaeological "Culture": Similarities and Differences in Early Paleo-Eskimo Cultures of Greenland. In *Fifty Years of Arctic Research: Anthropological Studies from Greenland to Siberia*, edited by R. Gillberg and H. C. Gulløv, p. 18. Ethnographic Series. National Museum of Denmark, Copenhagen.

Arge, S.

2008   The Faroe Islands. In *The Viking World*, edited by S. Brink in collaboration with N. Price, pp. 579–587. Routledge, London.

Arge, S., G. Sveinbjarnardóttir, K. J. Edwards, and P. Buckland

2005   Viking and Medieval Settlement in the Faroes: People, Place and Environment. *Human Ecology* 33(5):597–260.

Arge, S., M. Church, and S. D. Brewington

2009   Pigs in the Faroe Islands: An Ancient Facet of the Islands' Paleoeconomy. *Journal of the North Atlantic* 2(2009):19–32.

Arneborg, J.

1993   Contact between Eskimos and Norsemen in Greenland: A Review of the Evidence. In *Beretning fra tolvte tværfaglige vikingesymposium: Forlaget Hikuin og Afdeling for Middelalder-arkæologi*, edited by E. Roesdahl and P. M. Sørensen, pp. 23–35. Aahrus Universitet, Aahrus.

1996   Burgunderhuer, baskere og døde nordboer i Herjolfsnes, Grønland. Nationalmuseets arbehjdsmark: 75–883.

2003   Norse Greenland: Reflections on Settlement and Depopulation. In *Contact, Continuity and Collapse: The Norse Colonisation of the North Atlantic*, edited by J. Barrett, pp. 163–181. Studies in the Early Middle Ages. Brepols, Turnhout, Belgium.

Arneborg, J., M. B. Hebsgaard, N. Lynnerup, C. Koch Madsen, C. P. Paulsen, and K. Smiarowski

2008   *Resources, Mobility and Cultural Identity in Norse Greenland, Vatnahverfi Project: Report from Field Work, 2008*. National Museum of Denmark, Copenhagen.

Arneborg, J., N. Lynnerup, and J. Heinemeier

2012   Human Diet and Subsistence Patterns in Norse Greenland AD c. 980–AD c. 1450: Archaeological Interpretations. *Journal of the North Atlantic* 301:119–133. DOI:10.3721/037.004.s309.

Arnósdóttir, A. S.

2010   Property and Virginity: The Christianization of Marriage in Medieval Iceland 1200–1600. Aarhus University Press, Aarhus.

Arwill-Nordbladh, E.

1991   The Swedish Image of Viking Age Women: Stereotype, Generalization and Beyond. In Social Approaches to Viking Studies, edited by R. Samson, pp. 53–64. Cruithne Press, Glasgow.

Ashby, S. P.

2010   A Typological Guide for the Spot-Identification of Medieval Bone/Antler Combs from the British Isles and Northern Europe. Unpublished datasheet, ICAZ Worked Bone Research Group.

Badalanova Geller, F.

2006   The Spinning Mary: Towards the Iconology of the Annunciation in the Slavonic Tradition. Cosmos 20(2004):211–260.

Bankhead, G.

2016   A Report on Four Lead Cloth Seals Found in Iceland on Behalf of Professor Gavin Lucas, Professor of Archaeology, Dept. of Archaeology, University of Iceland. University of Durham, Durham, UK.

Barnes, T. M., and K. A. Greive

2017   Topical Pine Tar: History, Properties and Use as a Treatment for Common Skin Conditions. Australasian Journal of Dermatology 58(2):80–85. DOI:10.1111/ajd.12427.

Barrett, J. H.

1997   Fish Trade in Norse Orkney and Caithness: A Zooarchaeological Approach. Antiquity 71:616–638.

Barrett, J. H., C. Johnstone, J. Harland, W. Van Neer, A. Ervynck, D. Kakowiecki, D. Heinrich, A. K. Hufthammer, I. B. Enghoff, C. Amundsen, J. S. Christiansen, A. K. G. Jones, A. Locker, S. Hamilton-Dyer, L. Jonsson, L. Lougas, C. Roberts, and M. Richards

2008   Detecting the Medieval Cod Trade: a New Method and First Results. Journal of Archaeological Science 35(4):850–861.

Bek-Pedersen, K.

2007   Are the Spinning Nornir Just a Yarn? Viking and Medieval Scandinavia 3:1–10.

2009   Weaving Swords and Rolling Heads: A Peculiar Space in Old Norse Tradition. Viking and Medieval Scandinavia 5:23–39.

2013   The Norns in Old Norse mythology. Dunedin, Edinburgh.

Bender Jørgensen, L.

1986   Fornhistoriske textile i Skandinavien. Nordiske Fortidsminder 9, Series B.

1992   North European Textiles until AD 100. Aarhus Universitetsforlag, Aarhus.

2003   Scandinavia, AD 400–1000. In Cambridge History of Western Textile, edited by I. D. Jenkins, pp. 132–138. Cambridge University Press, Cambridge.

2007   The World according to Textiles. In Ancient Textiles: Production, Crafts, and Society, Proceedings of the First International Conference on Ancient Textiles held at Lund, Sweden, and Copenhagen, Denmark, March 19–23, 2003, edited by Carole Gillis, pp. 7–12. Oxbow, Oxford.

2012   The Introduction of Sails to Scandinavia: Raw Materials, Labour and Land. In *N-Tag Ten, Proceedings of the 10th Nordic TAG Conference at Stiklestad, Norway, 2009*, edited by R. Berge, M. E. Jasinski, and K. Sognnes, pp. 173–181. BAR international series 2399. BAR, Oxford.

Berglund, J.

1998   The Excavations at the Farm Beneath the Sand. In *Man, Culture, and Environment in Ancient Greenland: Report on a Research Programme*, edited by J. Arneborg and H. C. Gulløw, pp. 7–13. Danks Polar Centre, Copenhagen.

Berlo, J. C.

1992   Beyond Bricolage: Women and Aesthetic Strategies in Latin American Textiles. *Anthropology and Aesthetics* 22:115–134.

Berman, Constance H.

2007   Women's Work in Family, Village, and Town after 1000 CE: Contributions to Economic Growth? *Journal of Women's History* 19(3):10–32. DOI:10.1353/jowh.2007.0052.

Bernharðsson, H., M. L. Magnússon, and M. Jónsson

2015   *Járnsíða og Kristniréttur Árna Þorlákssonar*. Sögufélag, Reykjavik.

Bigelow, G. F.

1984   Subsistence in Late Norse Shetland: An Investigation into a Northern Island Economy of the Middle Ages. PhD dissertation, Wolfson College, University of Cambridge, Cambridge, UK.

Blake, N. F. (translator)

1962   *The Saga of the Jomsvikings*. Thomas Nelson and Sons, London.

Bolender, J. D., J. M. Steinberg, and E. P. Durrenberger

2008   Unsettled Landscapes: Settlement Patterns and the Development of Social Inequality in Northern Iceland. In *Economies and the Transformation of Landscapes*, edited by L. Cliggett and C. A. Pool, pp. 217–238. AltaMira Press, Lanham, Maryland.

Boyer, R.

1992   *Les vikings: Histoire et civilisation*. Plon, Paris.

Brewington, S., M. Hicks, Á. Edwald, Á. Einarsson, K. Anamthawat-Jónsson, G. Cook, P. Ascough, K. L Sayle, S.V Arge, M. Church, J. Bond, S. Dockrill, A. Friðriksson, G. Hambrecht, A. D. Juliusson, V. Hreinsson, S. Hartman, K. Smiarowski, R. Harrison, and T. H. McGovern

2015   Islands of Change vs. Islands of Disaster: Managing Pigs and Birds in the Anthropocene of the North Atlantic. *The Holocene* 25(10):1676–1684.

Bronk Ramsey, C., M. Scott, and H. Van der Plicht

2013   Calibration for Archaeological and Environmental Terrestrial Samples in the Time Range 26–50 ka cal BP. *Radiocarbon* 55(4):2021–2027.

Brown, K. M.

2007   *The Far-Traveller: Voyages of a Viking Woman*. Harcourt, New York.

Bryggens Museum

1975   *Tekstilfragmenter fra nr. 4873, nr. 12438 fiberprøver*. Bryggens Museum, Bergen.

Buckland P. C., T. Amorosi, L. K. Barlow, A. J. Dugmore, P. A. Mayewski, T. H. Mc-
Govern, A. E. J. Ogilvie, J. P. Sadler, and P. Skidmore

1996   Bioarchaeological and Climatological Evidence for the Fate of Norse Farmers in
Medieval Greenland. *Antiquity* 70(267):88–96.

Burge, K.

2009   Negotiations of Space and Gender in Brennu-Njáls Saga. In *Á Austurvega: Saga
and East Scandinavia (Papers from the Department of Humanities and Social Sciences, No. 14)*, edited by A. N. Henrik Williams and F. Charpentier Ljungqvist,
pp. 144–150. Gävle University Press, Gävle.

Byock, J.

1982   *Feud in the Icelandic Saga.* University of California Press, Berkeley.

1988   *Medieval Iceland: Society, Sagas, and Power.* University of California Press, Berkley.

2001   *Viking Age Iceland.* Penguin Books, London.

Callow, C.

2010   Iceland's Medieval Coastal Market Places: Dögurðarnes in Its Economic, Social
and Political Context. In *Strandsteder, utvikinglingssteder og småbyer i vikingtid,
middelalder og tidlig nytid (ca. 800–ca.1800)*, edited by J. Brendalsmo, T. Gan-
sum, and F. E. Eliassen, pp. 213–229. Interface Media, Oslo.

Carr, C., and R. F. Maslowski

1995   Cordage and Fabrics: Relating Form, Technology, and Social Processes. In *Style,
Society, and Person: Archaeological and Ethnological Perspectives*, edited by C.
Carr and J. R. Neitzel, pp. 298–343. Plenum Press, New York.

Cartwright, B.

2015   Making the Cloth That Binds Us: The Role of Textile Production in Producing Viking Identities. In *Viking Worlds, Things, Spaces and Movement*, edited by
M. H. Eriksen, U. Pedersen, B. Rundberget, I. Axelson, and H. Lundberg, pp.
160–178. Oxbow Books, Oxford.

Christensen, A. M., and M. Nockert

2006   *Osebergfunnet bind IV, Tekstilene.* Vol. 4. Museum of Cultural History, University of Oslo, Oslo.

Church, M. J, A. J. Dugmore, K. A. Mairs, A. R. Millard, G. T. Cook, G. Sveinbjarnardóttir, P. A. Ascough, and K. H. Roucoux

2007   Charcoal Production during the Norse and Early Medieval Periods in Eyjafjal-
lahreppur, Southern Iceland. *Radiocarbon* 49(2):659–672.

Cleasby, R., G. Vigfusson, and W. Craigie

1957   *An Icelandic–English Dictionary.* 2nd ed. Clarendon Press, Oxford.

Clover, C.

1993   Regardless of Sex: Men, Women and Power in Early Northern Europe. *Speculum*
68:363–387.

Colic, E.

2010   Analysis of Pottery from Gilsbakki. Unpublished report.

Conkey, M. W.

2003   Has Feminism Changed Archaeology? *Signs* 28(3):867–880.

Conkey, M.W., and J. M. Gero

1997   Program to Practice : Gender and Feminism in Archaeology. *Annual Review of Anthropology* 26:411–437.

Cooke, B., C. Christiansen, and L. Hammarlund

2002   Viking Woolen Square-Sails and Fabric Cover Factor. *International Journal of Nautical Archaeology* 31(2):202–210. DOI:10.1006/ijna.2002.1039.

Cox, N.

2006   Tudor Sumptuary Laws and Academical Dress: An Act against Wearing of Costly Apparel 1509 and an Act for Reformation of Excess in Apparel 1533. *Transactions of the Burgon Society* 6(1). DOI:10.4148/2475-7799.1047.

Crowfoot, E., F. Pritchard, and K. Staniland

2006   *Textiles and Clothing, c. 1150–c. 1450.* New ed. Boydell Press, Woodbridge.

Damsholt, N.

1984   The Role of the Icelandic Women in the Sagas and in the Production of Homespun Cloth. *Scandinavian Journal of History* 9:75–90.

Dennis, A., P. Foote, and R. Perkins (translators)

1980   *Laws of Early Iceland, Grágás.* Vol. 1. University of Manitoba Press, Winnipeg.

2002   *Laws of Early Iceland, Grágás.* Vol. 2. University of Manitoba Press, Winnipeg.

Dommasnes, L. H.

1982   Late Iron Age in Western Norway: Female Roles and Ranks as Deduced from and Analysis of Burial Customs. *Norwegian Archaeological Review* 14(1–2):70–84.

Douglas, M.

1966   *Purity and Danger: An Analysis of the Concepts of Pollution and Taboo.* Routledge and Kegan Paul, London.

Drooker, P. B.

1992   *Mississippian Village Textiles at Wickliffe.* University of Alabama Press, Tuscaloosa.

Dugmore, A., C. Keller, and T. H. McGovern

2005   Have We Been Here Before? Climate Change and the Contrasting Fates of Human Settlements in the Atlantic Islands. Human Security and Climate Change, conference paper, pp. 1–15. Oslo.

2007   Norse Greenland Settlement: Reflections on Climate Change, Trade, and the Contrasting Fates of Human Settlements in the North Atlantic Islands. *Arctic Anthropology* 44(1):12–36.

Durrenburger, E. P.

1992   *The Dynamics of Medieval Iceland: Political Economy and Literature.* University of Iowa Press, Iowa City.

Edwards, K. J., P. C. Buckland, A. J. Dugmore, T. H. McGovern, I. A. Simpson, and G. Sveinbjarnardóttir

2004   Landscapes Circum-landnám: Viking Settlement in the North Atlantic and Its Human Ecological Consequences: A Major New Research Programme. In *Atlantic Connections and Adaptations: Economies, Environments and Subsistence in Lands Bordering the North Atlantic*, edited by R. Housely and G. M. Cole, pp. 260–271. Oxbow Books, Oxford.

Egan, G.

1987   Provenanced Leaden Cloth Seals. PhD dissertation, Department of Medieval Archaeology, University College, University of London.

Eicher, J. B.

2000   The Anthropology of Dress. *Dress* 27(1):59–70. DOI:10.1179/036121100803656954.

2004   A Ping-Pong Example of Cultural Authentication and Kalabari Cut-Thread Cloth. *Textile Society of America Symposium Proceedings*, 103–109.

2001   The Cultural Significance of Dress and Textiles. *Reviews in Anthropology* 30(4):309–323. DOI:10.1080/00988157.2001.9978289.

Eicher, J. B., and M. E. Roach-Higgins

1992   Definition and Classification of Dress: Implications for Analysis of Gender Roles. In *Dress and Gender: Making and Meaning in Cultural Contexts*, edited by R. Barnes and J. B. Eicher, pp. 1–28. Berg, New York.

Einarsdóttir, S. S.

2015   The Ketilsstaðir Burial from the Archaeological Perspective. In *Bundled Up in Blue: The Re-investigation of a Viking Grave, National Museum of Iceland Exhibit Catalogue*, pp. 17–21. National Museum of Iceland, Reykjavik.

Einarsson, B. F.

2008a   *The Settlement of Iceland: A Critical Approach, Granastaðir and the Ecological Heritage*. Hið íslenska bókmenntafelag, Reykjavik.

2008b   Blót Houses in Viking Age Farmstead Cult. *Acta Archaeologica* 79(1):145–184. DOI:10.1111/j.1600-0390.2008.00112.x.

Eldjárn, K.

1956   *Kuml og Haugfé úr heiðnum sið á Íslandi*. Norði, Reykjavik.

Eldjárn, K., and G. Gestsson

1952   "Rannsóknir á Bergþórshvoli." *Árbók hins Íslenzka forn leifafélags*, 5–75.

Eldjárn, K., and A. Friðriksson

2000   *Kuml og Haugfe úr heiðnum sið á íslandi*. Mál og Menning, Reykjavik.

Ellis Davidson, H. R.

1990   *Gods and Myths of Northern Europe*. Penguin, London.

Erekosima, T. V.

1979   *The Tartans of Buguma Women: Cultural Authentication*. Paper presented at the African Studies Association Annual Meeting, Los Angeles.

Erekosima, T. V., and J. B. Eicher

1981   Kalabari Cut-Thread and Pulled-Thread Cloth. *African Arts* 14(2):48. DOI:10.2307/3335728.

Ewing, Thor

2006   *Viking Clothing*. History Press, Stroud.

Faerden, G.

1990   *De Arkeologiske Utgravninger i Gamlebyen, Oslo. 7: Dagliglivets gjenstander; Del 1*. Universitetsforl, Oslo.

Falk, H.

1919   *Altwestnordische Kleiderkunde: Videnskapsselskapets skrifter II. Hist.-Filos. Klasse 1918(3)*. Kristiania, Oslo.

Fitzhugh, W. W., R. Jordan, J. Adovasio, and D. Laeyendecker

2006   Cordage and Wood from the Avayalik Dorset Site in northern Labrador. In *Dynamics of Northern Societies: Proceedings of the SILA/NABO Conference on Arctic and North Atlantic Archaeology, Copenhagen, May 10–14, 2004*, edited by J. Arneborg and B. Grønnow, pp. 153–177. Publications from the National Museum of Denmark, Studies in Archaeology and History 10. National Museum of Denmark, Copenhagen.

Flowers, S. E.

2010   *Runes and Magic: Magical Formulaic Elements in the Older Runic Tradition*. Runa-Raven Press, Smithville, Texas.

Frei, K. M.

2014a   Provenance of Archaeological Wool Textiles: New Case Studies. *Open Journal of Archaeometry* 2(5239):1–5.

2014b   *Strontium Isotope Analyses of Ancient Wool Thread Samples from Viking Age to Early Modern Retrieved from Iceland*. Unpublished preliminary report. National Museum of Denmark, Copenhagen.

Frei, K. M., A. N. Coutu, K. Smiarowski, R. Harrison, C. K. Madsen, J. Arneborg, R. Frei, G. Guðmundsson, S. M. Sindbæk, J. Woollett, S. Hartman, M. Hicks, and T. H. McGovern

2015   Was It for Walrus? Viking Age Settlement and Medieval Walrus Ivory Trade in Iceland and Greenland. *World Archaeology* 47(3):439–466. DOI:10.1080/004382 43.2015.1025912.

Fridriksdottir, J. K.

2013   *Women in Old Norse Literature: Bodies, Words, and Power*. 1st ed. Palgrave Macmillan, New York.

Friðriksson, A.

2013   La Place du Mort: Les tombes vikings dans le paysage culturel Islandais. PhD dissertation, l'Université Paris-Sorbonne, Paris.

Gabra-Sanders, T.

1998   A Review of Viking-Age Textiles and Fibres from Scotland: An Interim Report. In *Textiles in European archaeology report from the 6th NESAT Symposium, 7–11th May 1996 in Boras* 1(6). Göteborg University, Göteborg.

Galbi, D.A.

1996   Through the Eyes in the Storm: Aspects of the Personal History of Women Workers in the Industrial Revolution. *Social History* 21(2):142–159.

Gale, Colin, and J. Kaur

2002   *The Textile Book*. Berg, Oxford.

Garðarsdóttir, V.

2010   *Alþingisreiturinn, Bindi 1 og 2*. Unpublished excavation report. University of Iceland, Reykjavik.

Gardela L.

2013   "Warrior-Women" in Viking Age Scandinavia? A Preliminary Archaeological Study. In *Analecta Archaeologica Ressoviensia: Funerary Archaeology*, edited by S. Kadrow, 8:pp. 273–314. Institute of Archaeology Rzeszów University, Rzeszów.

Geijr, A.

1938   *Birka III, die Textiflunde aus den Gräbern*. Almqvisat &Wiksell, Stockholm.

Gelsinger, B. E.

1972   The Mediterranean Voyage of a Twelfth Century Icelander. *Mariner's Mirror* 58(2):155–165. DOI:10.1080/00253359.1972.10658648.

1981a   *Icelandic Enterprise: Commerce and Economy in the Middle Ages*. 1st ed. University of South Carolina Press, Columbia.

1981b   Some Unusual Ships in Thirteenth Century Norway. *Mariner's Mirror* 67(3):173–180. DOI:10.1080/00253359.1981.10655816.

Gero, J., and M. W. Conkey

1991   *Engendering Archaeology: Women and Prehistory*. Blackwell, Oxford.

Gestsdóttir, H.

1998   *Kyn- og Lífaldursgreiningar á Beinum úr Íslenskum Kumlum (Sex and Age Determinations on Bones from Icelandic Graves)*. Fornleifastofnun Íslands, Reykjavik.

Gilchrist, R.

1999   *Gender and Archaeology: Contesting the Past*. Routledge, London.

Gjerset, K.

1924   *History of Iceland*. MacMillan, New York.

Goldwater, E.

1998   What Do Men Fear? *Modern Psychoanalysis* 23:211–224.

Gosden, C., and C. Knowles

2001   *Collecting Colonialism, Material Culture and Colonial Change*. Berg, Oxford.

Graham-Campbell, J. (editor)

2011   *Silver Economies: Monetisation and Society in Scandinavia, AD 800–1100: . . . Symposium Held on 5–6 December 2008 at Aarhus University*. Aarhus University Press, Aarhus.

Graham-Campbell, J., and C. E. Batey

1998   *Vikings in Scotland: An Archaeological Survey*. Edinburgh University Press, Edinburgh.

Gras, N. S. B.

1918   *A Documentary Study of the Institutional and Economic History of the Customs from the Thirteenth to the Sixteenth Century*. Harvard University Press, Cambridge.

Grautoff, F.

1871   *Urkundenbuch der Stadt Lübeck*. Vol. 3. Lübeck.

Gräslund, A.-S.

1995   The Christianization of Central Sweden from a Female Perspective. In *Rom und Byzanz im Norden: Mission und Glaubenswechsel im Ostseeraum Während des 8.-14 Jahrhunderts BandI*, edited by M. Müller-Wille, pp. 313–328. Akademie Der Wissenschaften und der Litteratur, Mainz.

1999   Is There Evidence of Powerful Women in Late Iron Age Svealand? In *Völker an Nord-und Ostsee und die Franken,* edited by U. Von Freeden, U. Kock, and A. Wieczorek, pp. 91–98. Dr. Rudolf Habelt GmbH, Bonn.

2001   The Position of Iron Age Scandinavian Women: Evidence from Graves and Rune Stones. In *Gender and the Archaeology of Death,* edited by B. Arnold and N. L. Wicker, pp. 81–102. AltaMira Press, Walnut Creek, California.

2003   The Role of Scandinavian Women in Christianisation: The Neglected Evidence. In *The Cross Goes North: Processes of Conversion in Northern Europe A.D. 300–1300,* edited by M. Carber, pp. 483–496. Woodbridge, Suffolk.

Gräslund, A. S., and D. Quast

2011   Female Elites in Viking Age Scandinavia during Christianization. In *Weibliche Eliten in der Frühgeschitchte (Female Elites in Protohistoric Europe),* pp. 267–278. Verlag des Römanisch Germanischen Zentralmuseums, Mainz.

Grønlie, Siân (editor)

2006   Íslendingabók: *The Book of the Icelanders.* Viking Society for Northern Research, London.

Guðjónsson, Else

1962   Forn röggvarvefnaður. *Árbók hins Íslenzka Fornleifafélags,* 12–71.

1964   Um skinnsaum. *Árbók hins Íslenzka Fornleifafélags,* 66–87.

1970   *The National Costume of Women in Iceland.* Litbrá, Reykjavik.

1973   Íslenzk útsaumsheiti og útsaumsgerdir á miðöldum. *Árbók hins Íslenzka Fornleifafélags,* 131–150.

1980   Note on Medieval Icelandic Shaggy Pile Weaving. Bulletin de liaison du centre international d'études des textiles anciens. CIETA, Lyon.

1989   Jarnvarðr Yllir. *Textile History* 20:2.

1990   Some Aspects of the Icelandic Warp Weighted Loom, Vefstaður. *Textile History* 21(2).

1992   Um rokka, einkum med tilliti til skotrokka. *Árbók hins Íslenzka Fornleifafélags,* 11–52.

1994   Um vefstóla og vefara á Íslandi á 18. og 19. öld. *Árbók hins Íslenzka Fornleifafélags,* 5–50.

1998a   Kljásteinavefstaðir á Íslandi og á Grænlandi. *Árbók hins Íslenzka Fornleifafélags,* 95–120.

1998b   Um vefstóla á Íslandi á 18. öld. Nokkrar athugasemdir. *Árbók hins Íslenzka Fornleifafélags,* 129–140.

Guðmundsson, Ó.

2016   *Sex in the Sagas: Love and Lust in the Old Icelandic Literature.* Skrudda, Reykjavik.

Gullbekk, S. H.

2011   Norway, Commodity Money, Silver and Coins. In *Silver Economies:, Monetisation and Society in Scandinavia AD800–1100,* edited by J. Graham-Campbell, S. M. Sindbaek, and G. Williams, pp. 93–111. Aarhus University Press, Aarhus.

Hagen, K. G.

1994   *Profesjonalisme og urbanisering.* Vol. 16. Universitetets Oldsakssamling Skrifter Ny rekke, Oslo.

Hägg, I.
1974   *Kvinnodräkten i Birka*. Vol. Aun 2. Institutionen för arkeologi Gustavianum, Uppsala Universitet, Uppsala.
1984a   Birkas orientaliska praktplagg. *Fornvännen* 78:204–233.
1984b   *Die Textilfunde aus dem Hafen von Haithabu, mit Beiträgen von G. Grenander Nyberg und H. Schweppe*. Vol. 20. Berichte über die Ausgrabungen in Haithabu. Neumünster.
1986   *Die Tracht*. Vol. 2. Birka II. KVHAA, Stockholm.
1991   *Textilfunde aus der Siedlung und aus den Gräbern von Haithabu: Beschreibung und Gliederung, Berichte* über *die Ausgrabungen in Haithabu, herausgegeben von K. Schietzel*. Vol. Bericht 29. K. Wachholtz, Neumünster.

Haines, R.
1677   *Proposals for Building in Every County a Working-Alms-House or Hospital, as the Best Expedient to Perfect the Trade and Manufactory of Linnen Cloth*. Printed by W. G. for H. Harford, Lonson.

Hajdas, I., C. Cristi, G. Bonani, and M. Maurer
2014   Textiles and Radiocarbon Dating. *Radiocarbon* 56(2):637–643. DOI:10.2458/56.17757.

Halldórsson, J.
1903   *Biskupasögur Jóns Prófasts Halldórssonar 1´ Hítardal: Med Viðbæti I. Skálholts- biskupar 1540–1801 (The Bishops' Histories of Jón Halldórsson from Hítardalur)*. Sögufélag, Reykjavik.

Hambrecht, G.
2009   Zooarchaeology and the Archaeology of Early Modern Iceland. *Journal of the North Atlantic* 1:3–22.

Hamilton, J. R. C.
1956   *Excavations at Jarlshof, Shetland*. Her Majesty's Stationery Office, Edinburgh.

Haraldur Bernharðsson (editor)
2005   *Járnsíða og kristinréttur Árna Þorlákssonar*. Smárit Sögufélags. Sögufélag, Reyk- javik.

Harris, M.
1995   *Cultural Anthropology*. 4th ed. HarperCollins, New York.

Harrison, R., and R. Maher (editors)
2014   *Human Ecodynamics in the North Atlantic: A Collaborative Model of Humans and Nature through Space and Time*. Lexington, New York.

Harrison, R., H. Roberts, and W. P. Adderley
2008   Gásir in Eyjafjörður: International Exchange and Local Economy in Medieval Iceland. *Journal of the North Atlantic* 1:99–119.

Hastrup, K.
1990   *Culture and History in Medieval Iceland*. Clarendon, Oxford.

Hayeur Smith, M.
2004   *Draupnir's Sweat and Mardöll's Tears: An Archaeology of Jewellery, Gender and Identity in Viking Age Iceland*. BAR international series 1276. Hedges, Oxford.

2012   "Some in Rags and Some in Jags and Some in Silken Gowns": Textiles from Iceland's Early Modern Period. *International Journal of Historical Archaeology* 16(3):509–528.

2014a   Dress, Cloth and the Farmer's Wife: Textiles from Ø172 Tatsipataa, Greenland with Comparative Data from Iceland. *Journal of the North Atlantic* 6:64–81.

2014b   Thorir's Bargain: Gender, Vaðmal, and the Law. *World Archaeology* 45(5):730–746.

2015a   Weaving Wealth: Cloth and Trade in Viking Age and Medieval Iceland. In *Textiles and the Medieval Economy: Production, Trade, and Consumption of Textiles, 8th–16th Centuries*, edited by A. Ling Huang and C. Jahnke, pp. 23–40. Ancient Textile Series. Oxbow Books, Oxford.

2015b   Dress, Jewellery and Textiles. In *Bundled Up in Blue: The Re-investigation of a Viking Grave*, pp. 24–42. National Museum of Iceland, Reykjavik.

2016a   Ethnicity and Cultural Influence in Dress from Scandinavia and the North Atlantic. In *A Cultural History of Dress and Fashion*, vol. 2, Medieval Age (800–1450), edited by S.-G. Heller, pp. 125–140. Bloomsbury, London.

2016b   Textiles. In *The Reykholt Church Excavation*, edited by Guðrún Sveinbjarnardóttir. Snorrastofa and Þjóðminjasafn Íslands, Reykjavik.

2018   Vaðmál and Cloth Currency in Viking and Medieval Iceland. In *Silver, Butter, Cloth: Monetary and Social Economies in the Viking Age*, edited by Jane Kershaw and Gareth Williams, with consultant editors Soren Sindbaek and James Graham-Campbell. Oxford University Press, Oxford.

2019a   *Preliminary Textile Report from the Stóraborg Excavations, 1979–1990.* Unpublished textile report. Haffenreffer Museum of Anthropology, Brown University, Providence.

2019b   Rumpestiltsken's Feat: Cloth and Hanseatic Trade with Iceland. In *German Trade in the North Atlantic, c. 1400–1700: Interdisciplinary Perspectives*, edited by N. Mehler, M. Gardiner, and E. Elvestad, Arkeologisk Museum Stavanger, Stavanger.

Hayeur Smith, M., J. Arneborg, and K. P. Smith

2016   The "Burgundian" Hat from Herjolfsnes, Greenland: New Discoveries, New Dates. *Danish Journal of Archaeology* 4(1):21–32. DOI:10.1080/21662282.2016.1151615.

Hayeur Smith, M., K. P. Smith and G. Nilsen

2018   Dorset, Norse, or Thule? Technological Transfers, Marine Mammal Contamination, and AMS Dating of Spun Yarn and Textiles from the Eastern Canadian Arctic. *Journal of Archaeological Science* 96:162–174. DOI:10.1016/j.jas.2018.06.005.

Hayeur Smith, M., G. Lucas, and Q. Mould

2018   Men in Black: Performing Masculinity in 17th- and 18th-Century Iceland. *Journal of Social Archaeology* 19(2):229–254. DOI:10.1177/1469605318793798.

Hayeur Smith, M., K. P. Smith, and K. M. Frei

2019   "Tangled Up in Blue": A Case Study of Death, Dress and Identity for an Early Viking Age Female Settler from Ketilsstaðir, Iceland. *Medieval Archaeology* 63(1):95–127.

Hays-Gilpin, K.

2000   Feminist Scholarship in Archaeology. *Annals of the American Academy of Political and Social Science* 571(1):89–106.

Hays-Gilpin, K., and D. S. Whitley (editors)

1998   *Reader in Gender Archaeology.* Routledge, London.

Hedenstierna-Jonson, C.

2015   She Came from Another Place: On the Burial of a Young Girl from Birka. In *Viking Worlds, Things, Spaces and Movement*, edited by M. H. Eriksen, U. Pedersen, B. Rundberget, I. Axelson, and H. Lund Berg, pp. 90–101. Oxbow Books, Oxford.

Hedenstierna-Jonson, C., and A. Kjellström

2014   The Urban Woman: On the Role and Identity of Women in Birka. In *Kvinner i Vikingtid*, edited by N. L. Colemand and N. Løkka, pp. 183–204. Scandinavian Academic Press, Oslo.

Heide, E.

2007   "Spinning Seiðr." In *Old Norse Religion in Long-Term Perspectives, Origins, Changes and Interactions: An International Conference in Lund, Sweden, June 3–7, 2004*, edited by A. Andren, K. Jennbert, and C. Raudvere, pp. 164–170. Nordic Academic Press, Lund.

Helgadóttir, S.

2013   *Faldar og Skart Faldbúningurinn og aðrir íslenskir þjóðbúningar.* Miðstöð Íslenskra Bókmennta, Reykjavik.

Helgason, A., E. Hickey, S. Goodacre, V. Bosnes, K. Stefánsson, R. Ward, and B. Sykes

2001   mtDNA and the Islands of the North Atlantic: Estimating the Proportions of Norse and Gaelic Ancestry. *American Journal of Human Genetics* 68(3):723–737. DOI:10.1086/318785.

Helle, K.

2019   Bergen's Role in the Medieval North Atlantic Trade. In *German Trade in the North Atlantic, c. 1400–1700: Interdisciplinary Perspectives*, edited by N. Mehler, M. Gardiner, and E. Elvestad, pp. 43–51. Arkeologisk Museum, University of Stavanger, Stavanger.

Hingley, R.

1996   Ancestors and Identity in the Later Prehistory of Atlantic Scotland: The Reuse and Reinvention of Neolithic Monuments and Material Culture. *World Archaeology* 28(2):231–243.

Hittinger, D.

2008   Auswertung der Tuchplombenfunde der Teerhofgrabung. *Bremer Archäologische Blätter* 7:111–144.

Hjálmarsson, J. R.

1993   *History of Iceland: From the Settlement to the Present Day.* Iceland Review, Reykjavik.

Hoffmann, M.

1974   *The Warp-Weighted Loom: Studies in the History and Technology of an Ancient Implement.* Universitets forlaget, Oslo.

Holtved, E.

1944   *Archaeological Investigations in the Thule District, II*. Meddelelser om Grønland, Copenhagen.

Ingstad, A. S.

1982   The Functional Textiles from the Osberg Ship. In *The Functional Textiles from the Osberg Ship*, edited by L. Bender Jørgensen and K. Tidow, pp. 85–96. Textil symposium Neumünster, Neumünster.

Jakobsson, Á.

2008   The Trollish Acts of Þorgrímr the Witch: The Meanings of Troll and Ergi in Medieval Iceland. *Saga-Book* 32:39–68.

Jensen Beder, N.

2010   *Seyður, ull, tøting*. Sprotin, Tórshavn.

Jesch, J.

2005   *Women in the Viking Age*. Boydell Press, Woodbridge.

Jochens, J.

1995   *Women in Old Norse Society*. Cornell University Press, Ithaca.

Johnson, W. C., and D. S. Speedy

1991   Cordage Twist Direction as a Tool in Delineating Territorial Boundaries and Demonstrating Population Continuity during the Late Prehistoric Periods in the Upper Ohio River Valley. Annual Meeting of the Middle Atlantic Archaeological Conference, Ocean City, Maryland.

1996   *Old Norse Images of Women*. University of Pennsylvania Press, Philadelphia.

Jones, G.

1986   *The Norse Atlantic Saga: Being the Norse Voyages of Discovery and Settlement to Iceland, Greenland, and North America*. 2nd ed. Oxford University Press, Oxford.

Jónsson, M.

2004   *Jónsbók, Lögbók Íslendinga*. Háskólaútgáfan, Reykjavik.

Kapp, E.

2013   *Rigmaroles and Ragamuffins: Unpicking Words We Derive from Textiles*. Cardiff, Oxford.

Karlsson,G.

2000   *The History of Iceland*. University of Minnesota Press, Minneapolis.

Keller, C.

1986   Nordboern på Grønland 985–1350. *Bidrag til en demografisk økologisk diskusjon* (1984/1985):145–157.

2010   Furs, Fish, and Ivory: Medieval Norsemen at the Arctic Fringe. *Journal of the North Atlantic* 3:1–23. DOI:10.3721/037.003.0105.

Kershaw, J., and G. Williams (editors)

2019   *Silver, Butter, Cloth: Monetary and Social Economies in the Viking Age*. Oxford University Press, Oxford.

Kimmel, M.S.

2012   Masculinity as Homophobia: Fear, Shame, and Silence in the Construction of

Gender Identity. In *Theorizing Masculinities*, edited by H. Brod and M. Kaufman, pp. 119–141. Sage, Thousand Oaks, California.

Kirjavainen, H.

2009   A Finnish Archaeological Perspective on Medieval Broadcloth. In *The Medieval Broadcloth*, edited by K. Vestergård Pedersen and M. L. Nosch, pp. 90–99. Oxbow Books, Oxford.

Kjellberg, A.

1979   Tekstilmaterialet I Oslogate 7. In *De arkeologiske utgravninger, in Gamlebyen, Oslo, bind 2, Feltene Oslogate 3 og 7*, pp. 83–105. Bebyggelsesrester og funngrupper, Øvre Ervik.

Kjellberg, A., and M. Hoffman

1991   Tekstiler. In *De arkeologiske utgravninger i Gamlebyen, Oslo*, pp. 13–81. Alvheim & Eide, Øvre Ervik.

Koch Madsen, C.

2014   Pastoral Settlement, Farming, and Hierarchy in Norse Vatnahverfi, South Greenland. PhD dissertation, University of Copenhagen.

Kupiec, P., and K. Milek

2015   Roles and Perceptions of Shielings and the Mediation of Gender Identities in Viking and Medieval Iceland. In *Viking Worlds, Things, Spaces and Movement*, edited by M. H. Eriksen, U. Pedersen, B. Rundberget, I. Axelson, and H. Lund Berg, pp. 102–123. Oxbow Books, Oxford.

Kutcha, D.

2002   *The Three-Piece Suit and Modern Masculinity: England, 1550–1850*. University of California Press, Berkeley.

Kuttruff, J. T.

1988   Textile Attributes and Production Complexity as Indicators of Caddoan Status Differentiation in the Arkansas Valley and Southern Ozark Regions. PhD dissertation, Ohio State University, Columbus.

Larson, L. M. (editor)

2008   *The Earliest Norwegian Laws: Being the Gulathing Law and the Frostathing Law*. Lawbook Exchange, Clark, New Jersey.

Lárusdóttir, B.

2011   *Mannvist, Sýnisbók Íslenskra Fornleifa*. Opna, Reykjavik.

Lárusson, B.

1967   *The Old Icelandic Land Registers*. C. W. K. Gleerup, Lund.

Lawson, T. I., F. J. Gathorne-Hardy, M. Church, A. J. Newton, K., J. Edwards, A. J. Dugmore, and A. Einarsson

2007   Environmental Impacts of the Norse Settlement: Paleoenvironmental Data from Mývatnssveit, Northern Iceland. *Boreas* 36(1):1–19.

Lillios, K. T.

1999   Objects of Memory: The Ethnography and Archaeology of Heirlooms. *Journal of Archaeological Method and Theory* 6(3):235–262.

Linnamae, U.

1975   *The Dorset Culture: A Comparative Study in Newfoundland and the Arctic.* Department of Tourism Heritage Resources Division, St. John's, Newfoundland.

Long, C. D.

1975   Excavations in the Medieval City of Trondheim, Norway. *Medieval Archaeology* 19:1–32.

Lucas, G. (editor)

2009   *Hofstaðir: Excavations of a Viking Age Feasting Hall in North-Eastern Iceland.* Fornleifastofnun Íslands, Reykjavik.

Lucas, G.

2010   The Tensions of Modernity: Skálholt during the 17th and 18th Centuries. *Journal of the North Atlantic* 2009(1):75. DOI:10.3721/037.002.s108.

2012   *Understanding the Archaeological Record.* Cambridge University Press, Cambridge.

Lucas, G., and T. McGovern

2007   Bloody Slaughter: Ritual Decapitation and Display at the Viking Settlement of Hofstaðir, Iceland. *European Journal of Archaeology* 10(1):7–30.

Lynnerup, N.

1998   *The Greenland Norse: A Biological-Anthropological Study.* Meddelelser om Grønland Man & Society 24. Commission for Scientific Research in Greenland, Copenhagen.

Magnúsdóttir, A. G.

1988   Ástir og völd–frillulífi á Íslandi á þjóðveldisöld (Love and power: Mistresses in Commonwealth Iceland). *Ný Saga* 2:4–12.

2008   Women and Sexual Politics. In *The Viking World*, edited by S. Brink and N. Price, pp. 40–48. Routledge, London.

Magnusson, M., and H. Pálsson (translators)

1969   *Laxdaela Saga.* Penguin, Harmondsworth.

Maher, R.

2007   Kuml, Kyn, og Kyngervi (Graves, sex, and gender). *Árbók hins Íslenzka Fornleifafélags*, 153–170.

Maik, J.

2009   The Influence of Hanseatic Trade on Textile Production in Medieval Poland. In *The Medieval Broadcloth*, edited by K. Vestergård Pedersen and M. L. Nosch, pp. 109–122. Oxbow Books, Oxford.

Mainland, I., and P. Halstead

2005   The Economics of Sheep and Goat Husbandry in Norse Greenland. *Arctic Anthropology* 42(1):103–120. DOI:10.1353/arc.2011.0060.

Mann, M. E., Z. Zhang, S. Rutherford, R. S. Bradley, M. K. Hughes, D. Shindell, C. Ammann, G. Faluvegi, and F. Ni

2009   Global Signatures and Dynamical Origins of the Little Ice Age and Medieval Climate Anomaly. *Science* 326(5957):1256–1260. DOI:10.1126/science.1177303.

Már Jónsson (editor)

2004   *Jónsbók: lögbók Íslendinga hver samþykkt var á Alþingi árið 1281 og endurnýjuð um miðja 14. öld en fyrst prentuð árið 1578*. Sýnisbók íslenskrar alþýðumenningar 8. Háskólaútg, Reykjavik.

Martensen, L.
1987   Herjolfsnæs-dragterne på Grønland: Vdnesbyrd om et Europa udenfor periferien. *Konsthistorisk tidsrift/Journal of Art History* 56(3):87–95.

Mary-Rousselière, G.
2002   *Nunguvik et Saatut: Sites Paléoeskimaux de Navy Island, Ile de Baffin*. Mercury Series 162. Canadian Museum of Civilization, Archaeological Survey of Canada, Ottawa.

Maurer, B.
2006   The Anthropology of Money. *Annual Review of Anthropology* 35:15–36.

Maxwell, M. S.
1973   *Archaeology of the Lake Harbour District, Baffin Island*. Mercury Series 6. Canadian Museum of Civilization, Ottawa.

1985   *Prehistory of the Eastern Arctic*. Academic Press, Orlando.

McGhee, R.
1984   Contact between Native North Americans and the Medieval Norse: A Review of the Evidence. *American Antiquity* 49(1):4–26.

2003   Epilogue: Was There Continuity from Norse to Post-Medieval Explorations of the New World? In *Contact, Continuity, and Collapse: The Norse Colonization of the North Atlantic*, edited by J. H. Barrett, pp. 239–248. Brepols, Turnhout, Belgium.

McGovern, T. H.
1980   Cows, Harp Seals and Churchbells: Adaptation and Extinction in Norse Greenland. *Human Ecology* 8(3):245–275.

1985   Contributions to the Paleoeconomy of Norse Greenland. *Acta Archaeologica* 54:73–122.

McGovern, Thomas H., Gerald F. Bigelow, Thomas Amorosi, and Daniel Russell
1990   The Archaeology of the Norse North Atlantic. *Annual Review of Anthropology* 19:331–351.

1991   Climate, Correlation, and Causation in Norse Greenland. *Arctic Anthropology* 28(2):77–100.

1996   Northern Islands, Human Error, and Environmental Degradation. In *Case Studies in Human Ecology*, edited by Daniel G. Bates and Susan H. Lees, pp. 103–152. Springer, Boston.

2000   The Demise of Norse Greenland. In *Vikings: The North Atlantic Saga*, edited by W. W. Fitzhugh and E. I. Ward, pp. 327–339. Smithsonian Institution Press, National Museum of Natural History, Washington, DC.

McGovern, T. H., O. Vésteinsson, A. Fridriksson, M. Church, I. Lawson, I. A. Simpson, A. Einarsson, A. Dugmore, G. Cook, S. Perdikaris, K. J. Edwards, A. M. Thomson, W. P. Adderley, A. Newton, G. Lucas, R. Edvardsson, O. Aldred, and E. Dunbar
2007   Landscapes of Settlement in Northern Iceland: Historical Ecology of Human Impact and Climate Fluctuation on the Millennial Scale. *American Anthropologist* 109(1):27–51.

McGovern, T. H., R. Harrison, and K. Smiarowski

2014   Sorting Sheep and Goats in Medieval Iceland and Greenland: Local Subsistence, Climate Change, or World Systems Impacts? In *Human Ecodynamics in the North Atlantic: A Collaborative Model of Humans and Nature through Space and Time*, edited by R. Harrison and R. A. Maher, pp. 153–176. Lexington Books, New York.

McGregor, A.

1985   *Bone, Antler, Ivory and Horn: The Technology of Skeletal Materials Since the Roman Period*. Croom Helm, London.

McKenna, C.

2007   Performing Penance and Poetic Performance in the Medieval Welsh Court. *Medieval Academy of America* 82(1):70–96.

Mehler, N.

2009   The Perception and Interpretation of Hanseatic Material Culture in the North Atlantic: Problems and Suggestions. *Journal of the North Atlantic* 1:89–108.

2015   The Sulphur Trade of Iceland from the Viking Age to the End of the Hanseatic Period. In *Nordic Middle Ages: Artefacts, Landscapes and Society, Essays in Honour of Ingvild Øye on Her 70th Birthday*, edited by I. Baug, J. Larsen, and S. S. Mygland, pp. 193–212. University of Bergen Archaeological Series 8. University of Bergen, Bergen.

Mehler, Natascha, and M. Gardiner

2013   On the Verge of Colonialism: English and Hanseatic Trade in the North Atlantic Islands. In *Exploring Atlantic Traditions*, edited by P. E. Pope and S. Lewis-Simpson, pp. 1–14. Boydell Press, Woodbridge.

Meulengracht Sørensen, P.

1983   *The Unmanly Man: Concepts of Sexual Defamation in Early Northern Society*. Viking Collection 1. Odense University Press, Odense.

Milek, K.

2012   Gendered Space and the Role of the Pit House on Viking Age Farmsteads in Iceland. *Medieval Archaeology* 56:85–130.

Miller, W. I.

1983   Choosing the Avenger: Some Aspects of the Bloodfeud in Medieval Iceland and England. *Law and History Review* 1(2):159–204.

1996   *Bloodtaking and Peacemaking: Feud, Law, and Society in Saga Iceland*. University of Chicago Press, Chicago.

Minar, C. J.

2001   Motor Skills and the Learning Process: The Conservation of Cordage Final Twist Direction in Communities of Practice. *Journal of Anthropological Research* 57(4):381–405.

Moltke, E., and P. Foote

1985   *Runes and Their Origin: Denmark and Elsewhere*. 1st English ed. Nationalmuseets Forl, Copenhagen.

Moore, J. W., M. E. Roach, and J. B. Eicher

1966   Dress, Adornment, and the Social Order. *American Sociological Review* 31(6):896. DOI:10.2307/2091707.

Mortensen, M.

1997   For Women Only? Reflections on a Viking Age Settlement at Stedje, Sogndal, in Western Norway. *Studien zur Schsenforschung* 10:195–206.

Munro, J.

2003   Medieval Woollens: Textiles, Technology and Industrial Organisation, c. 800–1500. In *Cambridge History of Western Textiles*, edited by I. D. Jenkins, pp. 181–227. Cambridge University Press, Cambridge.

Murdock, G.

2000   Dressed to Repress? Protestant Clerical Dress and the Regulation of Morality in Early Modern Europe. *Fashion Theory* 4(2):179–199. DOI:10.2752/136270400779108807.

Mygland, S. S.

2014   *Gender and Material Culture: Women in Medieval Bergen, A Contextual Analysis of Gender-Related Artefacts from Bryggen in Bergen, 1170–1476.* University of Bergen, Bergen.

2015   "Female" Activities, "Female" Artefacts: A Theoretical Approach to Women and Gender in Medieval Bergen. In *Nordic Middle Ages: Artefacts, Landscapes and Society, Essays in Honour of Ingvild Øye on Her 70th Birthday*, edited by I. Baug, J. Larsen, and S. Samset Mygland, pp. 241–250. Archaeological Series 8. University of Bergen, Bergen.

Näsström, B. M.

2003   *Freyja: The Great Goddess of the North.* Clock and Rose Press, Cap Code.

Nelson, D. E., J. Heinemeier, N. Lynnerup, Á. E. Sveinbjörnsdóttir, and J. Arneborg

2012   An Isotopic Analysis of the Diet of the Greenland Norse. *Journal of the North Atlantic* 301:93–118. DOI:10.3721/037.004.s308.

Nelson, E., J. Heinemeier, J. Møhl, and J. Arneborg

2012   Isotopic Analyses of the Domestic Animals of Norse Greenland. *Journal of the North Atlantic* 3:77–92.

Nelson, S. M.

1997   *Gender in Archaeology: Analyzing Power and Prestige.* AltaMira Press, London.

Netherton, R.

2008   The View from Herjolfsnes: Greenland's Translation of the European Fitted Fashion. In *Medieval Clothing and Textiles*, edited by R. Netherton and G. R. Owen-Crocket, pp. 144–153. Boydell Press, Woodbridge.

Niessen, S., and J. B. Eicher

1998   Dress and Ethnicity: Change across Space and Time. *Anthropologica* 40(1):129. DOI:10.2307/25605877.

Nørlund, P.

1925   Unpublished diary. Antikvarisk-Topografisk Arkiv, National Museum of Denmark, Copenhagen.

2010   *Buried Norsemen at Herjolfsnes: An Archaeological and Historical Study.* Museum Tusculanum Press, Copenhagen.

Norrman, L. E.

2008   *Viking Women: The Narrative Voice in Woven Tapestries.* Cambria Press, Amherst, New York.

Odess, D.

1998   The Archaeology of Interaction: Views from Artifact Style and Material Exchange in Dorset Society. *American Antiquity* 63(3):417–435.

Ogilvie, A. E. J., J. M. Woollett, K. Smiarowski, J. Arneborg, S. Troelstra, A. Kuijpers, A. Pálsdóttir, and T. H. McGovern

2009   Seals and Sea Ice in Medieval Greenland. *Journal of the North Atlantic* 2(2009):60–80.

Østergård, E.

1998   The Textiles: A Preliminary Report. In *Man, Culture, and Environment in Ancient Greenland: Report on a Research Programme,* edited by Jette Arneborg and H. C. Gulløv, pp. 58–65. Dansk Polar Center, Copenhagen.

2004   *Woven into the Earth: Textiles from Norse Greenland.* Aarhus University Press, Aarhus.

2005   The Greenlandic Vaðmál in Northern Archaeological Textiles. In *Textile Symposium in Edinburgh, 5th–7th of May 1999,* pp. 80–83. NESAT 7. Oxbow Books, Oxford.

Øye, I.

2016   When Did Weaving Become a Male Profession? *Danish Journal of Archaeology* 5(1–2):34–51. DOI:10.1080/21662282.2016.1245970.

Park, R. W.

2004   All Quiet on the Eastern Arctic Front? 69th Annual Meeting for the Society for American Archaeology, Montreal.

Pedersen, I. R.

1982   *Ketilsstaðir, Hjaltastaðahreppur, Islands.* Bryggens Museum, Bergen Norway.

Petersen, J. B., and J. A. Wolford

2000   Spin and Twist as Cultural Markers: A New England Perspective on Native Fiber Industries. In *Beyond Cloth and Cordage: Archaeological Textile Research in the Americas,* edited by P. B. Drooker and L. D. Webster, pp. 101–117. University of Utah Press, Salt Lake City.

Price, N. S., C. Hedenstierna-Jonson, T. Zachrisson, A. Kjellström, J. Storå, M. Krzewińska, T. Günther, V. Sobrado, M. Jakobsson, and A. Götherström

2019   Viking Warrior Women? Reassessing Birka Chamber Grave Bj.581. *Antiquity* 93(367):181–198. DOI:10.15184/aqy.2018.258.

Price, N. S.

2002   *The Viking Way: Religion and War in Late Iron Age Scandinavia.* 2nd ed. Aun 31. University of Uppsala, Uppsala.

2011   Sorcery and Circumpolar Traditions in Old Norse Belief: Popular Religion in the Viking Age. In *The Viking World,* edited by S. N. Price Brink, pp. 244–248. Routledge Worlds, London.

Price, T. D., Karin M. Frei, and E. Naumann
2015   Isotopic Baselines in the North Atlantic Region. *Journal of the North Atlantic* 7:103–136.

Price, T. D., and H. Gestsdóttir
2006   The First Settlers of Iceland: An Isotopic Approach to Colonization. *Antiquity* 80(2006):130–144.

Reimer, P. J., E. Bard, A. Bayliss, J. W. Beck, P. G. Blackwell, C. Bronk Ramsey, C. E. Buck, H. Cheng, R. L. Edwards, M. Friedrich, P. M. Grootes, T. P. Guilderson, H. Haflidason, I. Hajdas, C. Hatté, T. J. Heaton, D. L. Hoffmann, A. G. Hogg, K. A. Hughen, K. F. Kaiser, B. Kromer, S. W. Manning, M. Niu, R. W. Reimer, D. A. Richards, E. M. Scott, J. R. Southon, R. A. Staff, C. S. M Turney, and J. van der Plicht
2013   IntCal13 and Marine13 Radiocarbon Age Calibration Curves 0–50,000 Years cal BP. *Radiocarbon* 55(4):1869–1887. DOI:10.2458/azu_js_rc.55.16947.

Ribeiro, A.
2003   Dress in the Early Modern Period, c. 1500–1780. In *The Cambridge History of Western Textiles*, edited by D. Jenkins, pp. 659–689. Cambridge University Press, Cambridge.

Ritchie, A.
1993   *Viking Scotland*. B. T. Batsford, Historic Scotland, London.

Roach-Higgins, M. E., and J. B. Eicher
1992   Dress and Identity. *Clothing and Textiles Research Journal* 10(4):1–8. DOI:10.1177/0887302X9201000401.

Róbertsdóttir, H.
2008   *Wool and Society: Manufacturing Policy, Economic Thought and Local Production in 18th-Century Iceland*. Centrum för Danmarksstudier 21. Makadam Förl, Göteborg.

Ross, J. M., and C. Zutter
2007   Comparing Norse Animal Husbandry Practices: Paleoethnobotanical Analyses from Iceland and Greenland. *Arctic Anthropology* 44(1):62–86. DOI:10.1353/arc.2011.0089.

Rovine, V. L.
2009   Colonialism's Clothing: Africa, France, and the Deployment of Fashion. *Design Issues* 25(3):44–61. DOI:10.1162/desi.2009.25.3.44.

Ryder, M. L.
1982   European Wool Types from the Iron Age to the Middle Ages. In *Archäologische Textilfunde, May 6th to May 8th, 1981, Textilsymposium Neumünster (NESAT 1)*, edited by L. Bender Jørgensen and K. Tidow, pp. 224–238. NESAT 1. Neumünster.

Sabo, D., and G. Sabo
1978   A Possible Thule Carving of a Viking from Southern Greenland. *Canadian Journal of Archaeology* 2:33–42.

Sabo, G., and J. H. Jacobs
1980   Aspects of Thule Culture Adaptations in Southern Baffin Island. *Arctic* 33(3):4987–504.

Saul, M.

2004   Money in Colonial Transition: Cowries and Francs in West Africa. *American Anthropologist* 106(1):71–84.

Sawyer, B.

1991   Women as Bridge-Builders; The Roles of Women in Viking Age Scandinavia. In *People and Places in Northern Europe, 500–1600*, edited by I. Wood and N. Lund, pp. 211–224. Boydell Press, Woodbridge.

Sawyer, B.

1992   Kvinnor och familj det forn- och medeltida Skandinavien. *Occasional Papers on Medieval Topics* 6.

2004   Viking Age Women. *Viking Heritage* 2:3–6.

Schledermann, P.

1980   Notes on Norse Finds from the East Coast of Ellesmere Island. *Arctic* 33(3):454–463.

Schneider J., and A. B. Weiner

1989   Introduction. In *Cloth and the Human Experience*, edited by A. B. Weiner and J. Schneider, pp. 1–29. Smithsonian Institution Press, Washington, DC.

Schneider, J.

1989   Rumpelstiltskin's Bargain: Folklore and the Merchant Capitalist Intensification of Linen Manufacture in Early Modern Europe. In *Cloth and the Human Experience*, edited by A. B. Weiner and Jane Schneider, pp. 177–213. Smithsonian Institution Press, Washington, DC.

Schulman, J. K. (translator)

2010   *Jónsbók: The Laws of Later Iceland: The Icelandic Text according to MS AM 351 fol. Skálholtsbók eldri*. Bibliotheca Germanica 4. AQ-Verlag, Saarbrücken.

Seaver, K.

1996   *The Frozen Echo: Greenland and the Exploration of North America, ca. AD 1000–1500*. Stanford University Press, Stanford, California.

Sigurðsson, J. V.

1999   *Chieftains and Power in the Icelandic Commonwealth*. Odense University Press, Odense.

Sigurjónsdóttir, Æ.

1985   *Klæðaburður íslenskra karla á 16., 17. og 18. Öld*. Ritsafn Sagnfræðistofnunar 13, Reykjavik.

Sinding, M.-H. S., J. Arneborg, G. Nyegaard, and M. T. P. Gilbert

2015   Ancient DNA Unravels the Truth behind the Controversial GUS Greenlandic Norse Fur Samples: The Bison Was a Horse, and the Muskox and Bears Were Goats. *Journal of Archaeological Science* 53:297–303. DOI:10.1016/j.jas.2014.10.028.

Sinding, M.-H. S., F. G. Vieira, and M. Hayeur Smith

2017   Unmatched DNA Preservation Prove Arctic Hare and Sheep Wool in Norse Greenlandic Textile from "the Farm beneath the Sand." *Journal of Archaeological Science* 14:603–608. DOI:10.1016/j.jasrep.2017.06.043.

Skre, D.
2011   Commodity Money, Silver and Coinage in Viking-Age Scandinavia. In *Silver Economies: Monetisation and Society in Scandinavia, AD 800–1100*, edited by James Graham-Campbell, S. M. Sindbaek, and G. Williams, pp. 67–92. Aarhus University Press, Aarhus.

Smiarowski, K.
2012   *E172 Tatsipataa Midden Excavation 2009 and 2010.* Unpublished preliminary excavation report. CUNY Hunter College, New York.

Smiarowski K., and T. McGovern
2012   *Zooarchaeological Investigations of Animal Husbandry and Communal Hunting in the Norse Eastern Settlement Greenland.* Paper presented at the Vatnahverfi Workshop. Copenhagen.

Smiarowski, K., R. Harrison, S. Brewington, M. Hicks, F. J. Feeley, C. Dupont-Hébert, B. Prehal, G. Hambrecht, J. Woollett, and T. H. McGovern
2017   *Zooarchaeology of the Scandinavian Settlements in Iceland and Greenland: Diverging Pathways.* Oxford University Press, April 5.

Smith, B.
2013   Wadmal. In *Shetland Textiles, 800 BC to the Present*, edited by S. Laurenson, pp. 44–51. Shetland Heritage, Lerwick.

Smith, K. P.
1995   Landnám: The Settlement of Iceland in Archaeological and Historical Perspective. *World Archaeology* 26(3):319–347.
2009   *Preliminary Investigations at Gilsbakki, Borgarbyggð, Western Iceland, 2008 Season,* Unpublished excavation report. Haffenreffer Museum of Anthropology, Brown University, Providence.
2015   Dating of the Ketilsstaðir Grave. In *Bundled Up in Blue: The Re-investigation of a Viking Grave*, pp. 38–42. National Museum of Iceland, Reykjavik.

Snaesdóttir, M.
1991   *Stóra-Borg Fornleifarannsókn, 1978–1990.* Þjóðminjasafn Íslands, Reykjavik.

Solberg, B.
1985   Social Status in the Merovingian and Viking Periods in Norway from Archaeological and Historical Sources. *Norwegian Archaeological Review* 18(1–2):241–256.

Soli, B.
2002   *Seid–Myter, sjamanisme og kjønn i vikingenes tid.* Pax Forlag, Oslo.

Steinberg, J., J. Bolender, A. Schreiner, E. L. Button, R. S. Shepard, and K. A. Catlin
2009   *Test Pits at Meiðalheimur.* Unpublished report. Skagafjörður Archaeological Settlement Survey, Fiske Center, Boston.

Steinberg, J. M.
2006   A Political Economy from Increasing Marginal Returns to Labor: An Example from Viking Age Iceland. In *Labor in Cross-Cultural Perspective*, edited by E. P. Durrenberger and J. Marti, pp. 217–244. Society for Economic Anthropology Monograph. AltaMira Press, Lanham, Maryland.

Straubhaar, S. B. (editor)

2011 *Old Norse Women's Poetry: The Voices of Female Skalds.* D. S. Brewer, Rochester, New York.

Sutherland, P.

2000 Strands of Culture Contact: Dorset-Norse Interactions in the Canadian Eastern Arctic. In *Identities and Cultural Contacts in the Arctic: Proceedings from a Conference at the Danish National Museum*, edited by M. Appelt, J. Berglund, and H. C. Gulløv, pp. 159–169. Danish National Museum and Danish Polar Center, Copenhagen.

2002 Nunguvik and Saatut Revisited. In *Nunguvik et Saatut: Sites Paléoeskimaux de Navy Island, Ile de Baffin*, by G. Mary-Rousselière, pp. 115–119. Archaeological Survey of Canada, Mercury Series 162. Canadian Museum of Civilization, Ottawa.

2009 The Question of Contact between Dorset Paleo-Eskimos and Early Europeans in the Eastern Arctic. In *The Northern World, AD 900–1400*, edited by H. Maschner, O. K. Mason, and R. McGhee, pp. 279–299. University of Utah Press, Salt Lake City.

Sveinbjarnardóttir, G.

2006 Reykholt: A Centre of Power, the Archaeological Evidence. In *Reykholt som makt-og lærdomssenter i den islandsk og nordiske kontekst*, edited by E. Mundal, pp. 25–42. Snórrastofa, Reykholt.

2009 Kirkjur Reykholts—byggingasaga. In *Endurfundir: Fornleifarannsóknir styrktar af Kristnihátíðarsjóði, 2001–2005*, edited by G. Ólafsson and S. Kristjánsdóttir, pp. 58–69. Þjóðminjasafn Íslands, Reykjavik.

2012 *Reykholt: Archaeological Investigations at a High Status Farm in Western Iceland.* National Museums of Iceland, Reykjavik.

2016 *Reykholt: Church Excavations.* National Museum of Iceland in Collaboration with Snorrastofa and the University of Iceland Press, Reykjavik.

Sveinbjarnardóttir, G, K. Dahle, E.Erlendsson, G. Gísladóttir, and K. Vickers

2012 The Reykholt Shieling Project: Some Preliminary Results. In *Viking Settlements & Viking Society: Papers from the Proceedings of the Sixteenth Viking Congress*, edited by S. Sigmundsson, pp. 162–175. Hið Íslenzka Fornleifafélag and University of Iceland Press, Reykjavik.

Thirsk, J.

2003 Knitting and Knitwear. In *Cambridge History of Western Textiles*, vol. 1, edited by D. Jenkins, pp. 562–584. Cambridge University Press, Cambridge.

Thursfield, S.

2001 *The Medieval Tailor's Assistant: Making Common Garments, 1200–1500.* Ruth Bean, Carleton Bedford.

Tidow, K., and E. Jordan-Fahrbach

2007 Woollen Textiles in Archaeological Finds and Descriptions in Written Sources of the 14th to the 18th Centuries. In *Ancient Textiles: Production, Crafts, and Society, Proceedings of the First International Conference on Ancient Textiles held at*

Lund, Sweden, and Copenhagen, Denmark, March 19–23, 2003, edited by Carole Gillis, pp. 97–103. Oxbow, Oxford.

Tranberg Hansen, K.

2004   The World in Dress: Anthropological Perspectives on Clothing, Fashion, and Culture. *Annual Review of Anthropology* 33 (2004):369–392.

Traustadóttir, R.

2015   Spindle Whorls from Urriðakot. In *Nordic Middle Ages: Artefacts, Landscapes and Society, Essays in Honour of Ingvild Øye on Her 70th Birthday*, edited by I. Baug, J. Larsen, and S. S. Mygland, pp. 317–329. Archaeological Series 8. University of Bergen, Bergen.

Turner, T. S.

1993   The Social Skin. In *Reading the Body Social*, edited by Jeffrey David Ehrenreich and Catherine B. Burroughs. University of Iowa Press, Iowa City.

Vedeler, M.

2004   Pleated Fragments of Clothing from Norway. *Acta Archaeologica Lodziensia* 50(1):61–65.

2007   Klær og Fromspråk i Norsk Meddlealder. Kulturhistorisk Museum, Universitetet i Oslo, Oslo.

2010   Dressing the Dead: Customs of Burial Costume in Rural Norway. In *Northern European Symposium for Archaeological Textiles*, vol. 10, pp. 252–255. Oxbow Books, Oxford.

2014   *Silk for the Vikings*. Ancient Textiles Series 15. Oxbow Books, Oxford.

Vésteinsson, O., T. H. McGovern, and C. Keller

2002   Enduring Impacts: Social and Environmental Aspects of Viking Age Settlement in Iceland and Greenland. *Archaeologia Islandica* 2:98–136.

Vollmer, J. E.

2010   Cultural Authentication in Dress. In *Berg Encyclopedia of World Dress and Fashion: Global Perspectives*, edited by J. B. Eicher and P.G. Tortora, pp. 69–76. Berg, Oxford.

Walser, J., III

2015   Reading the Bones. In *Bundled Up in Blue: The Re-investigation of a Viking Grave*, pp. 47–53. National Museum of Iceland, Reykjavik.

Walton, P.

1988   Dyes of the Viking Age: A Summary of Recent Work. *Dyes in History and Archaeology* 7:14–20.

Walton Rogers, P.

1989   *Textiles, Cordage and Raw Fiber from 16–22 Coppergate*. Vol. 15–17. York Archaeological Trust, Council for British Archaeology, York.

1998   The Raw Materials of Textiles from GUS—with a Note on Fragments of Fleece and Animal Pelts from the Same Site. In *Man, Culture, and Environment in Ancient Greenland: Report on a Research Programme*, edited by J. Arneborg and H. C. Gulløv, pp. 66–73. Danish National Museum and Danish Polar Center, Copenhagen.

2001   *Fibres in a Textile from Tjornuvik Faroe Islands.* Unpublished report, York.

2012   Textiles Wool and Hair. In *Reykholt: Archaeological Investigation at a High Status Farm in Western Iceland,* edited by G. Sveinbjarnardóttir, pp. 196–217. National Museum of Iceland, Reykjavik.

Walton Rogers, P., and Greaves, P.

2018   *The Ties That Bind: Fur-Fibre Cordage and Associated Material from Dorset Paleo-Eskimo Sites in Eastern Canada.* Pangur Press, York.

Wayland Barber, E.

1995   *Women's Work: The First 20 000 Years, Women, Cloth and Society in Early Times.* Norton, New York.

Weiner, A.

1989   Why Cloth? Wealth, Gender and Power in Oceania. In *Cloth and the Human Experience,* edited by A. B. Weiner and J. Schneider, pp. 33–72. Smithsonian Institution Press, Washington, DC.

Weiner, A. B., and J. Schneider (editors)

1989   *Cloth and the Human Experience.* Smithsonian Series in Ethnographic Inquiry. Smithsonian Institution Press, Washington.

Weiss, K. M.

1973   *Demographic Models for Anthropology.* Memoirs of the Society for American Archaeology 27. Society for American Archaeology, Washington, DC.

Welander, R. D. E., C. Batey, and T. G. Cowie

1987   A Viking Burial from Kneep, Uig, Isle of Lewis. *Proceedings of the Society of Antiquaries Scotland* 117:149–174.

Wiberg, C.

1977   Horn og beinmaterial fra "Mindets tomt." In *De arkeologiske utgravninger i Oslo.* Bind 1, Oslo.

Wilcox, D.

2016   Scottish Late Seventeenth-Century Male Clothing: Some Context for the Barrock Estate Finds. *Costume* 50(2):151–168. DOI:10.1080/05908876.2016.1165953.

Wolf, K.

2007   The Colour Blue in Old Norse-Icelandic Literature. In *Scripta Islandica, Isländska Sällskapets Årsbok, 57–2006,* edited by R. A. H. Williams, M. McCleod, E. Mundal, G. Nordal, R. Palm, H. Pálsson, and D. Sävborg, pp. 55–78. Swedish Science Press, Uppsala.

Wood, R. E., C. Bronk Ramsey, and T. F. G. Higham

2010   Refining Background Corrections for Radiocarbon Dating of Bone Collagen at Orau. *Radiocarbon* 52(2):600–611. DOI:10.1017/S003382220004563X.

Wylie, J.

2014   *The Faroe Islands: Interpretations of History.* University Press of Kentucky, Lexington.

Zoëga, G.

2009   Folkið í Keldudal. In *Endurfundir: Fornleifarannsóknir styrktar af Kristnihátiðarsjóði, 2001–2005,* edited by G. Ólafsson and S. Kristjánsdóttir, pp. 30–43. Þjóðminjasafn Íslands, Reykjavik.

Zori, D.

2014   Viking Age Archaeology in Iceland: Mosfell Archaeological Project. In *Viking Archaeology in Iceland: Mosfell Archaeological Project*, edited by D. Zori and J. Byock. Brepols, Turnhout, Belgium.

Þorláksson, H.

1988   Gráfeldir á Gullöld og Vodaverk Kvenna (Graycloaks in the golden age and women's work). *Ný Saga* 2:40–53.

1991   *Vaðmál og verðlag: Vaðmál í utanlandsviðskiptum og búskap Íslendinga á 13. og 14. öld.* Háskóla Íslands, Reykjavik.

1999   *Sjóran og Siglingar: Ensk-Íslensk Samskipti, 1580–1630.* Mál og Menning, Reykjavik.

2010   Saga íslands VI. *Historical Society and the Icelandic Literature* 144.

Index

Page numbers in *italics* followed by the letters *t* and *i* refer to tables and illustrations. The letter *n* refers to notes.

MICHÈLE HAYEUR SMITH is an archaeologist and research associate at the Haffenreffer Museum of Anthropology at Brown University, Providence, Rhode Island. She is currently completing a three-year National Science Foundation–funded research project, Archaeological Investigations of the Eastern North Atlantic Trade and Globalizing Economic Systems, which expands on two successful three-year archaeological collections–based projects also funded by NSF's Arctic Social Sciences program: Weaving Islands of Cloth: Textiles and Trade across the North Atlantic from the Viking Age to the Early Modern Period and Rags to Riches: An Archaeological Study of Textiles and Gender in Iceland, AD 874–1800. These projects are generating new information on the roles of men and women in Norse societies of the North Atlantic, the structure of Viking Age and medieval textile production in that region, the role of textiles and women in the medieval economy of Iceland and in international trade, and creative approaches developed by women as sustainable responses to climate change during the Little Ice Age in the North Atlantic.